TAKE BACK OUR FUTURE

TAKE BACK OUR FUTURE

An Eventful Sociology of the Hong Kong Umbrella Movement

Edited by Ching Kwan Lee and Ming Sing

ILR PRESS

AN IMPRINT OF CORNELL UNIVERSITY PRESS   ITHACA AND LONDON

First published 2019 by Cornell University Press

Library of Congress Cataloging-in-Publication Data

Names: Lee, Ching Kwan, editor. | Sing, Ming, editor.
Title: Take back our future : an eventful sociology of the Hong Kong Umbrella Movement / edited by Ching Kwan Lee and Ming Sing.
Description: Ithaca [New York] : ILR Press, an imprint of Cornell University Press, 2019. | Includes bibliographical references and index.
Identifiers: LCCN 2019006496 (print) | LCCN 2019009147 (ebook) | ISBN 9781501740930 (pdf) | ISBN 9781501740947 (epub/mobi) | ISBN 9781501740916 | ISBN 9781501740916 (cloth) | ISBN 9781501740923 (pbk.)
Subjects: LCSH: Umbrella Movement, China, 2014. | Protest movements—China—Hong Kong. | Civil disobedience—China—Hong Kong. | Democracy—China—Hong Kong. | Hong Kong (China)—Politics and government—1997–
Classification: LCC JQ1539.5.A91 (ebook) | LCC JQ1539.5.A91 T35 2019 (print) | DDC 322.4/4095125—dc23
LC record available at https://lccn.loc.gov/2019006496

For the Umbrella Generation

Contents

Acknowledgments

We are grateful for the generous support of the Hong Kong University of Science and Technology and the University of California–Los Angeles. A faculty collaboration grant jointly run by the two universities allowed us to organize two workshops in Hong Kong where authors presented their drafts and gained valuable feedback from invited discussants. We also benefited from the insights of movement activists, documentary filmmakers, journalists, and scholars in related fields. For their input and encouragement, we thank Joshua Wong, Kin-man Chan, Evans Chan, Tsz-woon Chan, Ming-sho Ho, Yuen-Chung Chen, Mirana Setzo, Jeffrey Martin, Shun-hing Chan, Thomas Davies, Stephan Ortmann, Lawrence Ho, and Ching Cheong. We are particularly indebted to Frances Benson, our visionary editor at Cornell University Press, for her ardent support of this project. It has been a delight to work with her and her colleagues Meagan Dermody and Karen M. Laun.

TAKE BACK OUR FUTURE

TAKE BACK OUR FUTURE

An Eventful Sociology of the Hong Kong Umbrella Movement

Ching Kwan Lee

The outbreak of the Umbrella Movement (UM) in fall 2014 took everyone by surprise, from the student leaders and the intellectual activists at the center of the mobilization, to the Hong Kong government, the Beijing leadership, and the world at large. It literally exploded into existence amid the eighty-seven canisters of tear gas shot by the Hong Kong police to disperse the tens of thousands of protesters. The confrontation between the humble umbrellas wielded by goggles-wearing students and citizens on the one side, and the police in full combat gear armed with pepper spray and batons on the other, enraged even more people to join, leading to seventy-nine days of occupation in three downtown districts. Protesters blocked eight-lane highways, pitched tents outside some of the world's most expensive commercial real estates, and built makeshift platforms for public deliberations and mobile democracy classrooms. At the peak of the movement, about 20 percent of Hong Kong's 7.2 million residents participated in one form or another.[1] It was a stunning and puzzling spectacle: a world financial center long known for its purportedly free-wheeling capitalism, materialistic lifestyles, and apolitical culture was being transformed by its citizens into a hotbed of mass defiance and civil disobedience, forcefully demanding democracy from its communist sovereign. Yet the irony of the Umbrella Movement was that despite its extraordinary scale and radical form as an event, the core demand was reformist, legalistic, and constitutional in nature: genuine universal suffrage for the election of Hong Kong's chief executive, a political right that has been enshrined in Hong Kong's mini-constitution but delayed in practice by Beijing.

What accounts for the Umbrella Movement's eventful and reformist characters? How did movement activists and civil society groups develop their capacity for collective action? What were the bases of solidarity and conflicts within the movement? How did the Chinese and Hong Kong governments mount a variety of countermobilizations to subdue it, and with what consequences for Hong Kong, China, and beyond? This book is a collective effort to answer these questions by a group of scholars with interdisciplinary theoretical tool kits and intimate local knowledge; all authors were either born or based in Hong Kong. Zooming in and out of the movement, we address both the historical and social structural conditions of Hong Kong politics as well as the fine-grained mobilization processes of street contentions.[2]

The Lens of "Event"

This introductory chapter uses the lens of "eventful sociology" to understand the duality of the movement (i.e. its eventful form and reformist demands). Historically and theoretically significant, "events" are concentrated moments of political and cultural creativity when the logic of historical development is reconfigured by human action but by no means abolished.[3] According to William H. Sewell, "events" is a rare subclass of happenings that, instead of being produced by structure, have the potential to significantly disrupt structure. "Events transform structures largely by constituting and empowering new groups of actors or by re-empowering existing groups in new ways," putting in motion social processes that are "inherently contingent, discontinuous and open ended."[4] High eventfulness incidents were usually singled out as symbols of entire movements, as the taking of the Bastille for the French Revolution, or the Montgomery bus boycott for the American civil rights movement. Their transformative impacts are realized through the cognitive, affective, and relational mechanisms that happened inside eventful protests.[5]

Events can emerge under different constellations of political and historical conditions whose contingencies make events difficult to predict. But unpredictable is not the same as inexplicable in that we can still discern the determinants shaping the character of specific events. How should we understand the Umbrella Movement's duality of radical form and reformist contents? As a first approximation, the blockage of democracy imposed by 150 years of British colonialism and Chinese authoritarianism today have had the effects of weakening civil society organizations, alienating citizens from civic and political participation, and channeling accumulated popular grievances to noninstitutionalized, disruptive events. We shall see in a later section that the event of 2014 was just one among several in Hong Kong's political history. Second, the pragmatic, reformist, liberal demands evident in Hong Kong's protests have roots in the entrenched collective experience with common law and liberalism in the late colonial period (from the 1970s), in the constant threat of a negative alternative that was Chinese communism. These historical conditions and collective lived experiences gave rise to "events"—not social movements, political parties, or civil society organizations prioritized by Western social science—as the crucible of popular power with liberal imaginations in Hong Kong.

Like other eventful protests, the Umbrella Movement has had a transformative impact and may trigger new imaginations and demands inspiring and informing the next "event." As the chapters in this book demonstrate, the 2014 protest has spawned new cultural categories and narratives of localism, autonomy and even independence, fueled the formation and expansion of grassroots and professional organizations and networks both for and against the regime, and spurred the regime's turn to repression and structural closure of dissent. All these post-UM developments have led to unprecedented polarization in Hong Kong, engulfing state and civil society in ever hardening antagonism.

An eventful sociological approach can also illuminate mass mobilizations beyond this particular instance of revolt. It opens a unique vista into a repeated feature of Hong Kong politics that is not captured by existing theorizations, be they structural, cultural, or institutional.[6] I am referring to the episodic, concentrated, massive but rare eruption of popular political action in an otherwise calm and uneventful ocean of political inactivity and rule-binding routine politics characteristic of Hong Kong in both the British colonial and Chinese authoritarian eras. Later in this introduction, I will illustrate this pattern using three other previous events of popular mobilizations in Hong Kong's history: the 1966–67 riots, the June 4th mass protests in 1989, and the July 1, 2003, mass rally, in addition to the Umbrella Movement of 2014. These protest events have historically compelled Britain and China to reorient their policies and relations with Hong Kong society, be it toward social reform and democratization, or repressive control. But first we will turn to the historical and political genesis, the formation of a variety of political actors, the microprocesses of mobilization and countermobilization of the Umbrella Movement. Along the way, we will see how both the historical structural conditions and the layered collective experience of politics in Hong Kong anchored the revolt's liberal reformist utopian vision.[7]

Genesis: Recolonization and its Discontents

The genesis of the Umbrella Movement can be traced to an intensification of popular discontent against the Hong Kong government and its principal, the government of the People's Republic of China (PRC). Since China's resumption of sovereignty in July 1997, the end of British colonialism has been experienced by many Hong Kong citizens as the beginning of another round of colonization, this time by the Mainland Chinese communist regime. Such recolonization, which proceeded with fits and starts in the early years after the handover and had become more aggressive since 2003, can be broken down into three constitutive processes: political disenfranchisement, colonization of the life world, and economic subsumption. Bearing the brunt of these adversarial processes were the millennials. As a political generation a la Karl Mannheim, these youngsters (under thirty in 2014) have come of age in an affluent, albeit highly unequal, Hong Kong that at the time of the handover had been set on a path of democratization by the last colonial administration and given tantalizing promises of autonomy by Beijing. They shared a particularly strong sense of belonging, identity, and pride in Hong Kong as their natural homeland. Quite naturally, they literally led the charge of a cross-class revolt; youthful student leaders of the movement stormed into the Civic Square outside the Hong Kong government headquarters on September 26, 2014. Protests against their arrests grew and sparked confrontation with the police, who resorted to tear gas and rubber bullets on September 28. Vowing to "take back our future,"[8] protesters began their months-long occupation.

Political Disenfranchisement

Let's look at the first of the three dimensions of recolonization: political disenfranchisement or de-democratization. The most ubiquitous slogan of the Umbrella Movement was "I want genuine universal suffrage," written on numerous bright yellow banners, often chanted loud and clear in rallies.[9] This signature slogan summed up protesters' common aspiration, much as "689," the derogatory nickname given to the then chief executive (CE), C. Y. Leung, personified everything that was wrong with the lack of universal suffrage. "689" refers to the number of votes Leung obtained from the CE election open only to 1,200 people out of a city of 7.2 million. Even though colonial Hong Kong had never known full democracy, the postcolonial electoral system was nevertheless experienced as a deprivation of political rights for several reasons. First, universal suffrage for electing the CE has been stipulated in the Sino-British Declaration (1984) and the Basic Law (Article 45 and Article 68), Hong Kong's mini-constitution promulgated by the National People's Congress in 1990. Yet Beijing has delayed its implementation several times since 1997. Then on August 31, 2014, when the National People's Congress Standing Committee once again limited the right to nominate candidates for the CE to a 1,200-person committee structurally constituted to ensure pro-Beijing results,[10] popular anger boiled over and jump-started students and political activists' mobilizations. The August 31 decision was for many a blatant abrogation by China of her own constitutional promise to Hong Kong. It was also an insult to many self-styled cosmopolitan Hong Kongers in an age when universal suffrage (meaning equal right to vote and run for public office) is considered a basic human right around the world.[11]

China's obstruction of Hong Kong's democratization has taken different forms and strategies. Constitutionally, China imposed the Basic Law, which keeps intact the executive-dominant system put in place under British colonialism, on a society that had developed from a "barren rock" 150 years ago to a global financial center. Holding the initiative to legislate, the power to veto the legislature, and to appoint all the major bureau secretaries, some judges, major government officials, and heads of many policy commissions, the special administrative region (SAR) CE is deemed "constitutionally more powerful than most presidents in the world."[12] The post-1997 executive branch is even more powerful than before the handover because the Basic Law greatly curtails the policy influence of the legislature. Article 74 of the Basic Law stipulates that legislators can only propose bills that do not involve public expenditure, political structure, or operation of the government. The CE's written approval is required if a legislator wants to propose a bill involving government policy.[13] Changes in electoral rules after 1997—proportional representation replacing first-past-the-post system; reducing the size of the electorate eligible to vote for functional constituencies seats; instituting the voting-by-group rule within the legislature to fragment lawmakers—allow pro-Beijing and pro-establishment elites to enjoy a secured majority capable of neutralizing the challenge from the minority of directly elected prodemocracy politicians.

Besides engineering political institutions and rules favorable to its control, Beijing has also constructed an elaborate system of patron-clientelist networks to aggressively groom a new corps of pro-China politicians and loyalists to fill appointed or elected political positions at different levels. To the Hong Kong business and professional elite, China entices their loyalty by incorporating them into various consultative and political institutions, conferring honorary titles and facilitating their access to Mainland markets and businesses.[14] At the grassroots, the Central Government Liaison Office (CGLO), Beijing's local agency in Hong Kong, has made a systematic effort to co-opt, finance, and infiltrate civil society groups, such as mutual aid committees in public housing estates, homeowners associations in private condominiums, women's groups, charity organizations, sports clubs, and recreational centers in different districts. Over the past decade, these grassroots groups have benefited from financial, staff, and material sponsorship given by pro-China organizations and individuals and have turned into a groundswell of volunteers and votes for pro-Beijing candidates in district and legislature elections.[15]

The overall result was a disarticulation and alienation of popular will from the political process. Even though the pan-democrats have won 55 to 60 percent of the votes on average for directly elected seats since 1997, the system is so stacked against them that they have not been able to represent their constituencies' interests and effect change in public policies and public finances. While the executive branch and establishment politicians make policies that placate Beijing's interests, the prodemocracy opposition could only obstruct by creating deadlocks, criticizing controversial policies, delaying budgetary approval for government projects, or mobilizing public opinion against the CE and SAR government officials. Frustrated by a pervasive governance crisis, the general public has registered consistently rising levels of discontent. Public opinion polls show a secular decline in citizen satisfaction with both the CE and SAR government over the past two decades, registering double-digit negative net satisfaction rates. On the eve of the Umbrella Movement, net popularity rating for the CE and the SAR government dipped to -35 percent and -20 percent respectively.[16]

Developing in tandem with de-democratization was a palpable erosion of Hong Kong's core political values: rule of law, independent judiciary, due process, civil liberty, and freedom of the press.[17] Rule of law was originally touted by British colonizers to establish Hong Kong as an attractive place of trade for Chinese and European merchants, as well as to attach Hong Kong Chinese to colonial rule. The rhetoric of rule of law allowed the British to establish themselves as both bringers of civilization to the East and to mark its moral superiority against Red China during the Cold War. In the 1960s, responding to social unrest and short of extending Hong Kong people the political right to vote, the colonial government gave them legal rights, or what one scholar terms "legal liberalism." The intent was to absorb "demands for political change by offering instead justice, rights and equality before the law."[18] Colonial governance indeed improved dramatically after the 1970s, the period also of fundamental re-engineering of social policies and civic life in Hong Kong. Most notably, rampant abuse of police power, official corruption, and cronyism were successfully wiped out by the Independent Commission Against Corruption established in 1974.[19] Several years before the handover, the late colonial government formally enshrined the basic freedoms and protections Hong Kong citizens have enjoyed for several decades in the Bill of Rights (1991). The last governor, Chris Patten, in particular constructed a narrative of colonialism that insisted that the rule of law was the foundation of Hong Kong's way of life as well as its economic success.[20]

These core liberal values are deeply entrenched in the mentality of Hong Kongers, who in opinion polls consistently rank "rule of law" and "freedoms" higher in priority than "one person one vote."[21] To their dismay, except for the first few years after 1997, China mounted serious assaults against these cherished ways of life. Chinese officials responsible for Hong Kong affairs and pro-establishment elite uphold "patriotism" as a cardinal principle to neutralize or trump "rule of law." In the communist lexicon, "patriotism" or loving the country is conflated with loving the party-state. Therefore, "unpatriotic" has become the standard condemnation used by Chinese officials against pandemocrats, social movement activists, and critics of Beijing. Patriotism has also been emphasized as a key qualifying criterion for filling positions of power in the government and, astonishingly, even the court in Hong Kong. Just a few months before the Umbrella Movement, the PRC State Council issued a White Paper on "one country two systems," reasserting the primacy of one country over two systems, Beijing's prerogative to define the meaning of "high degree of autonomy," and the basic political requirement that judges and government administrators must be "patriots."[22]

Aside from the visible hands of Beijing, the Hong Kong SAR government has curbed civil liberties by amending the Public Order Ordinance.[23] Its notoriously ill-fated attempt to enact a sweeping antisubversion law, alternatively called "Article 23 of the Basic Law," prompted half a million people to take to the streets in 2003. Yet Beijing insisted that the SAR government had no choice but to enact one, widely feared to restrict civil liberties in the name of national security. These two instances were among a series of "law wars" that sent a chilling message to the public about the erosion of the rule of law. These wars were waged publicly between the Hong Kong judiciary on the one side and the Hong Kong government seeking interpretation of the law by the National People's Congress (NPC) in Beijing. Legal scholars have found that the meaning and practice of "rule of law" have changed under Chinese rule. "Rule of law" now takes on a statist "rule by law" or "law and order" interpretation, rather than the common-law notion of legal checks on government discretion.[24] Perhaps the most sobering indicator of how much damage Hong Kong's rule of law has sustained is that the Hong Kong legal profession has taken to the street four times since 1997 to protest China's interference.[25]

Press freedom has also taken a hit, and not just in terms of censorship and self-censorship of mass media contents (see chapter 5). Control of the press has taken blatant forms of ownership takeover (e.g. pro-Beijing investors' takeover of the two major television stations and direct control over seven other major mass media outlets; the government's refusal to grant a free-to-air license to a liberal broadcaster) and violent attacks on media workers (e.g. the knife attack in broad daylight on an editor of a local newspaper printing stories about secret wealth and corruption in China, and physical attack and vandalism against outspoken radio talk show hosts). In April 2016, Reporters Without Borders summed this all up starkly and succinctly: Hong Kong has fallen spectacularly in press freedom ranking, from 18th in the world to 70th between 2002 and 2015.[26]

Colonization of Life World and Identity

Beyond the political and legal spheres, China casts an unwelcome and menacing shadow on many aspects of local culture and daily life. As Beijing steps up its "hearts and minds" project (i.e., to inculcate patriotism among Hong Kongers), Hong Kong academics and the media popularize the term "Mainlandization" to describe the colonization of everyday life by Mainland Chinese citizens arriving in Hong Kong as permanent residents and tourists via various policy channels opened up by Beijing. Although a boon to the tourism industry, the influx of tens of millions of tourists a year to one the world's most densely populated metropolises has pushed the carrying capacity of the city's transportation and public facilities to the brink. Birth tourism among pregnant Mainland women has aggravated the supply of hospital beds for local mothers. Shops catering to local residents' daily necessities went out of business and were replaced by jewelry stores and factory outlets of luxury goods. Pharmacies stocked their shelves with infant milk powder purchased in bulk by Mainland tourists rather than regular over-the-counter medications needed by locals. Overcrowded subway trains and long lines for local residents getting to work raised the ire of many. Verbal and physical skirmishes in public places between local residents and Mainland tourists over norms of civility, mannerisms and sanitation became frequent. Some of these episodes were recorded by smart phones and went viral, triggering sensational and inflammatory comments about "locust invasion" by Mainlanders. Residents in several New Territories locations even staged "reclamation action day" protests against suitcase-bearing tourists seemingly engaged in parallel border trade.

The most significant and politicized instance of identity politics that antagonized and emboldened the younger generation who would later play a leading role in the Umbrella Movement was the anti-national-education campaign in 2012. The repertoire of collective action that emerged in this campaign would reappear in the Umbrella Movement two years later. It originated in a new "moral and national education" curriculum for all primary and secondary schools announced by the Hong Kong SAR government in 2010–2011 and scheduled to be implemented in fall 2012, with the explicit goal of cultivating Hong Kong students' national identity from an early stage in their lives. Sample teaching materials touted the superiority of the "China model" and praised the Chinese Communist Party (CCP) as a progressive, selfless, and united party. The CGLO officials instigated this curriculum in response to their sustained failure to "win the hearts and minds" of Hong Kong people. But such a high-handed, top-down, propaganda-like effort backfired badly: it prompted secondary school students to form their own movement organization (Scholarism), provoked mass rallies by ninety thousand students, parents, and teachers who occupied the Civic Square in front of the government headquarters, and politicized secondary school students who staged hunger strikes from which Joshua Wong emerged as the public face of his generation and leader of their movement. The Hong Kong government was forced to concede and made the curriculum optional rather than mandatory.[27] Buoyed by overwhelming public support and encouraged by their stunning victory against the communist regime and its handmaiden in Hong Kong, Scholarism and its large and youthful constituency would try to repeat their feat two years later.

The anti-moral and anti-national-education campaign reveals two important aspects of identity politics in Hong Kong. First, it shows a fundamental and increasingly irreconcilable gap between young Hong Kongers' identification with a rule-of-law civic culture and Communist China's one-party authoritarian ethnonationalism. Students, parents, teachers, and the general public rejected the curriculum based on its "brainwashing" intent and the Chinese government's conflation of the nation with the communist party-state in its rhetoric of "patriotism." This civic model of identity construction coexists and competes with a more nativist, xenophobic ethnocultural model of localism, but both draw identity boundaries against the Mainland Chinese regime's demand for nationalistic identification (see chapter 4). Second, these localistic identities have emerged primarily out of relational struggles with the Chinese regime: the more Beijing seeks to inculcate patriotism in the hearts and minds of Hong Kongers, the more localist the latter become in defense, which in turn hardens China's resolve to control.

Economic Subsumption

A more subterranean current of popular discontent about the economy was palpable among participants in the Umbrella Movement. In surveys, about one-third of the protesters mentioned economic inequality, lack of social mobility, and uncertain employment prospects as their main concerns.[28] The Declaration by the Federation of Students also spotlighted economic injustice, so did rank-and-file protesters interviewed by the international media.[29] Still, economic distress as a cause of the movement played second fiddle to political disenfranchisement in this movement. This is consistent with Hong Kong's majority acceptance of the liberal creed, market rationality, and the privatization of economic trouble, which also explains the lack of popular support for the 2011 Occupy Central campaign initiated by a group of activists in solidarity with Occupy Wall Street. Rallying against capitalism, socioeconomic injustice, and corporate greed, pitching their tents under the Hong Kong Shanghai Bank Building in Central, the number of occupiers peaked at about one hundred but averaged not more than a few dozen throughout the seven months of its existence. The objective realities of economic inequality have always been a fact of life in Hong Kong, but they alone seldom fueled collective mobilization.[30]

Arguably, it was not economic inequality but the specter of economic subsumption by China that became a motivating factor for protest. Over the past decade, Hong Kong's economic integration with China has proceeded apace and has increasingly become a zero-sum game. In other words, China's visible hands, often assisted and executed by those of the Hong Kong government, in land transactions, the stock market, media ownership, and infrastructural projects lay bare Beijing's intent to subordinate the needs and interests of Hong Kong to those of China. Economic integration now portends Hong Kong's subordination to and dependence on the Mainland, eliminating the city's own source of competitiveness and a vision of its economic future along the way. For the younger generation in Hong Kong, the China factor has cast a long and gloomy shadow on their economic future.

Several instances with direct impact on Hong Kong people's economic well-being made particularly deep and emotional impressions in the public consciousness about the trend of economic subsumption. Of primary concern to all in this "tycoon city" is housing prices. Most of the super-rich billionaires made their fortunes in real estate and then developed oligopolistic control over other key economic sectors.[31] Forty-five percent of residents live in public housing because the price of private housing is out of reach; median housing prices are fifteen times median household incomes.[32] Price indexes for private residential units have doubled between 2007 and 2014, while salaries for managerial and professional employees have remained constant. This overheated market was supported by the influx of cash-rich Mainland Chinese investors, especially after the Chinese stimulus package of November 2008, who bought properties in Hong Kong as a way to move capital out of China. For instance, in 2011, 35.5 percent of new home sales under HK$12 million were by Mainland Chinese investors. Additionally, the HKSAR government's pro-China immigration policies after the handover resulted in a substantial increase in the population and demand for housing.[33] Red capital coming from China is not just threatening the home ownership dreams of ordinary Hong Kong citizens. Local real estate tycoons increasingly find themselves outcompeted by Mainland developers, who have grown from buying 23 percent of land sales in Hong Kong in 1997 to

100 percent in 2017.[34] Watching them snapping up the most expensive lands sold by the government for residential development, one of them remarked publicly that "Chinese money buying up land in Hong Kong at sky-high prices has left many local developers with no standing room. In the future, Chinese capital will seep into many livelihood sectors in our city."[35]

The property market is just one prominent sector that indicates Mainland China's control over Hong Kong's economic life. Several multibillion-dollar infrastructural megaprojects were widely criticized as "white elephants" under-written by Hong Kong taxpayers but serving China's national economic needs. The most notorious is the High Speed West Rail, which does not add any economic value to Hong Kong, where there are already adequate rail connections to the Mainland. Yet Beijing wanted a symbolic terminal in Hong Kong to affirm its sovereignty. Despite widespread criticisms by the pan-democrats and the public at large, the pro-establishment legislature has always approved its ballooned financing. Similarly, the Hong Kong-Zhuhai-Macao Bridge has been built to serve Mainland planners' vision of development, to absorb Hong Kong into the so-called Greater Bay Area regional economy.

On top of these recent policy initiatives to foster Hong Kong's economic sub-sumption to Chinese development, Hong Kong's dependence on Chinese supplies of water and food has also increased. "By the end of 2013, some 95 percent of live pigs, 100 percent of live cattle, 33 percent of live chickens, 100 percent of freshwater fish, 90 percent of vegetables and 70 percent or more of flour on the Hong Kong market had been supplied by the mainland."[36] Controlling water and food supplies ensures China's political leverage in Hong Kong but also generates high profits. Run by monopolistic Chinese companies, the unit price of fresh water in Hong Kong is among the highest in the world, and the rising cost of food has led to public outcry that does not find any response from the Hong Kong SAR government.[37]

In short, the Umbrella Movement was a collective self-defense (viz. the slogan "We alone can save our city"), led by the young and educated but with cross-class participation of the local populace, against what many consider Beijing's recolonization of the city after 1997.[38] But what prompted people used to British colonialism to rebel against China's internal colonization? British colonial Hong Kong was indeed no paradise. Early colonial rule was marked by blatant racism, residential segregation, criminalization, miscarriage of justice, and police brutality against the Chinese population.[39] As a matter of fact, Hong Kong possessed one of the most top-heavy governments and one of the largest police forces in the British Empire in the late nineteenth century and early twentieth century. Miscarriage of justice rather than the rule of law was the norm.[40] It was only in the post–World War II era, in light of the international anticolonial climate and strategic considerations during the Cold War, augmented by pressures generated by local social struggles, that the colonial government began implementing social and political reforms in the 1970s. As a refugee society in the shadow of the Chinese communist regime, radical political ideas had little purchase outside some Beijing-sponsored mass organizations. Hong Kong Chinese have long focused their energy on economic advancement and social mobility, which they saw was made possible by British rule of law and an open, competitive capitalist economy. For the majority of Hong Kong citizens today, early colonial despotism belongs to the history books. What has lived on prominently in their collective memories were the Golden Years of enlightened colonialism, the 1970s under the governorship of Sir Murray MacLehose and continued by his successors. Against this long process of gradual democratization, rule-of-law institutionalization, economic takeoff, social reform, and good governance, postcolonial Hong Kong has been widely seen as a time of degeneration, disenfranchisement, erosion of core values, and economic subsumption by its Chinese sovereign.

The Umbrella Activists: Forging Collective Capacity

Increasing encroachment by China to turn Hong Kong into an internal colony has spurred the rise of new political actors and groups to defend Hong Kong's way of life and liberal civic values. From these antecedent activisms arose the major political subjects, leaders, and strategies we would find in the Umbrella Movement several years later. But two background structural conditions for the emergence of these mobilizations need to be highlighted in order to understand why "events" rather than social movement organizations or civil society institutions are the crucible of popular politics in Hong Kong. First, Hong Kong has an enduringly weak civil society characterized by reformist orientations and limited mobilizing capacity. Civil society organizations are "content with self-defense and maintenance or at most enlargement of the public space, instead of seeking more fundamental institutional reforms."[41] Their preferred movement organizing format has been the ad hoc united front that entails little costs or long-term commitments. Like in the Umbrella Movement, episodes of mobilizations leading up to it were not the result of sustained organization building. "Event," not civil society, is the theoretical category for analyzing Hong Kong's political development.

Second, a structural contradiction inherent in Hong Kong's political regime will continue to sow the seeds of eventful protests. This is because the Hong Kong government has been increasingly caught in a bind between its colonial legacy as a liberal and global city administration and its current nationalistic authoritarian sovereign. As a liberal rule-of-law city, Hong Kong still provides the necessary political spaces for protests against authoritarian rule. But as a part of an authoritarian state, implementing policies engineered and imposed by Beijing inevitably provokes mass grievances against the Hong Kong government.

Let's turn now to the series of contentious mobilizations leading up to the Umbrella occupations, to trace how the contradiction constitutive of this Hong Kong regime in transition from liberalism to authoritarianism have contributed to nurturing and growing the collective capacity of at least three general categories of political actors who would converge during the Umbrella protests: the self-mobilized citizenry, the localists, and the student activists (or the millennials). In the process, we will also witness an expansion in the repertoire of collective action.

July 1st, 2003, Rally: Self-Mobilized Citizenry

Post-1997 Hong Kong witnessed its first major protest on July 1st, 2003, when half a million citizens (or one-twelfth of the population) poured onto the streets in scourging summer heat to register their discontent with the Tung Chee Hwa administration. They turned the occasion for commemorating the official establishment of the SAR government into a resounding rejection of the government's proposed National Security Law, widely deemed to be a means of curtailing civil liberty in the name of punishing subversion, treason, and secession. Many joined the protest also to express their accumulated grievances against government incompetence and unresponsiveness to public opinion in the wake of a sustained economic downturn after 1997 and the SARS outbreak that killed about three hundred people, in addition to other scandals and policy debacles.[42] For our purpose, what was remarkable about this event was not just its scale but its formation through "self-mobilization"; "the citizens themselves have constituted the most important mobilizing agents."[43] Even though the official organizer of the protest, the Civil Human Rights Front, was a coalition of forty-two civil society associations, their mobilization capacity was so weak that year after year they failed miserably to predict the turnout of the rally. Mobilization was achieved by citizens themselves through a two-step process, according to a study by two media scholars. "A portion of the public has served as participatory leaders. They occupied the more privileged position within the socioeconomic structure of the society, but they also had the strongest discontent toward the government. They had more experiences in political participation and consumed the news media to a larger extent. After acquiring the relevant information and messages from the media, they shared them with others and asked their acquaintances to participate in the protest together."[44] Through the process of participation in this event, Hong Kong citizens once again saw who they were collectively—peaceful, civil, and nonviolent protesters—and what they were capable of doing—the chief executive and the secretary for public security stepped down in due course. The historic July 1st, 2003, rally has gone down in the city's collective memory as an episode of empowerment, while its self-mobilization and direct expression of public opinion on the streets became enduring features in the city's protest culture.

2004–2010 Heritage and Anti-Express-Rail Campaigns: The Localists

If the 2003 rally constituted the Hong Kong citizenry as a society-wide political subject in defense of civil liberty, the series of struggles from 2004 to 2010 to preserve cultural heritage against urban developmentalism contributed to the making of a new political subject: the localists.[45] Making claims of local identities, community participation, and cultural autonomy, these activists spawned various strands of localist ideology that would congeal into a dominant political orientation of the millennials, the generational force behind the Umbrella Movement. Besides formulating new identities and ideologies, this cycle of protests also achieved a paradigm shift in protest tactics. Direct action (occupation of public space, confrontation with police, and civil disobedience)—to be distinguished from peaceful, lawful, and nonconfrontational marches—became a salient part of Hong Kong's repertoire of collective action.

The emergence of "heritage" as a cause of social movement in Hong Kong, a society known for its forward looking, prodevelopment, go-go ethos and its lack of preservation culture, was puzzling. It was also ironic that the Hong Kong government's response to global competition was a main facilitating factor in the rise of the heritage preservation movement. Even as Hong Kong became a city under Chinese rule, the post-handover government aspired to maintain Hong Kong's global city status and partook in the global trend of developing the cultural economy, that is, turning culture, arts, and heritage into business. Reeling from the 1997 Asian financial crisis and facing the collapse of the real estate market in its aftermath, the government turned to cultural and heritage tourism in a bid to make Hong Kong "Asia's World City."[46] Historical buildings were identified, restored, and preserved for cultural, community, and commercial uses, and the private sector was to share the cost of redevelopment. Inadvertently, the government's discourse and practice of cultural economy sparked community interests in their own local history, subverting and contesting the government's agenda of commercialization. Several prominent campaigns attracted widespread media coverage and popularized the notion of "collective memories" in public debates.[47] In a few years, the politics of heritage, space, and memories would transform into a vocal movement for community autonomy and democracy in policy making and urban planning.

Rather than movement organizations mobilizing their bases, these protests occurred haphazardly and then grew through interaction among accidental participants during the time and in the space of the campaign. Ethnographic and autobiographical accounts of the nine-month-long campaign (from April 2006 to July 2007) to oppose the demolition of the Star Ferry and Queen's Pier and the anti-express-rail campaign in 2009–2010 revealed several important impromptu dynamics of protests in Hong Kong. In 2006, the twenty or so initial activists, including students, social workers, and community artists, began discussing their goals and strategies only after they accidentally and spontaneously charged into the demolition sites, taking advantage of a gate opening for a dump truck. Their street action lasted for several months, escalated to a hunger strike, sparked public debates, and drew citizens to observe and participate in open forums, exhibitions, concerts, and guided tours. It revived the public memory of the Star Ferry as the site of resistance of another hunger strike against ferry fare in 1966.

While the campaign failed to reverse the government's demolition decision, the fifty or so activists formed a loosely organized group called Local Action, which re-emerged in 2009–2010 to wage another high-profile protest against the construction of an express rail system connecting Hong Kong with Mainland China. They joined with the 150 households in Tsoi Yuen Village, slated for removal to make way for the project, to oppose the government's forced relocation, urban bias, developmental ethos, and undemocratic planning process. Again, protesters occupied a public square outside the legislature and staged a "Fun and Greenery Cultural Festival." Amid rally speeches and music, groups of thirty to forty activists took turns to parade around the LegCo Building, kneeling down every twenty-six steps (a reference to the 26 km Hong Kong rail section) to indicate their determination to fight against the proposal, their respect for the land, and their humble demand to stop destroying village homes. Public sympathy and opinion began to sway in their favor, and in a matter of weeks the protest grew to about ten thousand people, while thousands of young protesters broke through the police line to stage a sit-in outside the Government House, the residence of the chief executive. In the meantime, inside the LegCo Building, the Finance Committee of the legislature approved the budget for the rail, despite opposition from professional groups and opposition political parties. Clashes broke out between protesters who forced their way into the LegCo Building and the police, who used pepper spray to disperse them.[48]

More importantly, occupying public sites around the clock allowed citizens to explore and discover in situ a "new form of political agency,"[49] making a distinct "localist" claim to reconstruct Hong Kong identity, history, and future as one made by people's struggles and actions. This discourse was a powerful counterpoint to the official narrative that reduces the Hong Kong experience as one of an economic miracle arising from a fishing village to a global financial center.[50] Engaging the public through performance and public deliberations, assisted by the timely popularization of social media, these campaigns from 2006 to 2010 ushered in the era of online mass mobilization and popularized the notion of identity politics that would galvanize a range of protest action in the next few years against the use of simplified Chinese, cross-border parallel trade and self-driving Mainland tourists, etc.

Another notable and consequential feature of the heritage and localist campaigns is their turn to "direct action" as the preferred alternative to formal democracy, party politics, and ritualistic polite demonstrations. Ironically, Hong Kong's status as a global city inadvertently contributed to this radicalization of action. Many of the activists reported that their inspiration came from observing how Korean farmers adopted confrontational "break in" tactics to protest when Hong Kong hosted the 2005 World Trade Organization ministerial meeting. Opinion poll data collected right after the anti-express-rail protests showed that 26 percent of the Hong Kong population endorsed the protesters' confrontational action and uncompromising rhetoric.[51]

Campaign against Moral and National Education 2012: Student Activists

High school and university students who would become the main political actors during the Umbrella Movement burst onto the political scene in 2012, to the surprise of the public and the activists themselves. At the height of the campaign, high school students successfully mobilized a series of mass protests, including a ninety-thousand-strong rally on July 29, 2012. Their campaign sought to stop the government from implementing a new mandatory moral and national education curriculum in Hong Kong's primary and secondary schools. While the government's goal was to inculcate identification with Mainland China among the post-handover generation, the public assailed the curriculum as "brainwashing education" after sample teaching materials were shown to include descriptions of the Chinese Communist Party as "progressive, selfless, and united." At the center of the campaign was the high school student organization Scholarism and its fourteen-year-old founder Joshua Wong, who would become the most recognized face of the Umbrella Movement two years later. They formed an alliance with parents, teachers, and the Hong Kong Federation of Students, a university student association and another prominent player in the Umbrella Movement. In stark contrast to the previous movements, after some high school students staged a hunger strike in front of the government headquarters at the start of the school year and thousands of protesters claimed the Civic Square as a site for public lectures and civic salons, the government conceded and announced the curriculum optional.

Again this episode of contention has roots in the hybridity of the Hong Kong political regime. On the one hand, the moral and national education curriculum was clearly dictated by Beijing's political agenda, meant to forge nationalistic subjects in Hong Kong and to manufacture consent and obedience to authoritarian rule. On the other hand, Hong Kong's staunchly liberal civic culture remained intact, prompting citizens' resounding resistance to an illiberal education proposal, leveraging the freedom of association and assembly that the Hong Kong government still upheld.

Within the political space allowed for protests and movements, growth, accumulation, and diversification of political actors happened over time. In this case, the capacity, strategy, and identity of the student activists during the campaign against moral and national education clearly built on those practiced by their predecessors in the heritage and anti-express-rail movements, while they also introduced new ideas and methods that would inspire the next movement. Joshua Wong traced his interest in social movement to the anti-express-rail campaign and actively sought the advice of its activists during his campaign. "These experienced activists played a role of a 'hub' linking Scholarism to the existing social movement activists' network," leading to the formation of an alliance to facilitate resource integration.[52] Movement alliance is another standard mode of organization in all major protests in Hong Kong.

In terms of mobilization, the tech-savvy students as avid users of Facebook and other online platforms successfully leveraged the power of the Internet as a tool of mobilization and fund raising, in addition to using traditional means of publicity such as street booths, flyers, and interpersonal self-mobilization such as that seen in the July 1st, 2003, rally. It was also through Facebook that the movement attracted global support; many photos from major cities around the world showing young people posing with crossed hands, the signature gesture of the movement, flooded into the websites of Scholarism and the parents' concern group.[53] The repertoire of action of this movement bears a strong resemblance to that of previous movements: rallies, public forums, festivities, direct action such as break-in and occupation of government premises and public spaces, and hunger strikes. Finally, the students made "anti-CCP" an explicit movement position, exposing the hidden agenda and interference of Beijing and calling for independence of the mind among the youth. Emboldened by their spectacular success in gaining public support and government concession in this movement, the two student bodies—Scholarism and the Hong Kong Federation of Students—would re-emerge as the leaders among an alliance of civil society organizations during the Umbrella Movement, making claims of "self-determination" for Hong Kong's future.

In short, even before the event in 2014, Hong Kong had acquired a new distinction as a "city of protests" in tourist guides and journalistic writings, in addition to its longtime fame as a shopping paradise.[54] During the fifteen-year period when Beijing stalled on its democracy promise, a variety of political actors have come of age. The SAR government's policy proposals provoked citizens' discontent, but its rule-of-law and civil liberty institutions offered them protection and opportunities to formulate new claims and new collective identities (various brands of Hong Kong localism), explore and expand their repertoires of action (from ritualistic demonstrations to direct action) and grow their capacities and influence (forming organizations and alliances in local communities and online social media).[55] In other words, one of the most salient political structural impetuses of contentious politics in postcolonial Hong Kong is paradoxically its hybrid regime. As chapter 8 will elaborate, the "hybridity" in this case is defined by two sets of contradictory tendencies: (1) executive-dominant authoritarianism vs. rule-of-law semidemocratic liberalism and (2) ethnonationalism imposed by China's view of Hong Kong as a Chinese city vs. liberal cosmopolitanism of Hong Kong as a global city.[56]

Inside the Movement: Street Politics and Countermobilizations

The August 31, 2014, decision by Beijing not to open up the nomination process for the 2017 election of the chief executive sparked widespread consternation and outrage. University students took the lead to stage a five-day class boycott, with participation from high school students, supporters of the intellectual-led "Occupy Central with Love and Peace" campaign, and other movement activists and citizens. Toward the end of the class boycott, some thirteen thousand students began relocating their protest from the Chinese University campus to an area near the government headquarters. When student leaders of the Hong Kong Federations of Students and Scholarism charged into the gated Civic Square in the evening of September 26, confrontation with and arrests by the police drew a massive number of citizens and students on the streets nearby. Under pressure from the growing crowds and student protesters, the OCLP leaders announced the impromptu launch of the civil disobedience action campaign in the wee hours of September 27. More protesters poured onto the streets on September 28, a Sunday, many wearing goggles and raincoats, with umbrellas in hand and cling wraps for eye protection against pepper spray. Around 6 p.m., to everyone's surprise, riot police wearing helmets and gas masks began firing a total of eighty-seven canisters of tear gas at the crowd.[57] The use of what many considered disproportionate force and unjust repression against unarmed citizens simply sent more protesters to the streets. It was difficult to overstate the role of moral shock in the initial mobilization of the Umbrella Movement; 52 percent of the respondents in an onsite survey reported that they were motivated by "dissatisfaction with police handling of the protest."[58]

During the ensuing seventy-nine days of occupation, several salient features of mobilization and countermobilization can be discerned. First, the movement displayed an inclusive, anticentralization ethos from which a decentralized, informal leadership emerged organically around the two student organizations: Scholarism and the Hong Kong Federation of Students. Chapter 2 depicts, from the standpoint of a key leader of the movement, the inherent contradiction between the movement's prefigurative practices of egalitarianism and democratic solidarity on the one hand and the movement's inability to assert effective leadership across activist groups on the other. Wing Sang Law reminds us in chapter 4 that the Umbrella Movement was not a unidimensional struggle pitting a unified democracy movement against Beijing's refusal to grant genuine universal suffrage. In chapter 4, Law analyzes the differences and tensions among ideological positions within the movement, along a spectrum from moderate liberals' "reunion with China in democracy," to radical democrats advocating social rights of the working class and confrontational methods, and progressive and right-wing localists advancing ideas of autonomy and independence for Hong Kong. Law maintains that their contentious dynamics allowed for the rapid mobilization of a large number of participants but also led to the problem of disorganization as a movement.

Besides ideological diversity, Occupy Mongkok, as chapter 3 documents, witnessed the participation of a variety of grassroots groups from different class backgrounds: blue-collar workers, retirees, housewives, students, intellectuals, self-styled "localists" advocating militant confrontations, and "leftards," traditional liberals advocating peaceful action. Across the three occupy sites, vividly captured by Oscar Ho's photo essay, there was an outburst of creative expressions and protest arts, reflecting the eclectic, fun-loving, and street smart spirit of Hong Kong culture. Popular cultural icons, ranging from Spider Man and Captain America to Winnie the Pooh and Totoro, rubbed shoulders with Chinese folk deities (e.g. Kwan Tei and Che Kung), Jesus Christ, and the Archangel St. Michael.

Religious rituals mingled with local political gestures such as holding up hands to signify "non-violent" resistance, crossing hand as saying "no" to a fake universal suffrage, "three walks nine kowtow" performed by secondary school students to show their determination and humbleness. Chapter 2 likewise depicts similar energy and yearning in the Umbrella Movement's prefigurative politics for an alternative commons based on mutuality, do-it-yourself, solidarity, and sustainable production and consumption. Such open, nonviolent demonstrations of worthiness, unity, numbers, and commitment are the hallmarks of protests in many liberal democracies.

Notwithstanding some violent skirmishes between gangsters and protesters in Mongkok, the orderliness and civility that largely prevailed during the seventy-nine days of occupation belied the weak mobilization capacity of political parties, trade unions, and churches. Most protesters were self-mobilized, and they converged at the sites to form spontaneous connections with other citizens without organizational support or coordinated agenda. Political party leaders, trade unionists, and churchgoers were among the participants as individuals, not as members of these organizations. For instance, chapter 7 discusses the persistent tension between the logic of movement activism and the logic of electoral politics, which resulted in the marginalization of democratic parties during the Umbrella Movement, even though individual democrats were prominent supporters of the movement. Similarly, Chris Chan's fine-grained analysis in chapter 6 of the trade unions' role during the Umbrella Movement also highlights the weakness of unions as agents of working-class mobilizations, even as some union leaders played a central role in the coalition of civil society groups and students associations. For both the political parties and the trade unions, Mainland China's interference and cooptation stymied their capacity before and during the Umbrella Movement.

As in other hybrid regimes, Hong Kong also saw the growth of a countermovement sponsored by the pro-Beijing establishment.[59] Chapter 8 describes how the pro-China civic organization Silent Majority of Hong Kong mobilized the conservative middle class against protesters, advocated for the official discourse that accused civil disobedience as causing disruption to order and livelihoods, and trivialized the protesters' democratic claims. Other groups, such as Caring Hong Kong Power and Voice of Loving Hong Kong, were more aggressive and appealed to the grassroots audience. Espousing physical contention and large-scale rallies to show their strength, many of their demonstrators were organized by the communist youth groups, paid by clan societies, and recruited from Mainland China. *SpeakoutHK* was an indigenous propaganda outlet that emerged during the Umbrella occupation. It used populist language and false data and functioned as an unofficial mouthpiece for the administration. Chapter 8 shows that these countermovement organizations represent the tip of an iceberg; the Hong Kong and Chinese regimes have developed different methods and targets of cooptation, infiltration, and ideological education, with the goal of silencing and attacking prodemocracy forces.

Eventful Hong Kong Politics: Transformative Consequences of Mass Protests

If the essence of an "event" resides in its transformative consequences, we have to assess how the Umbrella Movement has redirected the logic of historical development in Hong Kong. Arguably, the most salient transformative impact has been the rise of localism as a political agenda and political identity, especially among the younger generation. Signaling a radical departure from China's increasing absorption of Hong Kong into its national political economy, the Umbrella Movement crystallized a political imaginary that included independence for Hong Kong. Even though cultural localism among the general populace had witnessed a significant strengthening in the post-handover era, it had never found explicit political expressions in the formation of political parties running on platforms of various degrees of local autonomy and independence. Among the political commentary and party organizations, Youngspiration, Hong Kong Indigenous Party, Hong Kong National Party, and Demosistō have been the most prominent. Some of their candidates won seats in the general election held in September 2016. Six newly elected legislators (out of a total of thirty) were Umbrella activists until five of them were disqualified by the Hong Kong government, presumably under the auspices of the National People's Congress in Beijing in 2017. In short, if there were only an inkling of localist tendencies before 2014, the "localist" agenda has been clarified and consolidated after 2014, evincing a power that provoked Beijing's heavy-handed repression.

Beyond formal politics, new visions of localism also developed during the movement when occupiers forged new groups, built trust, and shared ideas of how to continue their fight for change. Many Umbrella participants interpreted "localism" as long-term, labor-intensive activism at the grassroots and community levels, leading to the formation of at least forty-five "post–umbrella movement organizations."[60] The community-oriented ones, such as "Umbrella-2Neighborhood," "Community Citizens Charter," "Fixing Hong Kong," and "Wan Chai Commons," built on the slogan "Return to the Community" during the Umbrella Movement. The idea was that democracy is not just about electoral and constitutional struggles or protests in crisis moment, but everyday engagement with local community affairs and mutual help. Among professionals—lawyers, therapists, nurses, medical doctors, artists, insurance and financial service professionals, accountants, architects, urban planners, traditional Chinese medical doctors, and information technology workers—at least eighteen post-Umbrella professional political groups were formed.[61] Professional organizations such as the Progressive Lawyers Groups and Medecins Inspires promote political concerns among professionals, whereas professionals in the information technology, architectural, surveying, planning, and landscape sectors actively participated in elections for the Functional Constituency (in the legislature) and Election Committee (that elects the chief executive).

Last but not least, the Umbrella Movement was a wakeup call to the political establishment as the central government under President Xi Jinping's leadership decidedly reversed course and departed from the constitutional blueprint of "one country, two systems" established by the Sino-British Joint Declaration. Seeing the Umbrella Movement as a menace to its sovereignty rather than a quest to preserve the "two systems" promised by China, Beijing and the Hong Kong government increasingly turned to public and coercive institutions—the police, prosecutors, and the courts—to intimidate, criminalize, and punish civil resisters and democratic activists. Chapter 8 offers many examples of the Hong Kong government's maneuvering of prosecution procedures, outsourcing the filing of injunctions to evict the occupiers to proregime citizens' groups, and exploiting its access to public coffers to file lawsuits and appeals against protesters. Patriotic education in primary and secondary schools is imposed using sanitized history textbooks to glorify the Communist Party–led Chinese regime. Four years after the outbreak of the 2014 event, academics and public commentators agree that Hong Kong has entered an era of authoritarian politics. Whether repression will silence or radicalize Hong Kong politics, only the future can tell. But polarization and hardening of antagonism between state and society, and fragmentation within civil society, have become obvious. And as institutional channels for political participation of the young localists are increasingly blocked, disruptive events will likely be the main channels for expressing their demands and leveraging their power.

Beyond the Umbrella Movement, the enduring blockage of democracy and civil society's weak organizational capacity in Hong Kong had long produced "events" that were distinctive in their effects as "turning points" in inducing fundamental change in some aspects of the body politic, whether state or society or their relations. All these eventful episodes entailed surprisingly massive popular participation in highly visible and public demonstrations, unanticipated by the political establishment or by the organizers themselves, but expressing intense and impassioned political demands that were otherwise disaggregated and dispersed. Here I briefly discuss three events to illustrate how "event" is an important theoretical category for understanding Hong Kong's popular politics.

1966–1967 Riots

In the wake of the Star Ferry riots of 1966, when a young hunger striker's protest against a ferry fare instigated social unrest propelled by socioeconomic grievances, more sustained riots erupted in 1967. Beginning as an industrial dispute in an artificial flower factory in Kowloon in April 1967, violent clashes ensued between the workers and the police in May. The intervention by the communist-dominated Hong Kong Federation of Trade Unions and a protest statement issued by the Chinese Ministry of Foreign Affairs, followed by a sympathetic editorial in the *People's Daily*, spurred local leftists to action. Influenced by the Cultural Revolution's call for rebellion, leftist activists seized the opportunity to launch a self-professed anticolonial movement, evidently supported by Beijing. A four-day general strike was called and the use of bomb attacks paralyzed and terrorized the entire city. The police responded with massive arrests of rioters and raids on communist premises, reinforced by emergency legislation and the deployment of British troops. All told, the riots led to fifty-one deaths, 4,500 arrests, and damage to hundreds of buildings, as well as a fundamental change in the colonial regime's social policy, if not its undemocratic structure.[62] Social reforms, ranging from labor rights, provision of public housing, expansion of education, and better communication between government and the people by a new city district officer system, laid the foundation for Hong Kong' economic takeoff in the 1970s. Historians agree that the 1966–1967 riots "marked a crucial turning point in the development of the colonial regime's irreversible awareness of and irrevocable commitment to a more conscientious and responsive social policy with greater care and concern for the grass-roots community."[63]

June 4th, 1989, Rally

Between May 20 and June 4, 1989, three large-scale demonstrations, involving from fifty thousand to one million participants, took place in Hong Kong in support of the Tiananmen protesters and against Beijing's military crackdown. In light of the city's impending return to Chinese rule and bearing witness to the massacre in Beijing, the Hong Kong public was thrown into a frantic crisis of confidence, with polls showing one-third of Hong Kong households and 64 percent of professionals and entrepreneurs planning to leave.[64] After these mass protests, the colonial government made a remarkable shift in its policy toward Beijing, from one of accommodation to confrontation over the issue of democratic development in Hong Kong leading up to the handover in 1997. Specifically, Hong Kong government officials reversed their previous position, and increased direct election seats from ten to twenty in 1991; the Executive and Legislative Councils agreed to propose direct election by universal suffrage of the chief executive and all seats of the legislature by 2003. Emboldened by a high tide of popular support for democratization, with four out of five Hong Kong citizens favoring a speedier democratization even at the risk of confrontation with Beijing, the political party United Democrats was formed in 1990, winning a landslide in Hong Kong's first direct election in 1991.[65] As another turning point similar to the 1966–1967 riots, the massive protests against Beijing's 1989 crackdown ushered in an era of unprecedented democratization of Hong Kong's political structure under Chris Patten, the last colonial governor. To date, the annual vigil commemorating June 4th has lasted for almost three decades and has become one of the most important dates in Hong Kong's political calendar.

July 1, 2003, Rally

Scholars of postcolonial Hong Kong concurred that the 2003 mass rally of half a million people against the SAR government's plan to pass a national security law (as Article 23 of Hong Kong's Basic Law) was a "critical" or a "watershed" event, another "turning point" in Hong Kong's history. "The July 1, 2003 protest was the starting point of a new type of political dynamics among the government, political parties, and public opinion in Hong Kong."[66] Hong Kong public discourse talked about a new era, a new spirit; "(s)uddenly, people began to imagine the previously unimagined or unimaginable";[67] people who took part in the rally felt that they have made history, and the political elite also admitted that "2003 was the turning point that prompted the CPG (Beijing) to change its policy from 'non-intervention' to 'proaction.'"[68] For instance, since 2003, a member of the Politburo Standing Committee, the most powerful body of the Chinese communist regime, had been designated to oversee Hong Kong and Macau affairs. Beijing had also stepped up its cooptation and infiltration machinery at both the elite and grassroots levels, increased its efforts at ideological education and nationalistic propaganda, and expended more resources in securing pro-establishment votes in successive LegCo elections. Not just on the side of the Chinese and Hong Kong political establishments, but for the Hong Kong citizenry too, the July 1, 2003, rally was a moment of mass empowerment and consciousness raising. The growth of a "July 1" discourse became a symbolic resource that prodemocracy activists had tapped in response to the ever-changing political reality. Like the June 4th vigil, the July 1 rally, despite ebbs and flows in scale, has become an annual political ritual (i.e., regular, repetitive, relatively stable, and sustainable) for Hong Kong citizens to self-mobilize and express publicly their grievances and criticism against the government.[69] A survey of Umbrella Movement participants found that 85 percent of them have participated in a July 1 rally and 74 percent in a June 4 Vigil.[70]

In a nutshell, these events and the Umbrella Movement illustrate that an eventful sociological approach reconciles the seeming contradiction that the Hong Kong populace is both politically apathetic in ordinary times but politically passionate in crisis moments. It also spotlights how even under structural and institutional constraints on Hong Kong's democratization, Hong Kong citizens can still muster their collective capacity in forging unpredictable events to transform society, sometimes toward democratic openness and other times toward authoritarian closure.

Beyond Hong Kong: Popular Revolts against the Power Elite

A key structural condition that has consistently shaped all the historical events in Hong Kong is the "China factor." But Hong Kong is not alone in this regard. The "China factor" was the trigger of the Sunflower Movement in Taiwan in 2014. As Jieh-min Wu explains in chapter 10, for the past thirty years, China's strategy of "using business to encircle politics" has given rise not just to Taiwan's structural economic dependence on the Mainland, but also cross-strait networks of business-political interests, with many local collaborators doing the bidding of Beijing in Taiwan in different arenas (NGOs, religion, the media, education, and legislature). The intensification of and resistance to China's economic influence in Taiwan were evident in the conflict over the Cross-Strait Service Trade Agreement that sparked the Sunflower Movement occupation. In stark contrast to the Umbrella Movement's failure to realize its key demand for genuine universal suffrage, mass mobilization in Taiwan was able to stall the passage of the agreement, thanks to Taiwan's political independence from Beijing. Still, Hong Kong and Taiwan share the contradiction between their deepening economic integration with Mainland China on the one hand and the youth's cultural and political alienation from it on the other. Since these two movements in 2014, young activists from Taiwan and Hong Kong have deliberately built networks and solidarity ties based explicitly on the common threat of the "China factor."[71]

Moving beyond Asia, it is worth noting some of the striking parallels between the Umbrella protests and recent protest movements around the world: the Arab Spring (beginning in Tunisia in December 2010; spreading to Egypt in early

2011; to Days of Rage in January in Algeria, Lebanon, Jordan, Mauritania, Sudan, Oman, and Yemen; in February in Bahrain and Libya; and in March in Saudi Arabia and Syria), Spain's 15-M or Indignados movement beginning in May 2011, Occupy Wall Street in September 2011, and Turkey's Taksim Square occupation in June 2013. Each protest movement was sparked by unique local contingencies and conflicts in their national contexts. But overall there was an articulation between political and economic frustrations, with relative emphasis on one or the other varying across different movements. Protests in the United States and Europe were sparked by economic distress in the wake of the 2008 financial crisis, with protesters shouting slogans denouncing the unfairness of an economic system where the 1 percent profits from the suffering of the 99 percent, opposing governments' budget cuts, and the shortage of jobs and affordable housing. Their critique was not just directed at predatory capitalism but also at the current form of democracy where political parties and elections were disconnected from popular interests and voices. On the other hand, in the Arab Spring uprisings and Hong Kong's Umbrella Movement, the primary target was political tyranny or the lack of democracy, with economic grievance a closely related but secondary motivation.

In almost all these cases, it was an aspiring educated middle class, what Goran Therborn calls the "white collar masses," crucially including the students, that led the protests, while they also drew on the support and participation of a broad cross-class populace.[72] The so-called "lumpen intelligentsia" in the Middle East and North Africa region were caught in the contradiction between the widening education opportunity offered by the postcolonial state and twenty-first-century global capitalism marked by overcredentializing, downward social mobility, and narrowing opportunities for high-skilled employment brought on by technological upgrading.[73] In Occupy Wall Street, polls of the participants reflected a similar profile: highly educated (76 percent of the Wall Street occupiers had college degree or higher), white, young adult.[74] The historical and political-economic circumstances for their participation varied across countries and regions, but in each case there was a shared fear of falling and strong moral indignation against grotesque inequality resulting from entrenched collusion of the economic and political elites.

Besides the social origins of the protesters, there are uncanny similarities between the Umbrella Movement and other protests in the mode of mobilization. First, these protests did away with formal leadership or mobilization by labor unions, political parties, or civil society associations. In many cases there was careful preparation by some activist groups that went on for weeks (Indignados and Occupy Wall Street) and protest networks emerged over a decade (Tahrir Square). The functions of formal movement organization have been taken over by the Internet and social media, particularly Facebook and Twitter, whose networking capacity helped to spread activism like wildfire.[75]

Another inadvertent but common trigger of mobilization was state repression; movements snowballed in response to police repression. In Gezi Park, when news spread about the brutal attack on protesters by the Istanbul police, a sea of protesters flooded the park and neighboring areas and began building barricades.[76] In Occupy Wall Street, the police's use of pepper spray on nonviolent participants and the arrest of seven hundred peaceful demonstrators also backfired. "These incidents drew enormous media attention to the Occupy protests, amplifying their appeal, and helped inspire other occupations around the country."[77] Similar dynamics took place in Hong Kong, with tens of thousands of enraged citizens pouring into and occupying the streets in Admiralty in response to the police's firing of tear gas and pepper sprays on peaceful demonstrators. Global media's sustained coverage of the clashes right at the heart of one of the world's financial centers spotlighted the David vs. Goliath imbalance of power between the authorities and the protesters and helped broaden the protesters' moral appeal beyond Hong Kong.

Once the occupation of public spaces began, protesters remarkably organized themselves into autonomous communities, spontaneously putting in place communal infrastructure for everyday life: medical care and supplies, sanitation, security patrols, food stands, library, rules and schedules for general assembly, songs, and speeches (see chapter 2). While the cleanliness, order, and politeness of the Umbrella protesters in Hong Kong have caught world media attention, similar spaces of mutuality and civility emerged in other occupy protests as well. On the "liberated" Tahrir Square, protesters organized temporary "autonomous communes where 'normal rules' of politics were suspended, Islamists and secularists organized the spaces together, even praying together—unthinkable before the revolution. Women could move relatively freely, without the usual harassment. Rubbish was collected efficiently and recycled. The borders of these temporary 'republics' were defended effectively against state thugs."[78] Antiausterity occupy protests in Europe also witnessed citizens' claiming city space from the control of the regime and the discipline of its institutional order.

Finally, these movements shared distinct protest cultures emphasizing nonviolent, nonhierarchical, nonrepresentational consensus building, or "horizontalism," nondemand, decentralized, and leaderless, all in opposition to traditional party and government systems.[79] Yet beyond the moments of rebellion, their visions for programmatic and institutional transformation remained murky. The sociologist Asef Bayat called the Arab Spring protests "refolutions" because these movements, despite their radical mode of actions, still counted on the existing order to reform itself, failing to forge an alternative ideology or organizational leadership.[80] Similarly, Hong Kong's Umbrella Movement sought constitutional and electoral reforms (genuine universal suffrage for electing the chief executive), which one observer remarked as a "utopian embrace of formal democracy."[81] Regardless of the divergent assessment of the impacts of this wave of protests, most observers also agreed that these movements had politicized a whole generation of people who had no prior experience in politics, changed the conversation about politics and economy, fashioned new subjects and identities, and awakened popular consciousness. These were no small feats, regardless of whether or not the participants could eventually take back their future.

NOTES

1. Francis L. F. Lee and Joseph M. Chan, *Media and Protest Logics in the Digital Era* (New York: Oxford University Press, 2018), 1.

2. Andrew Walder, "Political Sociology and Social Movements," *Annual Review of Sociology* 35 (2009): 393–412.

3. Douglas McAdam and William H. Sewell Jr., "It's About Time: Temporality in the Study of Social Movements and Revolutions," in *Silence and Voice in the Study of Contentious Politic*, ed. Ronald Aminzade et al. (Cambridge: Cambridge University Press, 2001), 102. The philosopher Alain Badiou also sees events as the unpredictable ruptures of the appearance of normality, created by the excluded, which open a space to rethink reality from the standpoint of its real basis in inconsistent multiplicity. Sewell's formulation, however, offers a better heuristic tool for social scientific inquiry.

4. William H. Sewell Jr. "Three Temporalities: Toward an Eventful Sociology," in *Logics of History: Social Theory and Social Transformation* (Chicago: University of Chicago Press, 2005), 110.

5. Donatella Della Porta, "Eventful Protest, Global Conflicts: Social Mechanisms in the Reproduction of Protest," in *Contention in Context: Political Opportunities and the Emergence of Protest*, ed. Jeff Goodwin and James Jasper (Stanford, CA: Stanford University Press, 2012), 256–76.

6. Major works include Siu-kai Lau, *Society and Politics in Hong Kong* (Hong Kong: Chinese University Press, 1982); Wai-man Lam, *Understanding the Political Culture of Hong Kong: The Paradox of Activism and Depoliticization* (Armonk, NY: M. E. Sharpe, 2004); Ngok Ma, *Political Development in Hong Kong: State, Political Society and Civil Society* (Hong Kong: Hong Kong University Press, 2007).

7. Sebastian Veg, "Legalistic and Utopian: Hong Kong's Umbrella Movement," *New Left Review* 92 (Mar/Apr 2015): 55–73.

8. Joshua Wong, "Taking Back our Future," *New York Times* op-ed, October 29, 2014, accessed September 30, 2018.

9. The most memorable and awe-inspiring display of this slogan was a giant 6 m x 28 m banner hung on a cliff face of the Lion Rock hill, long considered the symbol of the Hong Kong spirit, by a group of rock climbers called "Hong Kong Spidie," accessed September 30, 2018. https://sinosphere.blogs.nytimes.com/2014/10/23/a-banner-on-a-hong-kong-landmark-speaks-of-democracy-and-identity/?_r=0.

10. Brendon Scott et al., "How China Holds Sway over Who Leads Hong Kong," *Bloomberg*, February 28, 2017, accessed September 30, 2018, https://www.bloomberg.com/graphics/2017-hk-election.

11. Universal suffrage is enshrined in Article 21 (3) of the United Nations' Universal Declaration of Human Rights, http://www.un.org/en/universal-declaration-human-rights.

12. Ngok Ma, *Political Development*, 59.

13. Ngok Ma, *Political Development*, 117.

14. Brian C. H. Fong, "The Partnership Between the Chinese Government and Hong Kong's Capitalist Class: Implications for HKSAR Governance, 1997–2012," *China Quarterly* 217 (March 2014): 195–220.

15. Au Nok Hin, "Retreat of Democracy under Electoral Authoritarianism: A Study of Regime Consolidation and the Making of Elite Coalition in Hong Kong" (MPhil thesis, Chinese University of Hong Kong, 2014). In the 1970s and 1980s, the colonial government also used grassroots organizations to cement consent to its rule, but with the opening of the political opportunity structure in the 1990s, a hollowing out of grassroots organizations happened when their leaders became politicians. In the postcolonial era, pro-China patron clientelism has outgrown the colonial variant because of the large budgets now disbursed by the District Councils, which now thrive on pork-barrel politics to ensure re-elections of councilors. See Eliza W. Y. Lee, "Civil Society Organizations and Local Governance in Hong Kong," in *Repositioning the Hong Kong Government: Social Foundations and Political Challenges*, ed. Stephen W. K. Chiu and Siu-lun Wong, 147–64 (Hong Kong: Hong Kong University Press, 2012); Lo Shui Hing, "Party Penetration of Society in Hong Kong: The Role of Mutual Aid Committees and Political Parties," *Asian Journal of Political Science* 12, no. 1 (2004): 31–64, 45–46.

16. Ngok Ma, *Political Development*, 6; and Public Opinion Program, University of Hong Kong, various years, https://www.hkupop.hku.hk/english/release/release1187.html.

17. In 2004, calling for public defense against China's interference into Hong Kong, two hundred professionals and academics announced a Hong Kong Core Values Declaration. The core values include liberty, democracy, human rights, rule of law, fairness, social justice, peace and compassion, integrity and transparency, plurality, respect for individuals, and upholding professionalism. Ambrose Leung, "Push to Defend City's Core Values," *South China Morning Post*, June 7, 2004, accessed September 30, 2018, http://www.scmp.com/article/458500/push-defend-citys-core-values.

18. Carol A. G. Jones, *Lost in China? Law, Culture and Identity in Post-1997 Hong Kong* (Cambridge: Cambridge University Press, 2015), 2.

19. Ray Yep, "The Crusade against Corruption in Hong Kong in the 1970s: Governor MacLehose as a Zealous Reformer or Reluctant Hero?" *China Information* 7, no. 2 (2013): 197–221.

20. Jones, *Lost in China*, 25.

21. Ming Sing, *Hong Kong's Tortuous Democratization: A Comparative Analysis*. (New York: RoutledgeCurzon, 2004), 141; Kua Hsin-chi and Lau Siu-ka, "The Partial Vision of Democracy in Hong Kong: A Survey of Popular Opinion," *China Journal* 34 (1995): 239–64; and Wong Tsz Wai et al., "What Kind of Democracy Do Hong Kongers Support?" *Ming Pao*, July 26, 2014, accessed September 30, 2018, https://m.mingpao.com.

22. State Council, White Paper on "The Practice of the 'One Country, Two Systems' Policy in the Hong Kong Special Administrative Region, June 10, 2014, Section V (3), full text: http://www.scmp.com/news/hong-kong/article/1529167/full-text-practice-one-country-two-systems-policy-hong-kong-special.

23. Agnes S. Ku, "Negotiating the Space of Civil Autonomy in Hong Kong: Power, Discourses and Dramaturgical Representations," *China Quarterly* 179 (September 2004): 647–64.

24. Jones, *Lost in China*, 2015. These "law wars" include the 1999 case involving the right of abode for children born out of wedlock and those born before their parents became permanent Hong Kong residents; the 1998 case involving the defacement of the national flag; the antisubversion law in 2003; and the various NPCSC interpretations of democratic reform in 2004, 2005, and then 2014.

25. More than a thousand lawyers and barristers dressed in black participated in silent marches in downtown Hong Kong in 1999, 2005, 2014, and 2016 to protest China's legal interference, http://www.scmp.com/news/hong-kong/article/1541814/hong-kong-lawyers-stage-silent-march-oppose-beijings-white-paper; http://www.reuters.com/article/us-hong kong-china-lawyers-idUSKBN13315Q?il=0.

26. Ming Sing, "An Overview on Hong Kong's Politics and Government," in *Global Encyclopedia of Public Administration, Public Policy, and Governance*, ed. Ali Farazmand (New York: Springer, forthcoming).

27. Klavier Jie Ying Wang, "Mobilizing Resources to the Square: Hong Kong's Anti-Moral and National Education Movement as Precursor to the Umbrella Movement," *International Journal of Cultural Studies* 20, no. 2 (2017): 127–45; Karita Kan, "Lessons in Patriotism," *China Perspectives* no. 4 (2012): 63–69. See also the 2014 documentary *Lessons in Dissent*, by Matthew Torne.

28. In the onsite survey (N=1681) conducted by Samson Yuen and Edmund Cheng, 96 percent cited "genuine universal suffrage as the most important or important reason for their participation, http://www.chinafile.com/reporting-opinion/features/hong-kongs-umbrella-protests-were-more-just-student-movement. Another survey (N=1441) conducted by a civic group called Umbrellaprofiling also found 90 percent of respondents citing "genuine universal suffrage" as their motivation, https://docs.google.com/forms/d/17BHsKpLInRAKQ9vNTV9K2q2CpqGIxvisfBLUVRyHiyM/viewanalytics.

29. From a survey conducted among protesters by a Facebook group called Umbrellaprofiling https://docs.google.com/forms/d/17BHsKpLInRAKQ9vNTV9K2q2CpqGIxvisfBLUVRyHiyM/viewanalytics.

30. It was therefore inaccurate to see the 2014 Umbrella Movement as the revival of the 2011 Occupy Central, as suggested by David Graeber and Yuk Hui, "From Occupy Wall Street to Occupy Central: The Case of Hong Kong," *Los Angeles Review of Books*, October 14, 2014, https://lareviewofbooks.org/article/occupy-central-the-case-of-hong-kong/.

31. Alice Poon, *Land and the Ruling Class in Hong Kong* (Richmond, BC: A. Poon), 2005.

32. B. Wissink, S. Y. Koh, and R. Forrest, "Tycoon City: Political Economy, Real Estate and the Super-rich in Hong Kong," in R. Forrest, B. Wissink, and S. Y. Koh, *Cities and the Super-Rich: Real Estate, Elite Practices and Urban Political Economies* (London: Palgrave Macmillan, 2017), 229–52.

33. Wissink et al., "Tycoon City."

34. Prudence Ho, "Chinese Giants Are Taking Over Hong Kong," *Bloomberg*, June 6, 2017, accessed September 30, 2018, https://www.bloomberg.com/news/features/2017-06-06/chinese-giants-are-taking-over-hong-kong.

35. Yi-zheng Lian, "Red Capital in Hong Kong," *New York Times*, June 1, 2017, accessed September 30, 2018, https://www.nytimes.com/2017/06/01/opinion/red-capital-in-hong-kong-china-investment.html?_r=0.

36. State Council, White Paper on "The Practice of the 'One Country, Two Systems' Policy in the Hong Kong Special Administrative Region, June 10, 2014, Section IV (4), full text: http://www.scmp.com/news/hong-kong/article/1529167/full-text-practice-one-country-two-systems-policy-hong-kong-special.

37. Siu-Keung Cheung, "Reunification through Water and Food: The Other Battle for Lives and Bodies in China's Hong Kong Policy," *China Quarterly* 220 (2014): 1012–32.

38. According to one survey of the occupiers, 37 percent were below twenty-four years of age and 61 percent were under thirty. Students accounted for 26 percent of the participants, while 58 percent were white-collar employees and professionals; 55 percent reported having a bachelor's degree and 81 percent identified themselves as "Hong Kongers." Samson Yuen and Edmund Cheng, "Hong Kong's Umbrella Protests Were More Than Just a

Student Movement" *ChinaFile*, July 1, 2015, https://www.chinafile.com/reporting-opinion/features/hong-kongs-umbrella-protests-were-more-just-student-movement.

39. Steve Tsang, *A Modern History of Hong Kong* (London: I. B. Tauris, 2007), 48–50.

40. Christopher Munn, *Anglo-China: Chinese People and British Rule in Hong Kong 1841–1880* (Richmond, UK: Curzon, 2001), 3.

41. Ngok Ma, *Political Development*, 218.

42. Francis L. F. Lee and Joseph M. Chan, *Media, Social Mobilization, and Mass Protests in Postcolonial Hong Kong: The Power of a Critical Event* (New York: Routledge, 2011), chap. 2.

43. Lee and Chan, *Media, Social Mobilization*, 58.

44. Lee and Chan, *Media, Social Mobilization*, 63.

45. The Hong Kong press used term "the post-80s protesters" to describe the collective movement actors behind these campaigns. But it was a misnomer because the core activists came from different age cohorts, and there is no evidence showing that the post-1980s generation holds distinct political orientations as a group. See Chor-yung Cheung, "Hong Kong's Systemic Crisis of Governance and the Revolt of the 'Post-80s' Youths: the Anti-Express Rail Campaign," in *New Trends of Political Participation in Hong Kong*, ed. Joseph Y. S. Cheng (Hong Kong: City University of Hong Kong Press, 2014), 417–47.

46. Agnes S. Ku and Clarence Hong Chee Tsui, "The Global City as a Cultural Project: The Case of the West Kowloon Cultural District," in *Hong Kong Mobile: Making a Global Population*, ed. Helen F Siu and Agnes S. Ku (Hong Kong: Hong Kong University Press, 2008), 343–65; Agnes S. M. Ku, "Making Heritage in Hong Kong: A Case Study of the Central Police Station Compound," *China Quarterly* 202 (June 2010): 381–99.

47. Besides those reported here, other campaigns concerned the redevelopment of the Lee Tung Street or "wedding card" street, restoration of the Central Police Station, and "anti-reclamation and protect the harbor" in 2004.

48. Chor-yung Cheung, "Hong Kong's Systemic Crisis of Governance."

49. Agnes S. M. Ku, "Remaking Places and Fashioning an Opposition Discourse: Struggle over the Star Ferry Pier and Queen's Pier in Hong Kong," *Environment and Planning D: Society and Space* 30 (2012): 5–22, 12.

50. Ip Im Chong, *Nostalgia for the Present: The Past and Present State of Cultural Preservation* [in Chinese] (Hong Kong: Chinese University Press, 2010), 50.

51. Chor-yung Cheung, "Hong Kong's Systemic Crisis," 427–29.

52. Klavier Jie Ying Wong, "Mobilizing Resources to the Square: Hong Kong's Anti-Moral and National Education Movement as Precursor to the Umbrella Movement," *International Journal of Cultural Studies* 20, no. 2 (2017): 134.

53. Wong, "Mobilizing Resources," 136–37. The anti-express-rail movement was the first to use social media in mobilization, but it generated much less impact because mobile Internet was still not as prevalent as it would become.

54. "Lonely Planet's Best in Travel: Top 10 Cities for 2012," accessed September 30, 2018, https://www.lonelyplanet.com/travel-tips-and-articles/lonely-planets-best-in-travel-top-10-cities-for-2012/40625c8c-8a11-5710-a052-1479d277f54a; Antony Dapiran, *City of Protest: A Recent History of Dissent in Hong Kong.* (Melbourne: Penguin Specials, 2017).

55. For analyses of the many protests and campaigns prior to the Umbrella Movement that are not discussed in this chapter, see Daniel Garrett and Wing-chung Ho, "Hong Kong at the Brink: Emerging Forms of Political Participation in the New Social Movement," in *New Trends of Political Participation in Hong Kong*, ed. Joseph Y. S. Cheng (Hong Kong: City University of Hong Kong Press, 2014), 347–83; Agnes Ku, "Negotiating the Space of Civil Autonomy in Hong Kong: Power, Discourses, and Dramaturgical Representations," *China Quarterly* 179 (September 2004): 647–64; for campaign against the Northeast New

Territories Plan, see Tse Hiu Hin, "Contesting the Local: Identity Politics in Hong Kong" (MPhil thesis, Chinese University of Hong Kong, 2014).

56. Charles Tilly and Sidney Tarrow, *Contentious Politics* (New York: Oxford University Press, 2016), 89, correctly classified Hong Kong as an unstable hybrid regime.

57. For a journalistic account, see Jason Y. Ng, *Umbrellas in Bloom: Hong Kong's Occupy Movement Uncovered* (Hong Kong: Blacksmith Books, 2016).

58. Edmund W. Cheng and Wai-yin Chan, "Explaining Spontaneous Occupation: Antecedents and Contingencies in the Making of the Umbrella Movement," *Social Movement Studies* 6 (2017): table 3.

59. Graeme Robertson, *The Politics of Protests in Hybrid Regime: Managing Dissent in Post-Communist Russia* (New York: Cambridge University Press, 2010).

60. Wai-man Lam, "Changing Political Activism: Before and After the Umbrella Movement," in *Hong Kong 20 Years after the Handover: Emerging Social and Institutional Fractures After 1997*, ed. Brian C. H. Fong and Tai-Lok Lui (London: Palgrave, 2017).

61. Ngok Ma, "The Plebeian Moment and its Traces: Post-UM Professional Groups in Hong Kong." Paper presented at the conference on Sunflowers and Umbrellas: Social Movements, Expressive Practices, and Political Culture in Taiwan and Hong Kong, Berkeley, California, March 16–17, 2018.

62. Ray Yep and Robert Bickers, "Studying the 1967 Riots: An Overdue Project," in *May Days in Hong Kong: Riot and Emergency in 1967*, ed. Robert Bickers and Ray Yep (Hong Kong: Hong Kong University Press, 2009).

63. John Carroll, "A Historical Perspective: The 1967 Riots and the Strike-Boycott of 1925–26," in *May Days in Hong Kong: Riot and Emergency in 1967*, ed. Robert Bickers and Ray Yep (Hong Kong: Hong Kong University Press, 2009).

64. Joseph Y. S. Cheng, "The Tiananmen Incident and the Pro-Democracy Movement in Hong Kong," *China Perspectives* 2, no. 78 (2009): 91–100.

65. Ming Sing, *Hong Kong's Tortuous Democratization*, 116–17.

66. Lee and Chan, *Media, Social Mobilization*, 9.

67. Lee and Chan, *Media, Social Mobilization*, 12.

68. Edmund W. Cheng, "Street Politics in a Hybrid Regime: The Diffusion of Political Activism in Post-Colonial Hong Kong," *China Quarterly* 226 (2016): 383–406.

69. Lee and Chan, *Media, Social Mobilization*, 98.

70. Cheng and Chan, "Explaining Spontaneous Occupation."

71. Fei-fan Lin, "Today's Hong Kong, Today's Taiwan," *Foreign Policy*, October 1, 2014, accessed September 30, 2018, http://foreignpolicy.com/2014/10/01/todays-hong-kong-todays-taiwan; Tony Cheung, "The Sunflower and the Umbrella: Hong Kong Activists Travel to Taiwan, Call for Closer Ties, New Policies from Incoming Government," *South China Morning Post*, January 17, 2016, accessed September 30, 2018, http://www.scmp.com/news/hong-kong/politics/article/1901985/sunflower-and-umbrella-hong-kong-activists-travel-taiwan.

72. Goran Therborn, "The New Masses: Social Bases of Resistance," *New Left Review* 85 (Jan-Feb 2014): 7–16.

73. Kevan Harris, "Did Inequality Breed the Arab Uprisings? Social Inequality in the Middle East from a World Perspective," in *The Arab Revolution of 2011: A Comparative Perspective*, ed. Said Amir Arjomand (Albany: State University of New York Press, 2015) 87–112; Erdem Yoruk and Murat Yuksel, "Class and Politics in Turkey's Gezi Protests," *New Left Review* 89 (Sept–Oct 2014): 103–23.

74. Ruth Milkman, Stephanie Luce, and Penny Lewis, "Changing the Subject: A Bottom-up Account of Occupy Wall Street in New York City." 2013. https://www.russellsage.org/research/reports/occupy-wall-street-movement.

75. Manuel Castells, *Networks of Outrage and Hope: Social Movements in the Internet Age.* (Cambridge: Polity, 2012); Jeroen Gunning and Ilan Zvi Baron, *Why Occupy a Square? People, Protests and Movements in the Egyptian Revolution* (Oxford: Oxford University Press, 2014).

76. Yoruk and Yuksel, "Class and Politics," 104.

77. Milkman et al, "Changing the Subject," 22.

78. Gunning and Baron, *Why Occupy a Square?* 164–65.

79. Milkman et al., "Changing the Subject."

80. Asef Bayat, *Revolutions without Revolutionaries: Making Sense of the Arab Spring* (Stanford, CA: Stanford University Press, 2017).

81. Sebastian Veg, "Legalistic and Utopian: Hong Kong's Umbrella Movement," *New Left Review* 92 (Mar-Apr 2015): 55–73.

2

PREFIGURATIVE POLITICS OF THE UMBRELLA MOVEMENT

An Ethnography of Its Promise and Predicament

Alex Yong Kang Chow

The Umbrella Movement was a popular struggle to demand constitutional and electoral reforms. But like other occupy movements in recent years, it was also an instance of prefigurative politics. If the slogan "I want genuine universal suffrage" articulated the former, "No general assembly, only the masses" expressed the protesters' experimentation with the latter.

Prefigurative politics refers to political actions or movements in which political ideals are experimentally realized in the "here and now," in which activists attempt to construct aspects of the ideal society envisioned in the present, rather than waiting for them to be realized in a distant future. It means that political principles are embodied in current behavior, not put on hold until the time is deemed right for them to be deployed. Thus, in prefigurative practices, the means applied are deemed to embody or "mirror" the ends one strives to realize.[1] "The most distinctive feature of prefiguration is the emphasis on experimentation," the "willingness to explore alternatives, to create anew, to depart from and subvert conventions." Its ethos is the Gandhian principle "to be the change you want to see in the world."[2]

The occupation of Tahrir Square in Cairo during the 2011 Egypt revolution was a well-documented case of prefigurative politics that would reappear in other occupy movements. People cocreated many prefigurative practices in the square that "housed a complete alternative society under construction."[3] The occupiers distributed food, provided health care and first aid, improvised field hospitals, fortified barricades, wrote and circulated journals and pamphlets, published press releases on social media, and set up a radio station. In a nutshell, participants "formulated, realized, tested, improvised, and discussed" these political ideals as a "prefigurative experiment."[4] Other occupations, van de Sande argued, such as Indignados in Spain, the Israeli social justice protest movement, and Occupy Wall Street, gradually advocated a more explicitly prefigurative strategy.[5]

In this chapter, I will demonstrate how the occupied zone in Admiralty, one of Hong Kong's central business districts and the location of the Hong Kong government headquarters, was such a prefigurative "social [laboratory] for the production of alternative democratic values, discourse, and practices."[6] People did not only act "as if one is already free."[7] They also practiced a "do it together" culture that emphasized prefigurative participatory democracy, a collective sense of community resistance, and an alternative urban community. But the heralded political culture had conflicting values that were both amplified, contested, and, sometimes, synthesized. Analyzing the everyday culture of the seventy-nine-day occupation through the lens of prefigurative politics, I show two salient dynamics that propelled and fractured the movement. First, occupiers built an alternative urban commons that embraced equality, sharing, and solidarity in everyday life, envisioning a utopian socioeconomic order different from the existing one in Hong Kong. Second, throughout the movement, occupiers and leaders struggled with the idea and practice of leadership. The predicament of ambivalent, ambiguous, and fragmented leadership in what some protesters deemed a "leaderless" movement led to indecision at several critical junctures of the movement.

This ethnographic account is based on my participation in the movement as the spokesperson of the Hong Kong Federation of Students, the leading student organization during the occupation. From the beginning, the Occupy movement faced structural tensions and built-in dilemmas. From its attempts to resolve them came the movement's dynamics. As a key member of the Occupy movement, I am able to provide a close observation of the dynamics that concerned the leading organizations, generated the attempts to consolidate an effective leadership, and hindered the progress of the movement. Since I am also part of the decision-making body, I should add a caveat that this chapter is written from the position of a leader in the movement. It might still contain blind spots after a thorough examination by myself and others. I personally have sympathy for most of the parties in the movement, and I am particularly aware of the limited options and agency the student bodies and others had due to extraordinary circumstances. My position might tilt in favor of the students. That said, the analysis and reflections are based on the dialogue with many movement participants to re-evaluate the achievement and the limitation of the occupation. The most challenging dilemma I found is not a person's positionality, but whether the dynamic can be understood within a wider historical context. I attempted to place the tension, the effort, and the constraint in their own context to produce a meaningful analysis and reflection. The Umbrella Movement is a symptom as well as a response to the challenges posed to the democracy movement. It deserves a more nuanced analysis that captures the dynamics between the structure and the agency. This chapter, therefore, is written in the hope of explaining the rupture and connection between the leaders and the occupiers and of elucidating the dialectic and symbiotic performance and relationship between the traditional leaders, the informal leaders, and the occupiers.

An Alternative Urban Commons

The Umbrella Movement was not explicitly anticapitalist. But the prefiguration of an alternative urban commons during the occupation did express a collective desire for economic exchanges based on reciprocity, solidarity, and sustainability. Some protesters who preferred a more militant approach to the movement criticized these communal practices in the occupied zone as misguided distractions; but to others, experimentation with an alternative urban governance and way of life was an integral part of the movement. Several onsite surveys revealed that about one-third of the occupiers mentioned rising socioeconomic inequality as one of the grievances motivating their participation. This sentiment was reflected in the Hong Kong Federation of Students' declaration, issued during the weeklong class boycott right before the onset of the Umbrella Movement.[8] It assailed the "return" to Chinese sovereignty as a "recolonization" by the "party-state-capitalists bloc" and asserted that the combination of capitalistic exploitation and colonial rule had deprived Hong Kong people of time (as there is no law regulating maximum working hours), of space (as private space, real estate is too expensive, thus homes tend to be tiny and overcrowded, and public space has been increasingly commercialized), and of power and resources in the face of the many corporate monopolies in every aspect of Hong Kong people's daily lives, from transportation to supermarkets and mass media.[9] Even though most students did not share such a radical critique of capitalism in Hong Kong, and the HKFS's critique of economic polarization quickly subsided once the masses joined the occupation, the everyday street culture during the occupation did express a yearning for a different organization of the socioeconomic order.

During the movement, the occupied zones functioned in many ways like a utopian participatory democratic community. Poet Liu Wai Tong called the occupied zones Umtopia. These treasured temporary autonomous zones were wonderful places suspended from regimented time and space. Occupy participants in Admiralty, Mongkok, and Causeway Bay transformed multilane freeways and urban streets into habitable communities.[10] In early October, after the students made an appeal to the occupiers to bring the tents over, tent settlements spontaneously emerged in Admiralty. According to a survey during the movement, 2,348 tents were set up in Admiralty on November 1, about a month after the occupation began.[11] Many supporters donated tents to the occupied zone so people could get a tent onsite if they did not bring their own. Campers decorated their tents and named them in ways related to the movement: "I love HK," "Living in Truth," "Universal Suffrage Road, No. 2014," "D7689."[12] The occupiers also renamed the occupied zone in Admiralty as the Umbrella Square. Some even self-identified as "villagers" and gave a name to their cluster of tents, such as "the orange village," to show respect to an occupier wearing an orange headscarf and taking up the leading role in the square. Interestingly, postal workers could deliver mail to a correspondent's address in the occupied community. Spatially, these tents marked a nascent space with no strict urban rules imposed, readily open for collective imagination and improvisation.

During the prolonged occupation, occupiers had to build various communal facilities and infrastructure to satisfy people's everyday needs. Occupants set up supplementary electricity and lighting, advanced their craftsmanship through mentor-training, organized art, cultural and leisure activities, designated places for studying and reading, maintained public hygiene, cleaning, and recycling. They developed a system to share food and other material resources. For example, a group of office ladies turned the nearby public toilets into powder rooms stocked with overwhelming donations of feminine napkins, skin care products, and other beauty products. Volunteers kept the toilets clean when the government's subcontracting company ceased to maintain them. Occupiers also constructed an umbrella bathroom furnished with a bathtub, curtain, shower, and water supply.

Using reclaimed wood materials, occupiers built and placed staircases for people to climb over the three-foot-high concrete median strip in the middle of multilane roads. At peak hours, volunteers staffed both sides of the median and offered their hands to assist pedestrians with the crossing. To allow the many secondary school and university students to continue their studies during the weeks and months of occupation, and for any citizen to do leisure reading, a study room and a library were built. The library shelves were self-made and stocked with books ranging from politics, economy, and literature to cooking and manga. A self-study area was designated with a seating capacity of two hundred people, equipped with large communal tables and strong free Wi-Fi. To provide lighting to the study room, occupiers designed a generator powered by stationary exercise bicycles and a wind turbine. Free mobile phone charges were also available for whoever needed them.

Reciprocity was a norm permeating different aspects of occupation life. Craftsmen organized carpentry, sewing, leather, and metal workshops to teach occupiers how to make ribbons, T-shirts, umbrellas, political pennants, and banners related to the movement. Some occupiers volunteered as teachers to tutor students in the self-study room for different subjects. A group of environmentalists ran a station to collect recycled materials and use them to make batteries, plastic boxes, metal wires, erasers, and fruit wrappers. Others offered green and health education, including the 4R (reduce, recycle, reuse, and replace) principle of waste reduction. As the air quality improved in the car-free occupation zone, citizens seized the moment and came out to walk their pets.[13]

Self-organized groups improvised to provide security and defense, transportation, food, medical support, even psychological counseling. Defense teams were a response to the shock of police violence and were formed as much out of indignation as necessity to safeguard the occupied zones and to protect occupiers. They set up barricades to prevent the police, gangsters and anti-occupation supporters from assaulting or infiltrating the zones. Others formed groups to manage the supplies stations to receive and distribute resources, such as umbrellas, raincoats, food and drinks, and first-aid medications. Around ten first-aid booths organized by doctors, nurses, medical students, and other citizens were also set up in early October to provide first aid and psychological support. At one point, a dozen parents formed "Umbrella Parents" to protect and support their children and to accompany their kids to the occupied zone. One local restaurant owner delivered hundreds of meal boxes freely to Admiralty each day. A radio DJ recruited volunteers to cook and distribute meals to occupiers. Housewives served homemade soup or sweet soup to occupiers. A group of volunteers even planted tomatoes, potatoes, choy sum, and other vegetable, including in the cleavage of asphalt road of Admiralty. This urban farming experiment suggested a radical alternative to Hong Kong's extreme dependency on external food imports and the possibility of redesigning the landscape of the urban commons. These urban farmers even put up a banner arguing for a return of agricultural power to the citizens and a sustainable and equitable land policy. In a nutshell, occupiers utilized the occupied public spaces to forge reciprocal practices and communal initiatives envisioning a potential community that embraced the culture of do-it-together, collective well-being, fair and sustainable food production, and a clean environment.

Prefigurative politics also encompassed textual, visual, and aesthetic practices. Many iconic installation artworks in Admiralty cocreated by artists and ordinary citizens—from chalk art on the grounds and road surfaces to countless umbrella-made installations, such as the Umbrella Man, the Large Yellow Umbrella, the tree of Umbrella, a constellation of Umbrellas from a hundred families—all acknowledged the courage of the people to transform the streetscape into a place of community creativity (see chapter 9). The colorful Lennon Wall and the Water Horse Wall were spaces for citizens to display Post-it notes expressing their hopes and criticisms about politics and Hong Kong; the Wall of Shame displayed dark humor against the establishment; the add-oil machine was a wall on which messages from around the world were projected at night to empower the people.[14] Many banners with slogans in different languages were hung on the Harcourt Road flyover, many of which were responses to the topics that were often debated during the occupation.

On another level, publication, posters, stickers, songs, paintings, and photographs were produced to circulate ideas and to facilitate communication. A group of students self-published a magazine, *Recap*, to document the events and stories during the occupation.[15] Protesters composed songs and performed them on the big stage at Admiralty, like the preteen indie band Big Boyz Club, joined by famous pop stars such as Deanie Ip, Denise Ho, and Anthony Wong. Some artists used art to spark discussion and communication among occupiers. An Italian artist invited passersby to write their hopes on his painting of Hong Kong's skyscrapers. The idea was to embed everyone's good will into Hong Kong's cityscape and to present a future scenario of Hong Kong with people's ideas. Another example was the "I Am the Chief Executive" photographing event, reproducing a set of photos for occupiers that Chun-ying Leung, the then chief executive, had taken. A group of advertising designers, cultural workers, photographers, and documentary filmmakers took photos of occupiers, asking them to pose as the then chief executive and requested the participants to present a platform as if they were running in the election to be the head of Hong Kong. Through these "performative" occupations, Umbrella occupiers symbolically reclaimed their right to the city's space, time, and future, and they empowered the participants through artistic creation and expression. This was a collective rebuilding of the sense of entitlement and belonging through everyday habitations of public space/time.

Unlike many one-off rallies where participants just came and went without engagement with each other, deliberations were crucial parts of everyday life in occupied zones. Apart from the countless internal meetings held by self-organized groups to review their everyday operation, many platforms were built to share personal stories and to discuss strategies and postoccupy goals. Countless people prefigured an alternative civic life that allowed for attentive listening, expressions of emotion, and rational contemplations of the movement.

In Admiralty, the HKFS had a chitchat booth that ran from early October till the end of the occupation. The booth not only functioned as a place for social gathering, material storage, and volunteers recruitment, but it also served the purpose of discussing various topics and inviting people to brainstorm strategies and tactics. Students and grassroots organizers of the chitchat group would visit villagers at night and engage them in discussions that would last from half an hour to several hours. Political parties also set up their own platforms, such as "Democracy Square," to deliberate on themes such as the Umbrella Movement, finance and the economy, methods to get along with family members who had different political views, the means to enhance democratic participation through district council election, the relationship between democracy and housing, labor, and planning policies, the delegation's visit to the United Nation's human rights committee, etc. In the meantime, some occupiers conducted a daily survey for people to discuss immediate matters arising from the occupation. Some would even organize occupiers to move beyond the occupied zone to other nonoccupied communities for dialogue and to encourage supporters to eat out in neighboring local restaurants as a gesture of mutual support and compensation.

From the pre-occupation class boycotts, occupiers wanted to practice effective, equal, and mutually respecting debate, learning, and discussion. More than one hundred seminars were held during the five-day students' strike. Speakers, mostly academics, professionals, and NGO workers, were required to make the sharing sessions as concise as possible to allow time for dialogue. The aim was to maintain a more democratic power relation between speakers and listeners, rather than one-way teaching. The Umbrella Movement continued this practice in the form of the Mobile Democracy Classroom and the Siu Lai Democracy Classroom, both organized by teachers, professional, social workers, and volunteers. For the Mobile Democracy Classroom, the volunteers were responsible for the design of the classroom. As a core volunteer recalled, the goals of the classroom were to support students and demonstrate the spirit of democracy movement. To appeal to different audiences, plurality was a key to the selection of themes. Therefore, the only requirement for speakers was that their talks were related to democracy. As a result, the topics of classrooms ranged from spirituality and resistance, mathematical thinking and social justice, and the way documentaries transformed society to the development of political thought, the rule of law and society, history, literature and movies, and sexual minorities.

On the other hand, the Siu Lai Democracy Classroom stressed the importance of listening and rational response. The organizers found that although some occupiers were willing to express themselves, they were not accustomed to listening to others and constructive dialogue. Therefore, after a person expressed one's thought, the hosts would summarize it to facilitate the dialogue. Both classrooms were prefigurative experiments in which new political ideals were formulated, realized, tested, improvised, and discussed. Debates turned confrontational and rowdy at times, but such "public space strengthens a democratic polity by providing a forum for dissenting views."[16] Deliberation enhanced trust, knowledge circulation, and consensus building, and participants learned to handle conflicts and dissent. The democratic commons gave voice to a diverse cross-section of the population: old, young, uneducated, highly educated, professionals, poor, rich, immigrants, LGBTQ, and people of all faiths and ethnicities. They awoke their buried civic subjectivity and agency for public participation and the collective political project.

Not everyone was enthusiastic about the emergent urban commons. Yes, this experiment could possibly transform the thoughts and habits of many people as they participated in equal, fair, and reciprocal economic production and consumption in environmentally friendly and sustainable ways, and engaged in equal and mutually respecting social relations. But the temporary autonomous zone was a disturbance to many local residents, and there was always a risk that the police or gangsters would raid and demolish the occupied zones. Drunken brawls and quarrels also happened and the marshals had to patrol and mediate conflicts, especially at night. Another dark side of the movement consisted of physical, verbal, and cyber sexual assaults by occupiers and opponents. Discussions of gender, queer/sexuality, and biopolitics were interwoven in the movement, but insufficient attention and respect were paid to women and sexual minorities as members of a democratic community. Discourses that reinforced stereotypes of masculinity and femininity were not uncommon on social media, including such sentiments as "men go to Mong Kok, women stay in Admiralty," or "men who have defended Mong Kok are real men."[17]

Many protesters saw the occupy commons as too toothless and soft to extract any concession from the government. To those who longed for militant action, the sharing and singing in the occupied zone was a self-indulgent, feel-good distraction from the real political battle facing the movement. The emergence of these two approaches to social change in Hong Kong—generating pressure on the power elite by confrontational political action or nurturing everyday practices conducive to a democratic, equal, fair, free, just, and compassionate society—would outlive the Umbrella Movement. Adherents of each of these strategies have continued their fight in the postoccupation era.

Leadership in a Leaderless Movement?

Other than experimenting with an alternative urban commons, prefigurative politics during the Umbrella Movement also strived for a model of leadership that was compatible with the movement's democratic aspirations. The practice of leadership was a particularly thorny issue in occupy movements that celebrated horizontalism and inclusiveness, for these principles could hamper effective decision making and therefore the success of mobilization. As one of the student leaders, I personally observed up close the appeal and the challenge of realizing collaborative leadership. There were three major difficulties. First, many occupiers were self-mobilized participants unattached to any organization, with no loyalty, trust, or allegiance to any individuals or organizations that later emerged as leaders during the seventy-nine days of occupation. When the movement dragged on with no tangible results, the participants became skeptical of these leaders. The use of digital communication for mass self-mobilization meant that organizers had no idea who the participants were. Even though organic coordination happened in the occupied zones, where different new social circles formed and informal leaders emerged, polycentric leadership and tenuous connections between the masses and the leaders would come to fragment the movement from within as it unfolded.

The second difficulty was the pre-existing fragmentation of the opposition camp. Beijing has imposed on Hong Kong an election system that was intended to stymie the development of political parties. Proportional representation allows small parties to win seats, thus fracturing the opposition into multiple candidate lists and increasing internal competition.[18] For instance, by 2012, two years before the occupation, the legislative election returned twenty-eight pan-democrats who belonged to eleven different political organizations. Also, due to the lack of progress in democratization after the handover, aging leadership, routinization of protest repertoires, and the failure of the opposition to influence policy making, public distrust of the pan-democratic opposition was prevalent and extended into the Umbrella Movement.[19] According to a survey conducted during the movement, only 7.6 percent stated that political parties were their ideal leaders, while 40.5 percent and 31.8 percent preferred the student organizations or self-organized leadership, respectively.[20]

Aside from the opposition political parties, the most likely leaders of the protests would have been the Occupy Central trio: the two academics Chan Kin-man and Benny Tai and the pastor Chu Yiu-ming, who initiated a campaign called Occupy Central with Love and Peace (OCLP) a year and a half before the occupations. They vowed to organize a mass occupation of the central business district if Beijing refused to grant genuine universal suffrage in the 2017 election of the chief executive. But from the beginning, the leadership was ambivalent. On the one hand, Benny Tai emphasized that they were not leaders but "facilitators," whose job was to listen, to be humane, humble, inclusive, synergistic, and creative to integrate different ideas.[21] They organized the first deliberation day as a means to build a new platform for a wide spectrum of opposition groups to resolve differences, but they delegated the organization of the subsequent ones to different community groups: university students, teachers, social workers, women, labor groups, finance professionals, churches, and patients groups. On the other hand, some radical democrats and some grassroots organizations, including the League of Social Democrats and Scholarism, felt they were excluded, and they criticized OCLP for not being inclusive and proactive enough to leverage its influence to extract concessions from Beijing.

The failure to form an inclusive decision-making platform during the OCLP campaign was the third difficulty that would haunt the Umbrella Movement. Disagreements on strategies among major constituencies of the OCLP were never resolved. During the pre–Umbrella Movement stage, some activists and I realized that OCLP's major tactic was not to achieve a democratic transition through occupation, but was to use occupation as a bargaining chip to threaten the Beijing government. Benny Tai publicly articulated this thought in a media interview after OCLP launched an unofficial referendum on various schemes of nomination for the election of the chief executive.[22] People who belonged to the action groups under OCLP also told me that OCLP spent little time in planning the occupation scene and operational protocols. It was reasonable to say that the first two stages, the deliberation days and the referendum, exhausted most of OCLP's energy. Only in the face of internal tension did OCLP begin strategizing the operational protocols for the occupation and lay down five guidelines for occupiers who participated in the dry run of the occupation.[23] This ironically resulted in contemptuous responses online and among some allies, including the students and social workers. Meanwhile, the radical democrats, namely the League of Social Democrats, demanded that OCLP reform the decision-making body to incorporate more organizations in the process. The advice, nonetheless, was declined by OCLP. Consequently, the preceding uneasy relationship between OCLP, the radical democrats, the moderate democrats, the students, and the grassroots organizations extended into the Umbrella Movement and obstructed the functioning of what would later be the leadership body, the so-called Five-Party Platform—HKFS, Scholarism, pan-democrats, OCLP, and a pan-alliance of NGOs from civil society.

Leadership Unraveled: The Five-Party Platform, Mainstage, and Marshals

Initially, HKFS and OCLP reached a consensus that the occupation would start after the student's strike. But the two groups did not have any well-functioned mechanism to communicate, make decisions, and plan strategies together, and they were rivals in any case. When students, eager to jump-start the occupation, decided to occupy the civic square on September 26th, the two sides did not have any agreement about when to announce the beginning of Occupy Central. There was also no backup plan for effective leadership when students leaders were all arrested. Rumors complicated the situation. At midnight of September 28th, after eighty-seven cans of tear gas had been thrown into the street, students and OCLP advised people to retreat from the occupied zone because there was a rumor that rubber bullets would be used. The occupiers, however, remained firmly on the site, defying the leaders' command to withdraw. In the end no rubber bullet was fired, but the credibility of the purported leaders had been undermined. Although the concept of facilitator was appealing and idealistic, the lack of a clear chain of command and the resultant poor coordination between the students and OCLP severely impaired the capacity for direct action.

With the leadership under siege, maintaining a balance between security maintenance and democratic openness became problematic. For instance, because marshals were mostly volunteers of OCLP and sent from the Five-Party Platform, some occupiers criticized them for betraying the students and obstructing the movement. The Five-Party Platform leaders thus decided that marshals should not be wearing OCLP patches, and these volunteers were soon substituted with a new team of marshals consisting of members from the NGOs, the political parties, and the student organizations. Later, only students wearing HKFS and Scholarism T-shirts were accepted as the legitimate mediators and picketers.

These gestures did not stop many occupiers from criticizing the marshals, the OCLP trio, the two student organizations, and the Five-Party Platform as an authoritarian group whose "mainstage" (the platform from which people made speeches to the crowd in Admiralty) controlled everything and obstructed any direct action to bring about real changes. Some occupiers accused the leaders of monopolizing the microphone, depriving them of their right to address the occupiers, and for not relaying the details of confrontation in the front line and mustering support for occupiers confronting the police. In the eyes of these critics, most of the activities in Admiralty weakened the militancy of the movement by romanticizing the occupation as a peaceful utopia where people sang, enjoyed carnivalistic spectacles, and slept in the tents instead of fighting the police like their counterparts in Mongkok (see chapter 3). On November 21, a group of these critical occupiers, who self-organized through the Internet and sought to dismantle the mainstage, surrounded the stage and demanded that the leaders dismiss all the marshals. By then, there were many accusations that the marshals stalled the escalation of actions, assaulted other occupiers, and colluded with police to arrest protesters. By that time, these proescalation occupiers had taken things into their own hands by breaking into the LegCo Building. In light of such dissent, student leaders invited all the occupiers to contemplate and deliberate the matter by abandoning the "mainstage" and moving to a new stage outside the civic square, where discussions lasted till the middle of the night. No concrete resolution was proposed, however, and many issues remained unresolved.

These examples illustrate that as an extension of the democracy movement and the Occupy Central movement, the Umbrella Movement inherited the limitations of both: a fragmented opposition camp that could not resolve conflict and create a united front. The inability to formulate mechanisms of decision making was the Achilles' heel of the occupations. Take the simple act of voting. Within the Five-Party Platform, political parties could not reach a consensus on how to count votes. Did the pan-democrats count as a whole? But many did not consider moderate democrats and radical democrats as belonging to the same camp. Was it then better to assign each political party a vote? But doing so would allow political parties to claim more votes than other groups in the platform. On top of this, some NGOs were reluctant to share power with OCLP because they felt that they had been excluded in the pre–Umbrella Movement stage and could not trust OCLP.

Within HKFS, there was a discussion about whether pan-democrats and OCLP were trustworthy. Although HKFS did not vote down the proposal to share power with pan-democrats and OCLP, some members doubted the need to do so. Not every members of HKFS deemed it essential to create a mechanism to foster a formal decision-making process. Furthermore, when the student representatives disagreed or had reservation over the proposals made by the pan-democrats and OCLP, a recurring question would arise: Would HKFS be misrepresented by the pan-democrats and OCLP? Should HKFS take a firm stand and clarify the misunderstanding? The students usually did not ask the question explicitly, but the tension was prolonged if not intensified.[24] Radical democrats and NGOs were usually on the students' side.[25] In contrast, pan-democrats and OCLP found that HKFS was uncooperative and reluctant to share power with them, and to make "the right decision": to retreat from the occupied zones. These parties held different strategic priorities not merely on the deployment of tactics, but also on whether the supporters of respective groups agreed with their leader's decisions, which exerted indirect pressure on their leaders in the decision-making process. Every party had different core supporters in and beyond the occupy zones.

The conflict over "square voting" proved to be even more detrimental and consequential. In mid-October, after the dialogue between HKFS and the government ended in a deadlock, the majority of HKFS member unions decided to give up the idea of dialogue and seek a more advocacy- and action-oriented strategy. At the time, Benny Tai of OCLP proposed to conduct a civic square (Admiralty) vote for participants to endorse or reject the idea of reassuming negotiations with the government. If successful, such voting could be replicated in the occupied zones for further decision making. Other parties expressed concern regarding the scale and technical problem of the voting system (e.g., how not to be hijacked by nonoccupiers and how to avoid the misperception among occupiers that the vote was an exit mechanism). Besides, OCLP wanted to execute the voting only in Admiralty, but students and grassroots organizations pointed out the risk of not including Mongkok and Causeway Bay. Still, some parties rejected the idea of a square vote, insisting that the Five-Party Platform was only a consultative and communication platform with no mandate to make decisions and that each party could act upon its own will.

While bickering about voting mechanisms and procedure dragged on, student leaders and their constituencies confronted the challenge of sustaining their mobilization capacity and of scaling up action. Student leaders did not have the experience and skills to handle the massive student turnout during the first few days of the occupations. HKFS spent most of its time and energy negotiating with the Five-Party Platform, coordinating with occupiers across three occupation zones, all under the constant threat of assault by gangsters and the police. As a result, HKFS was disconnected from the students on campus and was only able to maintain minimal communication with its member unions.

Disputes over leadership were an everyday occurrence. One incident happened in early October. While the pan-democrats faced pressure and felt it would be wiser to reopen Admiralty Road, the few occupiers who were stationed in the road also recognized the burden when insufficient occupiers concentrated there. Then, pan-democrats asked HKFS to deliberate with the occupiers. Both parties agreed that they could reopen the road on the condition that the government reopened the Civic Square. The decision was much criticized by those who saw the combined scale of the occupied zones as the Umbrella Movement's most powerful bargaining chip in pressuring the government. The proposal to reopen Admiralty seemed like a suicidal act to some. These occupiers claimed that they were not consulted, while others questioned the right of anyone to give up a road and shrink the occupied zone.

Other times disputes were miraculously resolved by the principle of no-leadership. In mid-November, when the court granted the injunction for the police to clear particular zones, including the area outside Tim Mei Road, the defense team wanted to save the barriers for other use, rather than letting them be confiscated by the bailiffs. Both the Five-Party Platform and the occupiers consented to the early removal of the barriers. Nonetheless, when the occupiers removed the barriers, a group of university students said they were not consulted before the action was taken. In the end, a HKFS volunteer who acted as the mediator made the argument that everyone should have the right to act upon one's will and no one could stop others from taking or not taking down the barriers.

Although some occupiers did attempt to build a bottom-up decision-making body, no inclusive participatory process was put in place to facilitate coalition building and effective collaborative leadership. In the beginning of the movement, some occupiers of a booth station tried to elect their own representatives. They were heavily criticized online and gave up the plan. Other occupiers and students tried again when they found the communication between groups was insufficient and wanted to pre-empt the circulation of rumors. Some occupiers, however, did not want to institutionalize the practice or be the representatives of the movement or of a collective decision. Turning themselves into representatives or spokespersons, they deemed, was too risky if individuals were targeted and attacked by the authorities.

Besides the struggles surrounding the issue of leadership, protracted occupations easily succumbed to the social and economic pressures exerted on protesters and groups. Before the Mongkok occupation zone was cleared, occupiers making up the defense team told HKFS that they could not continue the occupation until mid-December because many of them had to resume work after months of unemployment. By that time, HKFS had made an abortive attempt to go to Beijing,[26] and noncooperation actions such as a general strike and class boycotts failed to take off. Furthermore, students and the pan-democrats could not reach a consensus on if a de facto referendum would be put forward.[27]

The Umbrella Movement was waning in energy and support. After Mongkok was taken down by the authorities, the only alternative left to keep the movement alive was to escalate the action at Admiralty by surrounding the government headquarters on November 30. Informed by the occupiers that, regardless of students' final decision, some impatient participants had planned an imminent violent action against the government, students felt the need to mediate the anger and direct it for a good cause. The students, therefore, decided to take the lead, organize the action in a nonviolent fashion, and yet be flexible about frontline confrontation with the police. Tragically, since no firm alliance and decision-making body had been created in the preceding two months, HKFS and Scholarism could only connect with a few radical democrats and grassroots organizations to plan the action. Many of the students' strike committees were already inoperative. Most importantly, the students failed to include many informal leaders in their action-planning meetings for a well-coordinated strategy, even as the police had escalated their use of violence after two months of nonstop confrontation. In the end, the escalation failed and caused many injuries since the coordination and planning were poor.[28] The students realized that they could only rebuild the movement by building stronger trust with occupiers. While Scholarism launched a hunger strike, HKFS spent the rest of the time visiting and apologizing to the occupiers. By mid-December, students were able to persuade the defense group not to engage in militant confrontation but to end the movement in a civilly disobedient way. But the feeling of anger, distrust, frustration, and discontent also reached a zenith, disempowering many young people and further splitting occupiers into many clusters.

In a nutshell, the birth of the Five-Party Platform and the rethinking of a bottom-up decision-making body were attempts to build a collective leadership, which ultimately and unfortunately failed dismally. Since the legitimacy of leadership and the decision-making body remained unresolved issues throughout the movement, leaders spent much time negotiating with each other through the Five-Party Platform, which was a closed system with no binding power and created distrust among many occupiers toward their leadership. Such a trust deficiency tied the hands of the leaders, who could at best only act as nominal leaders with limited connection to many occupiers. A vicious circle then perpetuated itself. People had doubt about such a closed system, making it difficult for the Five-Party Platform to operate or reach a consensus when it was most needed. In short, fragmented leadership, the masses' culture of self-mobilization, and a yearning for a more egalitarian political process that would also deliver outcomes were some of the major contradictions at the heart of the event of 2014, and perhaps other recent occupy movements as well.

Beyond Occupy

This chapter argues that the relationship between the fragmented leadership and self-mobilized participants was a pivotal weakness of the Umbrella Movement. But this problem has entrenched roots in Hong Kong's semidemocratic political system and liberal capitalist economic order. Citizens lack the experience to produce an effective, participatory, and adaptable leadership that some occupiers wished had happened during the occupation. People are not comfortable critiquing Hong Kong's hierarchical, competition-driven socioeconomic system, and some occupiers even agreed with pro-establishment critics that the occupation was detrimental to ordinary citizens' livelihood. Is occupation a bomb designed to disrupt the political-economic order so as to pressure the authorities to yield and agree to political reform? Or should the goal of occupation be to incubate a new political-economic vision and culture? Can the two ideas coexist? The participants did not deliberate much on these questions before the occupation and no consensus was ever reached after the occupation was underway. To many people, political reform alone was sufficient to ensure a fair, just, healthy, and competitive society. In the eyes of many occupiers, Hong Kong people would not be willing to sacrifice too much of their economic and social interest for democracy in the long run. The Umbrella Movement, thus, was a one-off battle, a last chance. Some occupiers therefore scorned the social experiment in the occupied zones as demoralizing and noncombative. Militant escalation of direct action was the only pragmatic tactic, because there was no alternative to counter the ruthless dictators and still retain momentum among the occupiers. This mentality is the result of the dominant political-economic order, which has not changed since the end of British colonialism. In view of the built-in pessimism of this idea, neither the occupiers nor the activists were capable of coping in a democratic way with the challenges in order to build trust, to navigate or prioritize the achievable goals, to strategize accordingly, and to restructure the organization of the movement. When Beijing and the Hong Kong government adopted delay tactics, the unresolved conflict and socioeconomic pressure overwhelmed the occupiers. The agency of occupiers, politicians, and activists were constrained by the wider socioeconomic structure.

To trace the cause of such a structural hurdle, one cannot but direct one's attention to the past. In what way did colonial and postcolonial governance not only dictate the political development, but also shape the democracy movement and mold people's understanding and practice of leadership strategies?[29] This important question is beyond the scope of this chapter, but it is relevant to the understanding of the ambivalent nature of the leadership of the Umbrella Movement and is pertinent to the development of future social movements. To address it, one has to extend the inquiry from the political to the social, cultural, and economic arenas to gauge the intersection of social movements and the everyday experience of the public in the colonial and postcolonial eras. From there, another landscape might come into the horizon and open up space for us to rethink the dialectic and symbiotic processes between formal political institutions, prefigurative politics, and socioeconomic change in the long run, including the interrelation of power, control, liberation, and everyday life. More nuanced analyses are needed to untangle the impact of economic inequality, colonial education, urban-rural development, welfare policies, and colonial and neo/postcolonial governance on leadership and social movements.

In spite of the unresolved challenges, the struggle to realize an alternative urban commons and the struggle over collaborative leadership have persisted since the Umbrella Movement. For example, the back-to-the-communities movement seeks to rebuild the foundation of a democratic culture through a bottom-up approach. There has been a blossoming of many new community-based organizations and professional groups committed to running community newspapers, leading community events and advocacies in the postoccupation stage, and proposing initiatives for more local handicraft productions, local markets, book stores, and street markets. Some people ran for District Council and

LegCo elections to implement the democratic project and amplify their influence on community advocacies and urban policies. In those elections, participants would not only think how to push forward democratic reform in different regards, they would also study the participatory practice elsewhere, like Spain's Podemos, to test if an online discussion platform could be established to facilitate mass participation. The OCLP leader, Benny Tai, proposed new schemes to encourage and coordinate candidates and to plan for strategic voting in local elections. Some occupiers sought to rebuild connections across political camps, while others sought spiritual guidance and mindfulness practice to contemplate the meaning of politics and forms of leadership compatible with the everyday practice of democracy. These experimental pursuits might not provide an immediate remedy to the dilemma of democracy and leadership. But the quest for a more visionary, decisive, responsive, and collaborative leadership and a resilient urban future have definitely continued in the postoccupation era.

NOTES

1. Mona Baker, ed., *Translating Dissent: Voices from and with the Egyptian Revolution* (London: Routledge, 2016); Marianne Maeckelbergh, *The Will of the Many, How the Alterglobalisation Movement Is Changing the Face of Democracy* (London: Pluto Press, 2009).

2. Baker, *Translating Dissent*, 6.

3. Mathijs van de Sande, "Fighting with Tools: Prefiguration and Radical Politics in the Twenty-First Century," *Rethinking Marxism* 27, no. 2 (2015): 189.

4. van de Sande, "Fighting with Tools," 190.

5. van de Sande, "Fighting with Tools."

6. Jeffrey S. Juris, *Networking Futures: The Movements against Corporate Globalization* (Durham, NC: Duke University Press, 2008), 3.

7. David Graeber, *Direct Action: An Ethnography* (Edinburgh: AK Press, 2009), 210, 257.

8. "The HKFS Declaration for Students' Strike: Seize our Future! In Solidarity We Strike to Open New Possibilities," last modified September 22, 2014, http://www.hkfs.org.hk/students-strike-declaration/?lang=en.

9. "The HKFS Declaration for Students' Strike."

10. Hui Yew-Foong, "The Umbrella Movement: Ethnographic explorations of communal re-spatialization," International Journal of Cultural Studies 20, no.2 (2017): 146–61, doi: 10.1177/1367877916683822.

11. "Umbrella Movement Tents Population Census," accessed June 15, 2018, https://www.facebook.com/umbrellacensus.

12. A Cantonese slang to curse Chun-ying Leung, the then Chief Executive, who obtained only 689 votes in the election. A Cantonese slang to curse Chun-ying Leung, the then Chief Executive, who obtained only 689 votes in the election.

13. Sarah Karacs, "Hong Kong's air quality falls after Occupy clearance puts traffic back on the roads," *South China Morning Post*, December 17, 2014.

14. The Water Horse Wall was made by water-filled barriers, a type of police barrier that was firmer than the usual one.

15. The publication was satirically named *Recap*, parodying a police officer who held a daily press conference at 4 p.m.

16. Margaret Kohn, *Brave New Neighborhoods: The Privatization of Public Space* (New York: Routledge, 2004), 156.

17. Tze-Man Wong, "Bio-politics and Power-relation in the Umbrella Movement," *Inmedia*, Jan 27, 2015. Non-binary gender roles and fluid sexuality also existed in the Umbrella Movement. Some discourses would claim women who participated in the occupation were marriageable. Occupiers, including the two student organizations and some politicians, also marched in the annual Hong Kong Pride parade in November to support the LGBTQ community.

18. Ngok Ma, "Increased Pluralization and Fragmentation: Party System and Electoral Politics and the 2012 Elections," in *New Trends of Political Participation in Hong Kong*, ed. Joseph Y. S. Cheng (Hong Kong: City University of Hong Kong Press, 2014), 185–210.

19. Edmund W. Cheng and Wai-Yin Chan, "Explaining Spontaneous Occupation: Antecedents, Contingencies and Spaces in the Umbrella Movement," *Social Movement Studies* 16, no. 2 (2017): 222–39, doi: 10.1080/14742837.2016.1252667.

20. Cheng and Chan, "Explaining Spontaneous Occupation."

21. Sin Lai Ting, "Savour the Apple: Unleashing Love and Justice from Desperation, Benny Tai: Do You Hear the People Sing?" *Applydaily*, June 29, 2014.

22. Sin Lai Ting, "Savour the Apple."

23. 1. Occupiers should adhere to orders from the stage; 2. Do not wear a mask; 3. No loudspeakers or exhibiting slogans that are inconsistent with the demand of the organizers; 4. Do not resist when arrested by the police; 5. Do not take over the barriers or assault the police.

24 There was a view shared among the students that reflected the sentiment of their discontent toward mainstream politics: "When no one was on the street, the politicians asked people to come and participate. When everyone was on the street, the politicians asked people to return home. Did the politicians really want to make any changes?" Although students did not successfully seek an alternative, they aspired to a more radical strategy that would reinvigorate the oppositional politics. See chapters 3, 4, and 8 on the discussion of the repertoire of social movements.

25. See chapter 6, in which Chris Chan sketches the tension between the students and the grassroots organizers.

26. The students originally planned to visit Beijing during the Asia-Pacific Economic Cooperation meeting but were told that it would result in a greater crackdown of China's civil society.

27. The thought ran as follows: By resigning from the seats, the pan-democrat lawmakers could trigger a by-election, which should be taken as a de facto referendum. If the plan rolled out, HKFS would urge occupiers to withdraw from the occupied zones or to shrink the occupied sites, thereby transforming the movement and directing the energy to the communities.

28. When HKFS had the meeting with some radical students on how to escalate, most of the student leaders were unable to engage in the planning of an action plan due to mobilization fatigue.

29. See chapters 6 and 10 on the nature of the oppositional camp in Hong Kong. While Chris Chan in chapter 6 explains how the old "left" (e.g., HKFTU) has been absorbed into the authoritarian regime, and the youth movement in Hong Kong is embedded in a strong liberal tradition, Jieh-min Wu argues in chapter 10 that the civic society in Hong Kong is "intrinsically moderate and decorous" because of its colonial past.

3

TRANSGRESSIVE POLITICS IN OCCUPY MONGKOK

Samson Yuen

Most research on the Umbrella Movement treats it as a singular protest, in which the three protest camps joined in unison by similar groups of participants fighting for the same cause. The Admiralty camp, where the movement started and where most protests leaders were based, is either explicitly or implicitly regarded as the main stage as well as the defining voice of the movement.[1] By contrast, the other two camps—Causeway Bay and Mongkok—are treated as offshoots of the Admiralty camp and are often neglected by researchers. This obfuscates the differences between three protest camps in terms of the demographics of the protesters as well as their actions and political orientations. It also overlooks the contentious dynamics between the protest camps and the implications of such differences. These differences must be carefully examined in order to gain a thorough and nuanced understanding of the Umbrella Movement, and also to shed light on the increasingly decentralized, networked nature of protest mobilizations in the contemporary era, where there is rarely a unified voice.

This chapter will unravel the complexities of the Umbrella Movement by shifting the focus to the Mongkok protest camp, known here as Occupy Mongkok. Drawing data from two onsite surveys, semistructured interviews, and documentary research, this chapter argues that Occupy Mongkok was not just an extension of the Admiralty camp where the Umbrella Movement originated. Instead, Occupy Mongkok developed a movement environment and dynamics that not only distinguished it from the Admiralty camp but also challenged the city's political culture. First, despite sharing similar demographic features with their Admiralty counterparts, Mongkok protesters showed greater inclination to behave militantly, eschewing the civic, nonviolent repertoires that were characteristic of previous protests. This militant behavior, which was much more salient in Mongkok than in Admiralty, involved not only defending the protest camp with barricades but also the use of physical violence in response to the assaults by the police, thugs, and counterprotesters. Protesters were also more likely to embrace the idea of self-mobilization, an action logic that emphasizes personalized participation without following a collective frame or leadership. Second, even though Occupy Mongkok drew cross-class participation, the protest camp also highlighted the role of the grassroots—defined more in cultural than socioeconomic terms—in political contention, which had been neglected in the city's protracted struggle for democracy.

To employ the terminology used by McAdam, Tarrow, and Tilly in *Dynamics of Contention*, Occupy Mongkok could be regarded as a transgressive episode of contention in Hong Kong's history of political activism. Distinguished from "contained contention," in which all parties are previously established actors employing well-established means of claim making, in transgression contention "at least some parties to the conflict are newly self-identified political actors, and/ or at least some parties employ innovative collective action." An action is considered innovative "if it incorporates claims, selects objects of claims, includes collective self-representations, and/or adopts means that *are either unprecedented or forbidden within the regime in question.*"[2] Such a distinction, according to the authors, is important for two reasons. First, transgression contention often grows out of existing episodes of contained contention. Second, episodes of transgressive contention are often more likely to lead to substantial short-term political and social change than contained ones, which tend more often to reproduce existing regimes.

The concept of transgression contention is useful for grasping the significance of Occupy Mongkok. Protest actions in Hong Kong had long subscribed to the civic and nonviolent principle and had confined themselves to mundane and nonconfrontational forms such as rallies and sit-ins. Although these protest norms had already been contested in protests prior to the Umbrella Movement, Occupy Mongkok, given the duration and the intensity of activities, was a critical juncture at which the path dependence of civic, nonviolent activism was disrupted by the inclusion of innovative means of claims making and new political actors. A case study of Occupy Mongkok will not only reveal the process of how transgressive contention grows from contained contention, but will also illuminate the potential impact on future activism.

This chapter will be divided into four parts. The first part will review the changing political and protest culture in Hong Kong to provide the context in which the Umbrella Movement, as well as Occupy Mongkok, broke out. The second part will trace the emergence of Occupy Mongkok and compare its participants with those in Admiralty in terms of demographics, reasons for participation, actions, and political orientations. The third part will rely on semistructured interviews with Mongkok protesters to analyze how their militancy and emphasis on grassroots citizens challenged established protest norms in Hong Kong. The last part will discuss the broader implications of Occupy Mongkok on the city's contentious politics.

Protest Culture in Hong Kong

Tracking the changes in Hong Kong's protest culture is crucial to understanding the transgressive nature of Occupy Mongkok. During the colonial era, citizens were said to be politically apathetic due to the dominance of their family-centric and utilitarian concerns, a strong sense of political powerlessness, and the administrative absorption strategy practiced by the colonial government.[3] Scholars, however, have challenged this view by citing various episodes of political activism throughout the colonial era.[4] As Lam argues, the nature of Hong Kong politics was in fact the paradoxical "combination of political activism and a culture of depoliticization."[5] Shortly before the handover, political activism further increased and diffused alongside the gradual but partial process of democratization.[6] This led to the emergence of a "political society" as party politics and protest participation both continued to grow even after the 1997 handover.[7] Becoming more politicized, citizens were said to have evolved from "attentive spectators"[8] into "attentive analysts and occasional activists."[9]

Despite an increase in frequency, protest actions remained circumscribed under the colonial ideology of "law and order."[10] They also tended to follow the principle of being "peaceful, rational, non-violent and non-profane" and were mostly conducted in accordance with the rule of law. Their primary objective was to engage in some sort of "pressure group politics," mainly to obtain policy influence from the government or maximize gains in elections through mass mobilization.[11] In these almost scripted actions, protesters were expected to perform their "civic quality" and avoid confrontation with the authorities.[12] The annual July 1 antigovernment rally, in which protesters march peacefully to the government headquarters (and leave immediately after the event), was regarded as an exemplar of civic, nonviolent protests.[13] In the recent spate of protests, such as the heritage movements of 2006–2007, the 2010 anti-high-speed-rail movement, and the 2012 anti–National Education movement, social activists have adopted direct and spontaneous actions aiming to disrupt government plans, direct in the sense that individuals are acting directly for themselves through radical tactics without the mediation of politicians or political parties. Despite their novelty, however, these protests still remained largely confined within the paradigm of civic and nonviolent activism.[14]

Another key aspect of Hong Kong's protest culture is its middle-class orientation. Although grassroots or working-class activism was on the rise from the 1960s to the 1980s, as evidenced by the social unrest in 1966–67 and the community movements in the 1970s and 1980s,[15] it had become weakened and fragmented since the mid-1980s due to the increasing role of the middle class in the political arena. Thanks to the city's rapid economic development, the middle class—managers, technicians, professionals, and administrators—had increased in both size and strength. They had also begun to become more enthusiastic in politics, particularly concerning the democratization of the political system.[16] As a result, they became the main leaders and participants of prodemocracy activism.[17] This is indicated by findings that participants in major protest mobilizations, such as the annual July 1 rallies, were made up of mostly the middle class.[18] (In the 2003 rally, for example, 54.4 percent of followers, 64.4 percent of co-initiators, and 69.9 percent of leaders identified as middle class.[19]) Although it is true that prodemocracy activism since the mid-2000s has witnessed renewed attention on class issues such as urban redevelopment, privatization of public assets, and income inequality,[20] grassroots activism remained limited in scale and was unable to develop a robust class-based politics that effectively appealed to the working class. By contrast, it was found that low-income citizens tend to support pro-establishment political parties, partly because these parties are better at providing social services as a result of their abundant resources.[21]

Despite its dominance in the 1990s and 2000s, this civic and middle-class-oriented protest culture has come under increasing challenge since the mid-2000s. This began with the establishment of the League of Social Democrats (LSD) in 2006, a grassroots political party formed by progressive democrats. Proclaiming that veteran democrats were too conservative in their fight for democracy, the LSD vowed to resort to "street actions" and "legislative struggles," a radical approach that became popular among voters who were seeking a new approach. In 2010, the party launched the "Five Constituencies Referendum," in which five prodemocracy legislators resigned and ran in by-elections in order to pressure the government to implement universal suffrage. With the referendum failing to achieve its intended outcome, the party splintered off a new political party, People's Power (PP), which vowed to employ a more confrontational approach to punish the veteran democrats for their compromise with the Beijing authorities over electoral reform. After 2012, PP continued to split due to ideological differences, leading to the formation of Civic Passion in 2012 and the breakoff of the Proletariat Political Institute in 2013. Both groups promoted militant political actions to confront both the veteran democrats and the government. This approach attracted many young people and prodemocracy supporters who had been disillusioned about the stagnated prodemocracy movement.

The political rows within the prodemocracy camp soon gave rise to the emergence of the localist movement, which comprises a loose set of political ideas that share the basic objective of protecting of Hong Kongers' interests, culture, and identity but who differ in their ultimate goal, which ranges from self-determination to independence.[22] Although also vowing to fight for democracy, localists differentiate themselves from veteran democrats by advocating a more confrontational approach in conducting political activism. They see the longstanding repertoires of civic, nonviolent protests as too ritualistic and unlikely to challenge the regime due to their routinization. Moreover, they argue that the prodemocracy camp had neglected how interests of the local populace have been damaged by the influx of mainland tourists and migrants under rapid social and economic integration with Mainland China, as shown in the shortages of local necessities ranging from infant formula to hospital beds. In a series of anti-mainlander protests between 2011 and 2013 in which they rallied against Chinese tourists and parallel traders who smuggled goods across the Hong Kong-Mainland border, localists already started to protest militantly. They shouted profane insults at their targets and sometimes even physically assaulted them, even though the extent of violence remained rather limited. While such violence was not prevalent later in Occupy Mongkok, the imperative of direct, militant actions, as I will show, did strongly influence protesters there.

In light of this changing political culture, law professor Benny Tai Yiu-ting proposed a civil disobedience campaign called "Occupy Central" in early 2013. Through blocking roads and paralyzing the financial district for several days, "Occupy Central" was intended to pressure the Beijing government into allowing Hong Kong to implement universal suffrage in electing the next chief executive. This provocative idea triggered mixed reactions. While some prodemocracy activists welcomed the idea, progressive democrats and localist activists gave a cold shoulder. They reasoned that the plan was too moderate, since participants were required to pledge to adhere to the principle of nonviolence and bear the ensuing legal responsibilities.[23] They also argued that the scale and duration of road blockage were too limited, making it unlikely to pose a real threat to the Beijing government. Despite its intention to transgress the limits of existing protests, the campaign was still regarded by critics as a follower of the civic protest tradition.

The Emergence of Occupy Mongkok

By this time, the long-established ethos that protests should be civic and non-violent had been profoundly contested. In this light, Occupy Central became a bizarre embodiment of both contained and transgressive elements, using the terminology of *Dynamics of Contention*. While it proclaimed to use innovative tactics such as road occupation, the campaign taken as a whole was moderate and constrained. Organizers even held a dress rehearsal for the campaign after the July 1, 2014, rally, in which a few hundred protesters occupied a section of Chater Road in Central until the police made arrests. Given its highly rehearsed nature, few had expected Occupy Central to be a significant "threat" to Beijing. As a result, the Hong Kong Federation of Students (HKFS), an activist student organization established by student unions of local universities, decided to organize a class boycott from September 22 onwards, hoping to inject momentum into the Occupy Central movement.

A spate of contingencies played a crucial role in transforming the class boycott and the preplanned Occupy Central movement into what came to be known as the Umbrella Movement.[24] On September 26, the fifth day of the class boycott, a group of student activists broke into the "Civic Square," the forecourt of the Central Government Office that was cordoned off with metal fences after a mass protest was held there in 2012 that successfully forced the government to shelve an unpopular patriotic education curriculum. Scores of students were detained in the action. On the next day, thousands flocked to Admiralty to support the detainees, prompting Occupy Central leaders to modify plans and announce the relocation of the campaign to the CGO area.

In the face of an unexpectedly large turnout, the government decided to deploy repressive actions. On September 28, as protesters flooded the streets around the CGO, riot police fired eighty-seven rounds of tear gas in an attempt to disperse the crowd. But the action provoked strong resistance as protesters held their ground, defending themselves by umbrellas, facemasks, and goggles. As the mass transit service was suspended at Admiralty because of the turmoil, protesters turned their attention to other districts. A group of protesters, pushed by riot police to the east of Admiralty, became the first to block the main traffic lane of Causeway Bay at around 10 p.m. Others gathered at Mongkok and besieged the intersection of Argyle Street and Nathan Road at around 11 p.m., marking the onset of Occupy Mongkok.

A protester recalled how Occupy Mongkok was formed:

> I was among the first group of people who sat down on Nathan Road. Originally I was in the Admiralty frontline, but it was too dangerous. I then saw people calling for occupying Mongkok on Internet chatrooms, so I decided to check it out. When I walked out from the MTR station, many people were already gathering outside Langham Place. A few guys were taking the lead to march out. But interestingly, we did not block the traffic immediately. We waited for the traffic lights to turn green before we went to the middle of the road and sat down.[25]

Throughout that night, protesters in Mongkok gradually grew into the thousands. Several trucks were driven in to block the road to shield the nascent encampment. In the following two days, more and more protesters joined, pushing the occupation beyond the road intersection. Some brought sleeping bags to stay overnight in case the police decided to evict the protesters; others set up supply and medical stations to provide logistical support. A stage was set up at the road intersection, where protesters took turns making public speeches. Barricades were erected to fend off the police and to mark the boundary of occupation. By now, a protest camp had been formed.

The occupation inadvertently mobilized actors who did not originally intend to participate in the OCLP campaign and brought innovative protest tactics into play, opening up a truly transgressive episode of contention. In this chain of events, Occupy Mongkok played a significant role. It expanded the geographical distribution of protest activities, diluted the police's resources, and gave better protection to the two other protest camps. The interconnected streets and high population density in Mongkok also made any immediate advances by the police difficult. Moreover, the cultural image of Mongkok also gave the protest camp a distinctive character. Located at the heart of the Kowloon Peninsula, Mongkok is a densely populated residential and shopping area, frequented by local youth and the working class due to its convenient location and low prices.[26] This has created an image that Mongkok is a place for the "common people," where they can enjoy themselves comfortably despite their class status and do not have to conform to social expectations. These features were crucial in differentiating Occupy Mongkok from the Admiralty camp, to which this chapter will now turn.

Comparing Participants in Mongkok and Admiralty

How were protesters in Mongkok different from those in Admiralty? Two onsite surveys conducted at different time periods during the Umbrella Movement allow us to examine some of their differences. The first onsite survey was conducted by researchers at the School of Journalism and Communication of the Chinese University of Hong Kong in Admiralty and Mongkok on October 4 and 5, 2014,[27] one week after the firing of tear gas and the formation of the protest camps. This survey helps to capture the early dynamics of the Umbrella Movement, particularly after anti-Occupy protesters and suspected triad members stormed the Mongkok camp on October 2, 2014.[28]

The descriptive statistics provide a snapshot of the Umbrella Movement protesters across the two protest camps. In terms of the basic demographics, as shown in table 3.1, Mongkok and Admiralty protesters were generally not qualitatively different, except that those in Mongkok were predominantly male. Although on average Mongkok protesters were slightly older and less educated, and a greater proportion of them identified as the lower or grassroots class, these variables were not statistically significant. In terms of their actions and political orientations, however, the two groups showed salient differences. Mongkok protesters tended to stay longer in the camp both in terms of the number of days and the number of hours. They were more likely to have built barricades, defended against anti-Occupy protesters, and helped to protect the protest camp when the police took action. These militant features, as will be further discussed in the next

TABLE 3.1   Demographics of Umbrella Movement protesters (CUHK survey)

	ADMIRALTY	N	MONGKOK	N
Age				
Under 18	8%		5%	
18–29	57%		58%	
30–39	21%		16%	
40–49	7%		10%	
50–59	5%		7%	
Above 60	2%	355	4%	182
Average age	28.2	355	30.6	182
Gender				
Male	52%		75%	
Female	48%	367	25%	184
Education				
Primary	10%		4%	
Secondary	28%		37%	
Tertiary	62%	366	59%	188
Socioeconomic class				
Lower or grassroots	44%		50%	
Middle class	51%		40%	
Upper class	4%	336	10%	161

TABLE 3.2 Actions and orientations of Umbrella Movement protesters (CUHK survey)

	ADMIRALTY	N	MONGKOK	N
Rationale* (degree of importance)				
Fight for genuine universal suffrage	60%	369	47%	187
Protest against the police's use of tear gas	79%	370	65%	188
Support and protect students	85%	371	76%	188
Support Hong Kong Federation of Students	19%	369	−6%	184
Support Scholarism	16%	367	−3%	184
Support Occupy Central Trio	−20%	370	−39%	183
Action				
Discussion about the movement direction and strategies	45%		43%	
Delivery of materials or maintaining order	59%		57%	
Setting up blockades	30%		38%	
Handling anti-Occupy protesters	39%		58%	
Help protecting the occupation area when police take action	56%		63%	
Do something to support the movement outside the occupied area	57%	371	46%	189
Views of self-mobilization* (degree of agreement)				
Self-mobilization makes the movement purer	62%	364	65%	186
. . . prevents the movement from being hijacked	58%	365	71%	187
. . . blurs movement focus	19%	365	−11%	186
. . . undermines movement leadership	35%	362	6%	185
Political belief* (degree of importance)				
Local interests	76%	361	88%	188
Universal values	81%	360	80%	187
Democratization of China	31%	361	20%	185
Party support				
Democratic Party	4%		3%	
Civic Party	15%		11%	
Labour Party	6%		3%	
League of Social Democrats	11%		10%	
People's Power	8%		15%	
Civic Passion	5%		17%	
Others	7%		10%	
None	41%		36%	
Don't know	17%	370	12%	188

* This question asked interviewees to rate the degree of importance/agreement, on a scale from 1 (very unimportant/utterly disagree) to 5 (very important/utterly agree), in participating in the Umbrella Movement. The above graph shows the "degree of importance," which is calculated by the following equation: Degree of importance = (% Very important/%Utterly agree + % Important/%Agree) − (% Unimportant/%Disagree + % Very unimportant/%Utterly disagree) section, were not surprising given that Occupy Mongkok was repeatedly harassed by counterprotesters and suspected triad members in early October, just before the survey was conducted.

Meanwhile, as shown in table 3.2, although demanding universal suffrage and protesting against police actions were important motivations for Mongkok protesters, their degree of importance were lower than that for their Admiralty counterparts. Across the board, Mongkok protesters were generally less motivated by specified rationales, an indication that they were skeptical of the agenda put forth by the leadership of the Umbrella Movement. This could be more pertinently illustrated by their responses that supporting the leadership—the Hong Kong Federation of Students, Scholarism, and the Occupy Central organizers—was not an important motivating cause. By contrast, they had more positive attitudes toward self-mobilization, seeing it as an element that made the movement pure and preventing it from being hijacked by political groups. They also tended to disagree that self-mobilization blurred the focus of the movement and undermined movement leadership. In terms of political belief, while protesters from both camps saw universal values as an important foundation of the movement, Mongkok protesters emphasized local interests more and the democratization of China less, an indication of localist political beliefs. Finally, even though protesters tended to have low support for political parties, Mongkok protesters had significantly greater support for radical and localist prodemocracy parties, namely People's Power and Civic Passion.

The second onsite survey was co-conducted by the author from October 20, 2014, to October 26, 2014.[29] It captures the period during which the protest camps had become stabilized, when there was substantially less risk of police clearance. This survey should be considered as supplementary data for the first one. The results corroborate some of the findings in the first survey. It shows that while Occupy Mongkok involved cross-class participation, it had a higher proportion of protesters self-identified as the lower class. In addition, a higher proportion of protesters in Mongkok claimed to live in public or government-subsidized housing, an indication of lower-income status.

Bringing Militancy into Contentious Politics

Why did militant protesters, who esteemed the virtue of self-mobilization, prefer to stay at Mongkok? How did Occupy Mongkok become a symbol of localism and form tension with the Admiralty camp? Since surveys can only provide a static and general picture of protesters' characteristics and orientations, one must also rely on ethnographic observation and interviews to better understand the dynamics of contention and the meanings that protesters attributed to their actions.

Although Occupy Mongkok was initially only an expedient tactic aimed at distracting the police, it soon grew into a protest camp erected with tents and demarcated by makeshift barricades. Unlike in Admiralty and Causeway Bay, protesters in Occupy Mongkok encountered more frequent incursions from counterprotesters and mobs, likely because proregime groups hoped to create an image of chaos and unruliness in a densely populated neighborhood.[30] The dramatic events of October 3 were illustrative. In the early afternoon, hundreds of facemask-wearing men, widely suspected to be gangsters, arrived at the Mongkok camp. Chanting anti-Occupy slogans, they began to remove barricades, dismantle tents and violently attack protesters and anyone who was around. Chaotic scuttles continued throughout the afternoon despite the presence of the police, which prompted speculation that they were colluding with the mobs. In response, pro-Occupy protesters staunchly defended the protest site. Toward the evening, more and more protesters returned to Mongkok after work. They began to outnumber the counterprotesters, forcing both them and the police to retreat.

Just as the counterprotests waned, the police took turns making advances on the protest camp, likely because they considered Occupy Mongkok to be a grave challenge to social order because the neighborhood is densely populated. In the early hours of October 17, when few protesters were stationed, the police dispatched elite units to evict the Mongkok camp, clearing the barricades and tents on the road. Traffic resumed for the first time in three weeks, but that did not last. By early evening, thousands of pro-Occupy protesters returned to Mongkok to "reclaim" the camp. They stopped the traffic again and removed police barricades to break into the cordoned area.[31] Facing the use of shields, batons, and pepper spray by police officers, protesters resisted with umbrellas and metal barriers. Many were injured through the clashes, and some were arrested. But their persistence eventually paid off. Within hours, Occupy Mongkok was recovered.

These dramatic events made "defending Mongkok" an imperative of the Umbrella Movement. Because of the counterprotests and police actions, Occupy Mongkok developed into more than just the spatial extension of the Admiralty protest camp. It became a place to defend proactively, with direct actions against proregime groups and the policemen. A protester described his encounter with the suspected gangsters:

> I was shoved and beaten by them, and they were merciless. I couldn't say for sure the police were collaborating with the triads, but I felt that at least they were not taking a neutral stance. At that moment I felt that

the police could no longer safeguard our freedom. We were at a "state of nature" where we were obliged to defend ourselves militantly.[32]

Another protester emphasized that being militant was not the same as using violence:

> I don't agree with using violence, but being militant is necessary given what we are facing. Violence means attacking your opponents for no reason. But militancy is different. It means protecting yourself against aggression.[33]

These militant actions presented a grave challenge for Occupy Central leaders, who considered Mongkok to be unsafe and repeatedly urged protesters to return to Admiralty. For many in Mongkok, however, chaos and danger did not stop them from defending the protest camp. By contrast, the more counteroffensives they experienced, the more necessary it became to fend off the enemies and protect the camp. As shown by the first survey, 38, 58, and 63 percent of the Mongkok protesters said that they had built barricades, handled counterprotesters, and protected the camp when the police took actions respectively, which are substantially higher than Admiralty protesters. Such militant actions made Occupy Mongkok a symbol of resistance against an unjust and repressive regime, offering an alternative solution to the use of civic, nonviolent activism for the sake of defending Hong Kong's liberal order.

Unsurprisingly, this militant ethos created a tense atmosphere in Occupy Mongkok. An activist recalled how he tried to offer a spare mattress to a fellow protester, who was dressed in full protective gears: "That person turned me down bluntly, and said that he was there to defend, not to sleep over."[34] Another protester described the atmosphere as nerve-wracking: "After the triad incident, people were alert all the time. Mongkok was a de facto war zone, and you always have a feeling that you might lose your life."[35] But rather than demobilizing protesters, this tense atmosphere produced reciprocal ties of solidarity. A volunteer of a supply station remarked:

> The constant threat brought us together as a group. In Admiralty, you could sleep in a tent for the entire night without worrying that people would disturb you. But in Mongkok, there were no tents because of the constant threat of being evicted, so we had to take shift to go to sleep. You can't sleep well, but it was this need to watch each other's back that we like about Mongkok.[36]

The militant discipline was, however, not enforced by the presence of a strong leadership in the camp. By contrast, such discipline—at least in the early stage—was more or less self-imposed by protesters who highly esteemed the virtues of self-mobilization. While self-mobilization had always been the basis of Hong Kong's popular protests,[37] it was further elevated and celebrated in Occupy Mongkok as a guiding ethos. Glorified by the slogan "no leaders, only the people," which became particularly popular among Mongkok protesters, self-mobilization was considered necessary for keeping the movement pure and preventing it from being hijacked by political forces. This also explained why support among Mongkok protesters for the Umbrella Movement leadership tended to be low, whereas support for radical political parties, such as People's Power and Civic Passion, which refused to follow the leadership of veteran democrats, tended to be relatively high.

Cross-Class Participation with Grassroots Manifestation

Other than their actions and political orientations, Occupy Mongkok protesters were also commonly assumed to be of a less privileged socioeconomic class. In media reports and firsthand accounts by activist journalists, they were often portrayed as grassroots citizens underrepresented and marginalized by the political and economic system.[38] This is an oversimplified portrayal, however. While the surveys did indicate a higher proportion of self-identified grassroots protesters in Mongkok (50 percent) than in Admiralty (44 percent), there were still 40 percent of Mongkok protesters who identified as middle class and 10 percent who identified as the upper class. Moreover, Mongkok protesters tended to be highly educated, with 59 percent of them having received tertiary education (compared with 62 percent in Admiralty). Even within the 50 percent Mongkok protesters who saw themselves as grassroots, 54 percent had attended tertiary institutions. This tallied with the author's observation that Occupy Mongkok protesters were from diverse backgrounds—students, office workers, blue-collar workers, artists, retirees, homemakers, self-styled rebels, and even the elderly. This eclectic composition differentiated Occupy Mongkok from the camps in Admiralty and Causeway Bay, but it fell short of upholding the mainstream portrayal of the camp as a grassroots protest.

Occupy Mongkok is more suitably characterized as a cross-class protest with a self-proclaimed grassroots identity. This characterization emphasizes that the working-class vibe in Occupy Mongkok was due less to the demographic composition of the protesters than to protesters' self-representation or identification as the grassroots. Here, "grassroots" took on a much broader meaning than the conventional economic understanding as class status. Rather than simply referring to people with a lower socioeconomic status, it embodied the identification with a plebeian culture under which protesters from all walks of life would be welcome, regardless of class status. This plebeian, inclusive atmosphere could partly be attributed to the cultural image of Mongkok as a place for the common people, of which interviewees often showed strong identification. A young protester said that Mongkok represents an "authentic Hong Kong" given its mixture of people from different class and cultural backgrounds:

> It was a utopia as you felt that all social norms and class boundaries were smashed, and all of us were fighting for the same goal—universal suffrage. People from different class can come together to fight for democracy. Our group has school drop-outs, construction workers, and taxi drivers who come every night at 3 a.m. I like the feeling a lot.[39]

Another protester, who lived on Hong Kong Island, explained why he came to Mongkok instead of Admiralty:

> People in Admiralty wear nice clothes. Grassroots like me would feel very uncomfortable in their gazes. They would suspect me as a spy. I feel much more at ease in Mongkok, and the people here speak my language. Admiralty doesn't need me. Mongkok does.[40]

The absence of a strict discipline was also what attracted protesters to come to Mongkok instead of Admiralty. Unlike in Admiralty, where pickets were organized to maintain order, no pickets were officially formed in Mongkok. As a protester said, "I can curse whenever I want, and I don't give a damn at how other people judge me."[41] Another protester said that he was originally staying in Admiralty, but decided to move to Mongkok because he thought the picket teams in Admiralty bossed around too much, whereas "Mongkok didn't give you that kind of attitude." He added, "There was even a smoking area in Admiralty. How ridiculous! In Mongkok, you could just smoke as you wish."[42]

The free-spirited, plebeian—almost anarchistic—atmosphere could also be seen in the eclectic mix of religious, folk, and cultural symbols in the protest camp. Protesters built a Christian chapel where believers held daily prayers. Others erected a shrine to worship Kuan Kung, a Chinese warrior god that symbolizes valiance, loyalty, and righteousness.[43] A young couple even held a wedding in front of the shrine, accompanied by a group of protesters wearing militant outfits and Guy Fawkes masks. Street hawkers, a symbol of the working class that had been largely outlawed by government authorities, would also frequent the protest camp, selling snacks, fruit juices, and herbal tea to the protesters. Tents that popped up on the road were given creative names parodying those given to the city's luxurious and increasingly unaffordable property developments.

For some protesters, defending against counterprotesters and police officers, and enjoying the plebeian atmosphere in Occupy Mongkok, was not enough. These protesters believed they should also reach out to the surrounding neighborhoods and explain to the residents about the aims of the Umbrella Movement, which had been criticized by the government and proregime media for adversely affecting people's livelihood. In mid-October, they formed groups and organized community visits, sending volunteers to residential buildings and shops around the protest camp. One group that participated was Woofer Ten, a Mongkok-based artist collective. It launched a campaign to map out shops and restaurants in Mongkok that had been affected in the hope that prodemocracy protesters could support their business.[44] These community initiatives were intended to send a message that the Umbrella Movement was not only about suffrage rights, but also about the everyday livelihood of the working class.

While these initiatives did not appear to be effective in soliciting mass support given the declining support for the Umbrella Movement in the opinion polls, protesters' efforts helped to emphasize the role of grassroots citizens in the middle-class-oriented prodemocracy movement. Even though grassroots, redistributive issues could be heard from time to time in local politics, Occupy Mongkok became a space to visualize and articulate the concerns of the common people. The importance of such space is further highlighted after it disappeared. A protester, who came from a wealthy family and was studying law in university at the time, recounted how her protest group fell apart after leaving Mongkok: "We still kept in contact, but our opinions became divergent. I used to be close to a fellow protester, Kit, who was a school dropout. But after Mongkok, we no longer talked to each other. Perhaps he was ashamed of being a school dropout, and that I am a 'privileged college student.'"[45]

Internal Strife, Court Injunction, and the Demise of Occupy Mongkok

Despite the distinctive character of Occupy Mongkok, tensions and conflicts became increasingly salient in the protest camp. One schism came from the debate of whether Occupy Mongkok should be a site for defending against the regime or for grassroots citizens to prefigure an alternative social order. Tension surfaced quickly after the counterprotests in early October, during the so-called hotpot incident. On October 9, left-wing activists, who tended to focus on redistributive issues and adhere to the civic, nonconfrontation protest tradition, organized what they called "Mongkok New Estate Opening Day." They brought

Ping-Pong tables, mah-jongg sets, a cotton candy maker, and hotpots into the camp, inviting protesters to join them. The idea was to do something imaginative on the road in order to create "more possibilities," such that public spaces could be "liberated for the public" rather than being "controlled by the government and real estate companies."[46] The event quickly provoked a backlash from critics who saw that the festive spirit would tarnish the image of Occupy Mongkok. An angry crowd showed up later, forcing the organizers to remove the hotpots and other equipment and to cancel the whole event. Some even threatened to call the food and hygiene department to "enforce the law."

Event organizers were criticized for not respecting the militant origin of the protest camp. As a protester said,

> It was morally inappropriate to have fun in Mongkok because people actually shed blood here when fighting the triads. I understand that people need to entertain themselves even during protests. But Mongkok isn't a place for that.[47]

Organizers and their sympathizers were labeled "leftards," a popular term used by pro-independence localists to criticize left-leaning, prodemocracy activists who were considered incompetent in protecting local interests because their strategies were too moderate and because they were too moralistic with Mainland Chinese. Usage of the term "leftards" could be traced to the anti-Mainlanders protests between 2011 and 2013, which saw the rise of the localists demonstrating against the influx of Chinese tourists, pregnant women, and parallel traders into Hong Kong.[48] Localists blamed veteran activists because they were unwilling to recognize Mainlanders as the problem of Hong Kong's political predicament. Early on in Occupy Mongkok, criticisms against the "leftards" were already prevalent. Posters urging protesters to "beware of the leftards" could be seen everywhere in the camp. Labeled activists who went into the camp were even harassed and told to leave.

Many localist groups that had been critical of the "leftards" were attracted to Occupy Mongkok. The most active one was Civic Passion, a localist political party that splintered off from People's Power in 2012. As shown in the first survey, among survey participants in Mongkok, support for Civic Passion was the highest of all political parties. A media report published in mid-October also found that two out of the four supply stations in Mongkok were run by Civic Passion supporters.[49] When the party left the Admiralty camp after failing to take control there, it moved to Mongkok, where it was able to build a sizeable base of support.[50] This allowed Civic Passion to actively promote the narrative that Occupy Mongkok was a localist stronghold that could confront an increasingly authoritarian regime. Such a narrative was promoted by the book *The Failure of the Umbrella Revolution*, in which Mongkok was characterized as being "isolated but dedicated to warfare":

> Occupy Mongkok was not like Admiralty. There was no elegance, no singing, no performances and no picket teams. For Mongkok occupiers, there was nothing but police attack and injuries. That was why Mongkok had an unyielding spirit. . . . In Mongkok, protesters kept on resisting against the enemies, and this allowed localist consciousness to gradually take over the protest camp. . . . From now on, localist consciousness will be unstoppable.[51]

The emphasis on militancy had a profound impact, igniting continual conflicts in Occupy Mongkok.[52] After the "hotpot incident," localist and militant protesters became intolerant of any leisure activities in the camp. The following evening, a group of students was screening *Ordinary Heroes*, a film about social activism in colonial Hong Kong, but militant protesters came to stop them. One of them was heard to say the following: "Do you know why Occupy Wall Street failed? It was because people kept doing useless things, singing, discussing and watching films, like what you guys are doing now!"[53]

These conflicts heightened the tense atmosphere in the protest camp, shifting the target for militant actions from counterprotesters and police officers to protesters who did not endorse the militant ethos. An air of insecurity became prevalent. The result was a gradual territorial partition of Occupy Mongkok, unlike in the early days when the protest camp was mixed and fluid. Localist and militant protesters, such as Civic Passion, occupied a central location: the area near the intersection of Nathan Road and Argyle Street. While many leftist protesters left the camp after the "hotpot incident," those who stayed moved to the peripheral areas. Due to the conflicts, groups that did not have a clear ideological stance also started to leave the camp in late October. A supply station volunteer said that their group decided to leave Mongkok in early November because they thought that the protest camp had been "hijacked" by the militant localists.[54]

By mid-November, the momentum for continuing the protest in Occupy Mongkok had become significantly weakened. As the police and counterprotesters stopped harassing the camp, protesters no longer faced a common enemy. As the weather turned chilly, fewer and fewer protesters stayed overnight in the camp. But the key turning point was the issuing of court injunctions. In late October, Hong Kong's court granted injunctions brought by taxi and public minibus industry associations to prohibit the continual occupation of the main road of Mongkok. Attempts by Occupy protesters to appeal the injunction were dismissed. Given that the court remains a highly revered institution in the semiautonomous city, its decision to grant injunctions against the protests placed constraints on the protesters, including the militant ones.[55]

Contrary to their earlier militant attitude against the counteroffensives, few protesters showed willingness to defy the court's order and accept the legal consequences, especially at a time when popular support for the Occupy protests continued to decline. When bailiffs enforced the court injunction in late November, with police officers working alongside them, the eviction effort did not provoke as much resistance as the previous attempt and the protest camp was evicted smoothly within hours. The clearance of Occupy Mongkok was a rehearsal for the Admiralty camp, which was later cleared under the enforcement of court injunctions two weeks later. The last protest camp in Causeway Bay was cleared on December 15, 2014, ending the seventy-nine-day Umbrella Movement.

Conclusion

This chapter analyzed the origins and dynamics of Occupy Mongkok to illustrate how it differed from the Admiralty camp and how it served as a critical juncture to challenge the paradigm of civic, nonviolent, and middle-class-oriented activism. As shown by the analysis, Occupy Mongkok attracted a group of protesters different from those in Admiralty, and their differences are more in terms of their actions and political orientations than in their demographic features. Mongkok protesters tended to be more militant, embrace self-mobilization, and support radical, localist political parties. Their skirmishes with counterprotesters and police officers allowed the legitimation of militant tactics, which had been discouraged under the city's protest culture. Moreover, despite drawing protesters of all socioeconomic classes, Occupy Mongkok was appealing to grassroots citizens who sought to emphasize the participation of the "common people" in political activism, countering the dominating role of the middle class in the prodemocracy movement.

These transgressions had a significant impact on Hong Kong's politics that has traveled beyond the Umbrella Movement. The perceived failure of the Umbrella Movement to achieve any tangible political concessions from the government has reinforced the self-fulfilling narrative that *more* militant tactics are required to create pressure on the authorities. Serving as the symbol of militant protest, Occupy Mongkok catalyzed a tactical shift in the organizational forms and repertoires of political activism. Demonstrations and mass rallies—tactics used by prodemocracy old guards—are no longer seen as effective in challenging the regime and helping Hong Kong to achieve democracy. The low turnouts in annual antigovernment protests after the Umbrella Movement, such as the New

Year rally and the July 1 rally—protests that typically attracted tens of thousands of participants—were testaments of that.

After Occupy Mongkok, localist protesters became increasingly estranged from veteran democrats and turned toward more militant and spontaneous protest actions. A pertinent example was the Mongkok unrest, also known as the Fishball Revolution, which broke out on the first day of Lunar New Year in February 2016, when localists showed support for street food vendors (hence the name Fishball, a popular local street food). On that night, after the police moved in to clear the vendors from makeshift stalls, hundreds of masked protesters, led by Hong Kong Indigenous, a localist party, fought against the police by throwing glass bottles and bricks dug out from the pavement. Some protesters even set fires in garbage bins. The unrest left dozens of people injured and arrested, some of whom were later charged with rioting and assaulting police officers. Meanwhile, the rise of militant activism has also changed the organizational ecology of the prodemocracy movement. After the Umbrella Movement, several university student unions initiated referendums to decide whether their universities should leave the Hong Kong Federation of Students (HKFS), which was blamed by the localists for failing to achieve any concessions from the government despite the phenomenal scale of the protest. One of the leaders of the Umbrella Movement, the HKFS was established in 1958 and had been a leading voice in local activism. After various referendums, four universities voted to withdraw from the HKFS, which implied its de facto dissolution and significantly weakened its leadership role. On the other hand, a number of new community-based organizations and political parties that champion ideas of localism have been established, such as Youngspiration, Hong Kong Indigenous, and the Hong Kong National Party, forming a "third force" in the political landscape. Distinguishing themselves from the veteran prodemocracy forces, these localist groups and parties advocated the use of militant protest tactics and espoused pro-independence ideas, renouncing the doctrine of "democratic reunification" promoted by veteran democrats.

While the localists managed to win seats in both the 2015 District Council election and the 2016 Legislative Council election, their meteoric rise has since then been met with increasingly harsh government measures. Soon after the 2016 election, two elected localist lawmakers, Baggio Leung and Yau Wai-Ching, were unseated because the court ruled their oaths, which contained pro-independence statements and remarks insulting China, as "unconstitutional." The ruling emboldened the government to disqualify another four prodemocracy lawmakers, three of whom had promoted "self-determination," or support for a referendum to decide Hong Kong's political future after 2047, when the fifty-year limit on Hong Kong's autonomy expires. Candidates who were accused of harboring pro-independence or self-determination ideas were also barred from entering the subsequent by-election in March 2018. In the meantime, some of those who were charged with rioting and assaulting police officers in the Fishball Revolution have been given lengthy jail sentences. These hardline legal measures have not only raised the cost of collective actions, but has also excluded both the localists and those who are perceived by the authorities to harbor similar ideas from entering the political system. The result is hardly a reinvigorated prodemocracy movement, as had been predicted shortly after the Umbrella Movement, but rather a fragmented and embittered struggle against an increasingly authoritarian regime over the long haul.

NOTES

1. For example, see Stephan Ortmann, "The Umbrella Movement and Hong Kong's Protracted Democratization Process," *Asian Affairs* 46, no. 1 (2015): 32–50; Sebastian Veg, "Legalistic and Utopian," *New Left Review* 92 (2015): 55–73.

2. Doug McAdam, Sidney Tarrow, and Charles Tilly, *Dynamics of Contention* (Cambridge: Cambridge University Press, 2001), 7–8.

3. Siu-kai Lau, *Society and Politics in Hong Kong* (Hong Kong: Chinese University Press, 1984); Ambrose King, "Administrative Absorption of Politics in Hong Kong: Emphasis on the Grassroots Level," *Asian Survey* 15, no. 5 (1975): 422–39.

4. Michael E. Degolyer and Janet Lee Scott, "The Myth of Political Apathy in Hong Kong," *Annals of the American Academy of Political and Social Science* 547, no. 1 (1996): 68–78; Elizabeth Sinn, *Power and Charity: A Chinese Merchant Elite in Colonial Hong Kong* (Hong Kong: Hong Kong University Press, 2003); Wai-man Lam, *Understanding the Political Culture of Hong Kong: The Paradox of Activism and Depoliticization* (Armonk, NY: M. E. Sharpe, 2004).

5. Lam, *Understanding the Political Culture of Hong Kong*, 4.

6. Ngok Ma, *Political Development in Hong Kong: State, Political Society, and Civil Society* (Hong Kong: Hong Kong University Press, 2007).

7. Hsin-chi Kuan, "Escape from Politics: Hong Kong's Predicament of Political Development?" *International Journal of Public Administration* 21, no. 10 (1998): 1423–48.

8. Siu-Kai Lau and Hsin-Chi Kuan, "The Attentive Spectators: Political Participation of the Hong Kong Chinese," *East Asia* 14, no. 1 (1995): 3–24.

9. Francis L. F. Lee and Joseph M. Chan, "Making Sense of Participation: The Political Culture of Pro-democracy Demonstrators in Hong Kong," *China Quarterly* 193 (2008): 84–101.

10. Agnes Ku, "Negotiating the Space of Civil Autonomy in Hong Kong: Power, Discourses and Dramaturgical Representations," *China Quarterly* 179 (2004): 647–64.

11. Stephen W. K. Chiu and Tai-Lok Lui, *The Dynamics of Social Movements in Hong Kong* (Hong Kong: Hong Kong University Press, 2000), 9.

12. Edmund W. Cheng, "Street Politics in a Hybrid Regime: The Diffusion of Political Activism in Post-Colonial Hong Kong," *China Quarterly* 226 (2016): 383–406.

13. Joseph Y. S. Cheng, ed., *The July 1 Protest Rally: Interpreting a Historic Event* (Hong Kong: City University of Hong Kong Press, 2005).

14. Cheng, "Street Politics in Hybrid Regime," 383–406.

15. Chiu and Lui, *The Dynamics of Social Movements in Hong Kong*, 185–202.

16. Ming K. Chan, "Grassroots Activism and Labour Electoral Politics under the Chinese Rule," in *Social Movements in China and Hong Kong: The Expansion of Protest Space*, ed.

Khun Eng Kuah and Gilles Guiheux (Amsterdam: Amsterdam University Press, 2009), 179–204; Ming Sing, "Weak Labor Movements and Opposition Parties: Hong Kong and Singapore," *Journal of Contemporary Asia* 34 (2004): 449–64.

17. Alvin So and Ludmilla Kwitko, "The New Middle Class and the Democratic Movement in Hong Kong," *Journal of Contemporary Asia* 20, no. 3 (1990): 384–298; Tai-lok Lui, "Rearguard Politics: Hong Kong's Middle Class," *The Developing Economies* 41, no. 2 (2003): 161–83; Agnes S. Ku, "Civil Society's Dual Impetus: Mobilizations, Representations and Contestations over the First of July March in 2003," in *Government and Politics in Hong Kong: Crises under Chinese Sovereignty*, ed. Ming Sing (London: RoutledgeCurzon, 2009), 38–57.

18. Francis L. F. Lee, and Joseph M. Chan, "Making Sense of Participation: The Political Culture of Pro-democracy Demonstrators in Hong Kong," *China Quarterly*, 193 (208): 84–101.

19. Francis L. F. Lee, and Joseph M. Chan, *Media, Social Mobilisation and Mass Protests in Post-Colonial Hong Kong: The Power of a Critical Event* (Abingdon: Routledge, 2010), 59.

20. Yun-chung Chen and Mirana M. Szeto, "The Forgotten Road of Progressive Localism: New Preservation Movement in Hong Kong," *Inter-Asia Cultural Studies* 16, no. 3 (2015): 436–53.

21. Stan Hok-wui Wong, "The Real Estate Elite and Real Estate Hegemony," in *Routledge Handbook of Contemporary Hong Kong*, ed. Tai-Lok Lui, Ray Yep, and Wing-kai Stephen Chiu (Abingdon: Routledge, 2018), 342–62.

22. Ying-ho Kwong, "The Growth of 'Localism' in Hong Kong," *China Perspectives* 3 (2016): 63–68; Malte Philipp Kaeding, "The Rise of 'Localism' in Hong Kong," *Journal of Democracy* 28, no. 1 (2017): 157–71.

23. "Letter of Intent," Occupy Central with Love and Peace, accessed April 3, 2018, http://oclp.hk/index.php?route=occupy/letter_detail&letter_id=11.

24. Edmund W. Cheng and Wai-Yin Chan, "Explaining Spontaneous Occupation: Antecedents, Contingencies and Spaces in the Umbrella Movement," *Social Movement Studies* 16, no. 2 (2017): 222–39.

25 Jason Chow, interview, Hong Kong, November 21, 2016.

26. Cannix Yau, "Inside Mong Kok: Hong Kong's Simmering Melting Pot Where Passions Can Boil Over," *SCMP*, February 16, 2016, http://www.scmp.com/news/hong-kong/law-crime/article/1913347/inside-mong-kok-hong-kongs-simmering-melting-pot-where.

27. I thank Professor Francis L. F. Lee for sharing the raw data of this survey.

28. The survey questionnaire comprised thirty-two questions, covering topics such as the duration of stay, reasons for participation, source of information, use of the Internet and social media, as well as political orientations. Among the sample of n=569, n=273 collected from Admiralty and n=296 from Mongkok. Table 1 presents the descriptive statistics of protest participants in Admiralty and Mongkok, focusing on their demographic features, reasons for participation, action taken in the camp, and political orientations. But rather than using the survey site (where a participant was interviewed) to categorize his or her location of participation, I use the location of the longest stay, which was also asked in the survey, as the marker for categorization. This leaves us with n=371 in Admiralty and n=189 in Mongkok. Although the sample size of Admiralty protesters is almost double those of Mongkok, this caveat will help to tackle the problem that protesters did not necessarily stay longer in the camp where they were interviewed, and that they tended to travel between different protest camps. Nine interviewees (who stated Causeway Bay as their location of longest stay) are excluded from the analysis to focus on the comparison between Mongkok and Admiralty.

29. The survey questionnaire comprised twenty-seven questions, covering similar topics but less focused on communicative aspects and more on the rationale for participation. While the sample size reached as many as n=1,681, the majority of the sample was collected at Admiralty (n=1,525). Only n=156 was collected at Mongkok.

30. Varese, Federico, and Rebecca W. Y. Wong, "Resurgent Triads? Democratic mobilization and Organized Crime in Hong Kong," *Australian & New Zealand Journal of Criminology* 51, no. 1 (2018): 23–39.

31. "Chaos in Mong Kok as Police Use Batons, Pepper Spray to Repel Surge of Protesters," *SCMP*, October 17, 2014, http://www.scmp.com/news/hong-kong/article/1618168/swift-police-operation-ends-occupy-mong-kok.

32. Jason Chow, interview, Hong Kong, November 21, 2016.

33. Oscar NG, protester, interview, Hong Kong, October 17, 2016.

34. Kim Chan, interview, Hong Kong, October 19, 2016.

35. Oscar NG, interview, Hong Kong, October 17, 2016.

36. Mr. Lee, interview, Hong Kong, November 24, 2016.

37. Francis L. F. Lee, "Internet, Citizen Self-mobilisation, and Social Movement Organisations in Environmental Collective Action Campaigns: Two Hong Kong Cases," *Environmental Politics* 24, no. 2 (2015): 308–25.

38. Kristine Kwok, "Never Retreat, a Mong Kok State of Mind," *SCMP*, October 12, 2014, http://www.scmp.com/news/hong-kong/article/1614747/never-retreat-mong-kok-state-mind.

39. Rachel Li, interview, Hong Kong, November 11, 2016.

40. Vivian Tam, "Zhangyi meiduo tugou bei" [The less educated have more sense of justice], *Pentoy*, October 10, 2013, http://www.pentoy.hk.

41. Keith Li, interview, Hong Kong, November 12, 2016.

42. Mr. Yeung, interview, Hong Kong, October 19, 2016.

43. Joseph Bosco, "The Sacred in Urban Political Protests in Hong Kong," *International Sociology* 31 (2016): 375–95.

44. For the interactive map, see https://hackpad.com/-411-znDGdo9EpB5, accessed December 28, 2016.

45. Rachel Li, interview, Hong Kong, November 11, 2016.

46. Facebook page of Mongkok New Estate, accessed December 28, 2016, https://www.facebook.com/341993955960982/.

47. Jason Chow, interview, Hong Kong, November 21, 2016.

48. Sebastian Veg, "The Rise of 'Localism' and Civic Identity in Post-Handover Hong Kong: Questioning the Chinese Nation-State," *China Quarterly* 230 (2017): 1–25.

49. "Xuelian zeng wangjiao canyu huan xinren" [Hong Kong Federation of Students increased presence in Mongkok to win more trust], *Mingpao*, October 19, 2014.

50. Anonymous protest leader, interview, March 28, 2018.

51. Passion Times, ed., *Yusan Shibailu* [The failure of the Umbrella Revolution: A record] (Hong Kong: Passion Times, 2016).

52. Holok Chen, "Hotpot, Gods and 'Leftist Pricks': Political Tensions in the Mong Kok Occupation," Libcom.org, October 15, 2014, accessed December 28, 2016, https://libcom.org/blog/mk-hotpot-tensions.

53. Mr. Lee, interview, Hong Kong, November 24, 2016.

54. Mr. Lee, interview, Hong Kong, November 24, 2016.

55. Samson Yuen and Edmund W. Cheng, "Neither Repression nor Concession? A Regime's Attrition against Mass Protests." *Political Studies* 65, no. 3 (2017): 611–30.

4

THE SPECTRUM OF FRAMES AND DISPUTES IN THE UMBRELLA MOVEMENT

Wing Sang Law

The Umbrella Movement is undoubtedly a pivotal event of the Hong Kong prodemocracy movement. It is therefore quite natural to explain the protests as a one-dimensional prodemocracy movement pitting Hong Kong against Beijing's denial of universal suffrage.[1] This approach, however, is quite insufficient for understanding the complexity of the event; neither can it explain how the occupation unfolded in the ways it did, nor is it helpful for coming to know the dynamics and tensions within the movement itself. This chapter, therefore, aims at situating the Umbrella Movement in the wider historical context, treating it as an occasion for activists in the diverse factions of the prodemocracy movement to play out their differences in terms of their divergent visions and actions. Contrary to some characterizations of the event as a "spontaneous" and "leaderless" campaign, this chapter stresses the importance of how the key campaign groups (and their key opinion leader(s)) contested each other through their efforts of "framing" the movement in different ways so as to realize their competing visions of social mobilization.

Part A will first track the trajectories of the struggle for democracy in Hong Kong, highlighting the internal rifts and fissures emerging in the past two decades and mapping out the current spectrum of ideological positions in the prodemocracy camp. I will borrow from the "frame analysis" of social movement studies the concept of "master frame" to describe the coherent set of ideas and practices of Hong Kong's prodemocracy movement before it started to be challenged after the 1997 handover of sovereignty.[2] I will then describe how the crisis of the "master frame" manifested itself in the rapid pace of radicalization, which led not only

TABLE 4.1 Framing prodemocracy movement by different political groups

	MODERATE DEMOCRAT	RADICAL DEMOCRAT	PROGRESSIVE LOCALIST	RADICAL RIGHT-WING LOCALIST
Ideology	Liberalism; Chinese nationalism	Radicalism; participatory democracy	Left-liberalism; antidevelopmentalism	Radicalism; populism
Master frame/ competing alternatives	Reunion-in-democracy	Radical activism	Progressive localism	Hong Kong nationalism; city-state theory
Diagnostic framing	Undemocratic government	Undemocratic government; corporate power; meek leadership of pro-democracy movement	Failing leadership of pan-democrats; underdevelopment of grassroots participatory democracy	Colonization of Hong Kong by China; pseudo-resistance by pan-democrats & leftards
Prognostic framing	Negotiation with the government & Beijing; democratic reforms; voting for democrats; persistence in nonviolent protests	Democratic reforms; voting for democrats; exert pressure on the regime by nonviolent radical actions	Urban-rural activisms; cross-sectoral mobilization at community level; combined use of moderate and aggressive direct action	Ethnic struggles against Mainlandization; Wiping out pan-democrats & leftards; militant spirit and actions
Motivational framing	Civic maturity	Reaction against oppression	Post-materialistic values of young generation; quest for local identity	Hong Kong ethnic identity; sense of cultural crisis

to the formation of different "pan-democrat' factions but also culminated eventually in a call for a total overhaul of the established convention of Hong Kong oppositional politics (see table 4.1). In Part B will look into the various aspects of "frame disputes" among activist factions before and during the occupation. Such disputes carried with them serious implications for the style of organizing the protests; these, in turn, resulted in substantial transformations of the civil disobedience action envisioned initially by Benny Tai. Part C will look particularly into the right-wing localists' extensive use of "adversarial framing" of the other occupiers.[3] I will discuss how these efforts to "frame" the "enemies within" are an extension of right-wing populist discursive tactics. With the effects of cultivating the "culture of distrust"[4] that split the occupation counterproductively—bordering on becoming a countermovement[5]—these tactics are, however, understandable as part of a desperate attempt to reinvent the existing prodemocracy movement's master frame.

Part A: The Making and the Crisis of "Reunion-in-Democracy"

Hong Kong's prodemocracy movement began in the early 1980s, when Hong Kong's future was the subject of Sino-British negotiation. In that period, both the British and the Chinese wanted to show that they welcomed some future form of democracy flourishing in Hong Kong. The British Hong Kong government opened up seats for direct election at the district level in 1982. The ideas of "one country, two systems" put forward by the Chinese government also allowed Hong Kong people to rule Hong Kong after the end of colonial rule in 1997. Although most people preferred to see the continuation of the status quo of British colonial rule, soon rejected by Deng Xiaoping, some opinion leaders tried to look forward to the future of Hong Kong's autonomous rule under the PRC's flag and argued that democratic rule was the best postcolonial political system for Hong Kong. They framed their cause as "reunion-in-democracy" meaning that they accepted the reunification with China but insisted on having a democratic system to be gradually built in Hong Kong.[6]

In face of the confidence crisis caused by Hong Kong's uncertain future, the discourse of "reunion-in-democracy" provided a comprehensive interpretive schema for the activists, across different sectors and political persuasions, to mobilize people to join the prodemocracy cause. It defined the handover of sovereignty as an opportunity to develop democracy in Hong Kong, as the city was going to end its colonial rule; it called for people's participation and political engagement to establish a sense of community and citizenship in order to stem the tide of emigration. Although the NGOs and the emergent political concern groups had different political orientations and even diverse views regarding the issue of 1997, they agreed that the best thing to do for Hong Kong was to push for genuine democratic reform. The leading democrat politicians and activists gradually adopted the rhetoric of "reunion-in-democracy," which became a "master frame" of the prodemocracy movement, giving shape to a cycle of protests for gradual democratic reform that lasted for almost two decades.[7] As an anchoring master frame, "reunion-in-democracy" also affected the tactical choices within a cycle of protest, screening out those not consistent with it.

The prodemocracy movement in Hong Kong gained massive momentum after the 1989 democracy movement in Beijing.[8] The sympathy for the protesting students and the grief about the June Fourth Massacre were soon transformed into an awareness about the need to protect Hong Kongers' preferred ways of life by democratic institutions and people's participation. The Chinese nationalistic feeling unleashed in 1989 soon joined the cause for local democracy as people increasingly perceived that a strong democracy in Hong Kong would help guard against the threats of the coming communist rule.[9] People's enthusiasm for democracy intensified; democrats won victory easily in most elections, although the overall political system was still undemocratic.

In social movement studies, "collective action frame" refers to a schemata of interpretation to code reality and enable individuals to locate, perceive, identify, and label occurrences within their life space as well as the world at large.[10] A collective action frame makes attributions regarding who or what is to blame (diagnostic framing), articulate an alternative set of arrangements (prognostic framing), and urge others to act in concert to affect change (motivational framing). In the face of a series of political crises in the 1980s and 1990s, "reunion-in-democracy" provided such a schemata of interpretation to mobilize Hong Kongers to take the prodemocracy movement as a realistic, pragmatic yet also proactive response to the uncertain future.

The prodemocracy movement, however, suffered a serious setback and lost steam and momentum after China derailed Governor Chris Patten's reform package by setting up a new Provisional Legislative Council (PLC) with largely Chinese-appointed or Chinese-selected delegates. Right after the handover on July 1st, 1997, the PLC abolished numerous reforms achieved in the last days of the British rule. The prodemocracy movement had a brief reinvigoration in 2003, when 500,000 people took to the streets on July 1st to protest against Article 23 (National Security Bill).[11] The democrats, however, failed to get more substantial gains for the prodemocracy cause.[12] The yearly march, organized thereafter by the Civil Human Rights Front (CHRF), turned itself into a kind of ritualistic protest, like just another June 4th commemoration.[13] Young people's frustration over the repeated rituals gradually accumulated and became the driving force for the radical turn of the prodemocracy movement.

Protest in New Style: The Rise of Radical Democrats

After 1997, the stagnancy of the prodemocracy movement was widely criticized; the emergent radical voices attributed it to the poor leadership of the moderate democrats. Most attacks targeted their conservative, unimaginative approach regarding actions. Since Hong Kong's prodemocracy movement in the 1980s and 1990s was not based upon a forceful mass movement of decolonization to back up claims for democracy, "reunion-in-democracy" adherents, therefore, had to rely on the good will of the British and the Chinese governments.[14] The leading democrats believed they could convince the Chinese authorities as well as the ruling corporate elites that democracy would not turn into a populist mob rule that jeopardized economic prosperity. To convince the people that democratic reforms for Hong Kong would be harmless, the democrats always had to rely on a "civic maturity" framing to describe Hong Kong citizens as being moderate and mature enough to run a stable democratic system. To put words into actions, the "civic-maturity" frame has to be reaffirmed time and again in almost every protest activity. Despite their anger, the protests have always been conducted in a highly civilized manner. The participants never resorted to extreme or emotional opinions; they were always law-abiding, peaceful, and nonviolent.

The first breakthrough was brought by the election of a well-known radical protester, ex-Trotskyite Leung Kwok-Hung, into the Legislative Council in 2004. It marked the initial moment of the challenge to the timidity of the old moderate democrats. His victory led to the formation of the populist party League of Social Democrats (LSD) in 2006, with Leung and Wong Yuk-man (a radio anchor) as the main leaders. In the years after the establishment of LSD, the prodemocracy movement was undergoing a split between its moderate and radical wings. The trend of radicalization also prompted People Power, a splinter group from LSD, to be formed in 2011.

The radical democrats broke the political culture of self-limitation by revising the codes of protest actions performed both on the streets and in the Legislative Council chamber. These new radical protests caused a stir in public opinion. But apart from that, the radical democrats did not differ much from the moderates in their diagnosis of the dire situation of Hong Kong and their blaming the Beijing authorities behind the scenes. They equally took to task the unelected government and its procorporate policies; they also upheld the belief that only an elected government could solve most of the problems and crises faced by Hong

Kong. Like the moderates, the radical democrats did not consider challenging the "one country, two systems" constitutional arrangement since it would do no good in advancing the prodemocracy cause. They differed from the moderates and disagreed with their middle-class, nonconfrontational approach, and they also criticized their blind belief in negotiation and communication with the real power holders.

Starting in 2009, however, the relationship between the moderate and radical camps turned increasingly sour over a strategic dispute concerning how the democrats should respond to the proposal of election reforms for both chief executive and the Legislative Council. The moderates could no longer lead the prodemocracy movement after the radicals started to challenge the moderates' long-held leadership. The radicals devised ever more aggressive protest actions and were increasingly eager to re-examine how the moderates' failing strategies were rooted in their ideological background and the ways they had been "framing" the prodemocracy movement.

Cognitive Liberation: The Emergence of Progressive Localism

The year 2006 also saw the emergence of the new urban-rural activism (new preservation movements, or NPM). Campaigners participating in the preservation of Star Ferry Pier, Queen's Pier, and a number of urban renewal projects took a new approach to social campaigns, aiming to realign campaigners, urban planning professionals, artists, media workers, and campaign constituents. NPM traversed the conventional boundaries between political parties and rights-advocacy NGOs.[15] The young NPM activists (the so-called post-80s generation) broke new ground in launching a new kind of activism that blurred the dividing lines between political movement and social movement through the formation of mobile and unconventional campaign groups, canvassing support from the newly emerging online media.[16]

In the name of progressive localism, this new activism espoused and nurtured a new sense of belonging to this city, challenging the official conceptions of both colonial and postcolonial history and reclaiming the ordinary people's rights to cultural memories. Although these campaigns did not carry with them a clear political agenda of replacing the existing oppositional politics with a new line, they helped to foster the new sense of local identity. In this regard, NPM opened up previously concealed avenues to conventionalized political practices in Hong Kong, loosening up the old movement's master frame, which set off a kind of "cognitive liberation"[17] for the emergence of a new master frame of Hong Kong oppositional politics to come.

In 2010, NPM reached its climax in the anti-express-rail-link (anti-XRL) movement. A new generation of activists thus emerged with more aggressive styles of action, innovative ideas, and more ambitious political goals. They were no longer loyal followers of the old democratic parties but were more emotionally attached to Hong Kong and much more concerned about the loss of Hong Kong identity in the face of the rapid pace of China–Hong Kong integration. Quite a number of them remain campaign activists for various urban, rural, and other social issues, but a substantial number of the newly mobilized youth have gradually been attracted by the right-wing turn of the localist movement.

Ethnic Struggle: The Right-Wing Localist Turn

The radical right-wing localism took advantage of the series of China–Hong Kong conflicts, such as the D&G photo ban incident[18], a flood of Mainland individual tourists, birth tourism, and the shortage of milk powder, among others, to articulate a version of radical-right localism that is in sharp contrast to the NPM discussed above.[19] They took the moderate democrats, the believers of "reunion-in-democracy," to task for their adherence to Chinese nationalism. Very soon, this branch of localism developed into a number of different political ideologies. The City-State cult is led by Wan Chin, who is famous for his provocative writings.[20] In his essays, he calls on Hong Kongers to wage an ethnic struggle against the intrusion of Mainland communist culture, working together to build Hong Kong into a city-state.[21] In contrast, the faction seeking Hong Kong independence from China goes for Hong Kong nationalism and complete separatism.[22]

Yet however diverse these ideologies may be, the core belief of the right-wing localists is that Hong Kong has to maintain its separation from China in many key areas. Politically, Hong Kongers' interests should be the first priority for any policy issue. Economically, Hong Kongers should reject hasty integration plans and infrastructure projects that facilitate the cross-border integration with China. Culturally, Hong Kong people should have their own identity, defined as substantially different from the Mainlanders. The most imminent danger for Hong Kong is the loss of its distinct identity; therefore, Hong Kong people should stand up and guard against the infiltration of new Chinese Communist Party (CCP) culture propagated by the current Chinese regime and its accomplices in Hong Kong.[23]

Theoretical debates of all these different positions have attracted a small number of politically fervent netizens. They are usually young, high school students or in subdegree programs in colleges, or graduates with casual jobs. Apart from these young people, who are usually fresh in terms of experience in social activism, right-wing localism also attracts frustrated and angry middle-aged veteran protesters and disgruntled members of various democratic parties. But they would not be effective enough to change the world without their doctrines being translated into collective action frames. It was indeed through the incidents of the China–Hong Kong conflicts mentioned above that the right-wing localists could evolve into a political faction with significant influence.

Many scholars of social movement research point out that "framing" is not just about coding reality and devising tactics; it also links closely with collective identity. That means framing would either assert something about a group's consciousness or make claims about aspects of a group's character.[24] In that regard, "adversarial framing" has usually been used by the campaign organizer to give an account of who or what is responsible for causing the problem or failing to prevent it from being solved.[25] The concept of "adversarial framing," however, is usually applied in cases involving mutually antagonistic camps. Attention has seldom been paid to situations in which serious "frame disputes" happened among campaigners apparently aiming at similar goals. Clearly missing from the perspective of these studies is the cases of populist mobilization, which is normally based on a Schmittian conception of the political, namely friend-enemy distinction.[26] The sometimes sweeping allegations and unsubstantiated claims of the right-wing localists in Hong Kong offer plenty of examples of adversarial framing that mark off the pan-democrat leaders as the enemies within:[27]

(1) they have Chinese nationalistic fantasies and thus have unconditionally accepted China's claim to Hong Kong sovereignty;
(2) they adhere to the "reunion-in-democracy" line, which sets a fatalistic self-limitation to Hong Kong prodemocracy struggles;
(3) they have a flawed and fatalistic assumption that Hong Kong will only have democracy after China is democratized;
(4) they exert a monopoly over the leadership in prodemocracy movements;
(5) they have betrayed local people's interests in accommodating new immigrants;
(6) they are complicit with China in endorsing regional economic integration with China;
(7) they are middle-class cosmopolitan elites holding foreign passports without any real sense of what is happening in the local society.

In a nutshell, pan-democrats (regardless of the moderates or the radicals) are "framed" as no more than a bunch of demagogues who exploited the people and turned them into politicians' pawns. They never dare to go beyond the safe zone to launch real struggles against the CCP. That is the reason why oppositional politics led by pan-democrats in the past had never succeeded.

ATTACKS ON THE "LEFTARDS"

The enemy list of the radical right does not stop at vilifying the politicians but also includes the social activists. Although the NGO organizers or other grass-roots activists are also very critical of the gradualist and nonconfrontational approach of the old, moderate democrats, (right-wing) radicalism does not spare these veteran activists from attack. In other words, these old hands of the social movement, together with the younger NPM activists (the progressive localists), are equally guilty in blocking Hong Kong from developing genuine resistance against the impending Chinese colonial rule over Hong Kong. Collectively, they are labeled as the "leftards." Who exactly is being referred to by this label, however, became increasingly blurred. Sometimes, it refers to media workers, intellectuals, or anyone who holds any view against the radical right. The leftards are guilty because of:[28]

(1) their pro-Mainland immigrant stance in human rights or welfare issues;
(2) their lack of sympathy with the plight of the local populace;
(3) their high-sounding moral claims of tolerance and multicultural-ism detached from the residents' perception of being besieged by the Mainlanders;
(4) their blind observance of nonviolent principles, which allows them to throw away any chance of escalating the struggle to a higher level;
(5) their tricks to exclude participants who adopt confrontational measures in the face of the police or institutional forces;
(6) their tendency to disband the crowd prematurely by making protests pure self-congratulatory and symbolic events before the peoples' struggle can be escalated.

The right-wing localists consider the leftards to be career activists who through social movements avoid using confrontational actions or tactics because they always want to save room for themselves to make deals with the authorities. These routinized practices have guaranteed their status of being the permanent representative "agents" of the people. For them, protests are just occasions for their own advancement in the career path co-established by the NGO industry and the universities. Because of this, the right-wing localists see the leftards as neither their competitors nor their fellow travelers in the same journey but rather their enemies. The most popular doctrine made by Wan Chin is: If the leftards are not eliminated, there will be no end to the suffering of Hong Kong.

Indeed, from 2012 onward, the right-wing localists repeatedly launched attacks on the leftards. All of the three campaigns, which drew out a substantial number of protesters, eventually turned into occasions for scandalous stories about the alleged betrayals by the leftards.[29]

Part B: Tensions and Contentions Among Activists

After examining the spectrum of political factions, in this part I will analyze the development of the Occupy Central plan, the main ideas of which were initially proposed by Benny Tai. Rev. Chu Yiu-ming and Prof. Chan Kin-man were later invited to join Tai to form the OC trio. My focus is on how Benny Tai's original ideas have created differential impacts upon the political spectrum of the oppositional camp. I will examine how the radical democrats radicalized the ideas by transforming the original frame. I will also analyze how the right-wing localists made the best use of the collapse of the OCLP plan in an attempt to mount an alternative "master frame" through populist discursive practices and adversarial framing in a number of dimensions (see table 4.2).

Frame Disputes of Occupy Central

Benny Tai's initial idea of Occupy Central was appealing to veteran democrats who were eager to find a breakthrough for the stagnant prodemocracy movement. He described Occupy Central as an action that adopted a new paradigm of social movement organizing.[30] He tried to organize it in such a way that both the radicals and the moderates would have motivation to join. He chose first to mobilize the middle-class professionals with the assumption that radicalization of this usually cautious moderate class would create the greatest impact upon the rest of society and the government. To appeal to the cautious moderates, every step of the civil disobedience action strictly followed the principles of non-violent action. Preceding the actual occupation of the central business district, there were series of democratic procedures, including the Deliberation Days and Civic Referendum; every participant had to be registered and classified. The aim of these measures was to reach a consensus about the political reform proposal that the civil disobedience action could support, and everything would be risk-proof as well as neat and tidy. As Benny Tai wished, the representative of the pan-democrat camp would then have a strong bargaining chip on the negotiation table with the government.

In order to make the plan appealing to different sectors, he described the character of the plan differently at different stages. When the campaign began, he used the metaphor of "weapon of mass destruction" to describe the occupation, which excited many radical minds in Hong Kong.[31] Yet when the whole plan was later tagged with the descriptors of "love and peace"—and, accordingly, OC was renamed as OCLP (Occupy Central with Love and Peace)—many radical activists started to have doubts about the nature of this event and wondered if it might

TABLE 4.2 Action repertoires and framing activities of different activist factions

	OCCUPY CENTRAL TRIO	RADICAL DEMOCRATS	STUDENT BODIES	RIGHT-WING LOCALISTS
Organization (year of emergence)	Occupy Central with Love and Peace (2013)	Supporters of Occupy Central (2013)	Hong Kong Federation of Students (1958) Scholarism (2011)	Civic Passion (2012) Hong Kong Resurgence (2014)
Principle of collective action	Nonviolent civil disobedience	Nonviolent civil disobedience	Nonviolent civil disobedience	Militant resistance
Action repertoire	Deliberation days; civic referendum; regimented occupation	Trial run of mobile occupation	Occupation rehearsal; class-boycott; surprise occupation of civic square	Spontaneous occupation; crack the main platform; vigilante patrol; symbolic militancy
Framing activities	**Diagnostic framing:** Pseudo-universal suffrage will kill prodemocracy movement **Prognostic framing:** Negotiation backed up by direct action **Frame alignment:** With radicals: OC is not ritualistic protest; With moderates: OC is chaos-free	**Frame transformation:** OC is for everybody; massive mobilization is the key to success; holding OC in check	**Frame transformation:** Civil disobedience should be learned through practices; massive mobilization is the key to success; protect or support the students	**Adversarial framing:** Umbrellas revolution is discontinuous with OC; elites' conspiracy to sabotage a spontaneous revolution; OCLP Trio, student leaders and leftards hijack the occupation; grassroots' real resistances happen only in Mongkok

just be another "big show" without real political effects. To attract the support of the moderates, Benny Tai even, at some points, openly said to the public that the purpose of planning an occupation was not for real occupation but to use the talking of it as a bargaining chip in negotiations with the government. The skeptics conceived of this as the strongest proof of the lack of commitment to give occupation real teeth.

For the radical activists, however, only a shocking number of people through mobilization could exert enough pressure on the government to force it to make concessions. Thus the issues they were concerned most with were: Who would be eligible to participate? How could they participate? What kind of reform package would be backed by the whole action? They did not think that OCLP had provided them with convincing answers.

Indeed, OCLP took a cautious approach and tried to manage the occupation scene with strict discipline and order, to the point of even suggesting a ban on any unapproved loudspeaker. The purpose was to make sure that the whole action was strictly nonviolent; no unexpected event and no chaos would occur. Such a high caution against any possible disruption, however, also raised the degree of exclusivity, which in turn aroused more suspicion concerning the real goals of the whole operation. Many skeptics were concerned that the design was, indeed, to exclude the radical groups and that the plan was merely a moderates' ploy to strike a highly compromised deal with the government.

Frame Transformation: Holding OC in Check

The skeptics' criticisms of OCLP illustrate some of the difficulties of "frame alignment" between the OCLP initiators and the radical activists. What followed the criticisms was a process of "frame transformation," which usually occurs when the proposed frame "may not resonate with, and on occasion may even appear antithetical to, conventional lifestyles or rituals and extant interpretive frames."[32] In the case of OC, the transformation of frame materialized in a notion of "holding OC in check," which was put forward by Tam Tak-chi, an activist in People's Power.[33] Accordingly, Tam formed and led a concern group called Supporters of Occupy Central (SOC). Although SOC were organizationally unconnected with the official OCLP office, they saw themselves as a stand-in organizer of OC actions in case the OCLP plan was given up for whatever reasons. SOC also set up street booths to make contact with the public so that common people could have the chance to be involved. They also initiated small-scale protest actions to demonstrate to the public that there were other ways to take the idea of street occupation into people's own hands.[34] In terms of frame analysis, the transformed frame proposed by SOC had indeed reframed the motivation to join OC: not just to be an obedient participant but to prepare to take over the whole action.

Radical democrats, like Tam, also held the view that only a simple method such as civic nomination could ensure that the future chief executive election would not be manipulated by Beijing. They threw all their efforts to support reform proposals with the element of civic nomination; they also worked in collaboration with like-minded student leaders, such as Joshua Wong.[35] In the third Deliberation Day, the radicals and the students successfully pushed the Deliberation Panel to put up for civic referendum three reform proposals, all tagged with civic nomination. The result upset the moderate democrats, as it became harder for them to narrow their gap with the conservatives sitting at the pro-establishment side. The intervention of SOC was annoying for OCLP; even the far-right Civic Passion accused them of hijacking the OCLP campaign for opportunistic purposes. This initiative, however, had somehow redressed the problem of the elitist exclusivity of the OCLP and its overreliance on "deliberative democracy," which was inimical to the grassroots.

Occupation without a Plan: HKFS and Scholarism

The two student bodies—HKFS and Scholarism—held similar skeptical views about OCLP's plan. They were particularly impatient about the lack of actual involvement of the potential participants of occupation, as the leaders seemed to have spent most of the time talking about the ideas and organizing the Deliberation Days, which were indeed attended only by a few.[36] They worried that the whole campaign would cool down before it could really have a chance to start. To demonstrate their determination to make the actions real, they insisted on holding an "occupation rehearsal" in the Central after the July 1st Handover Day march, although OCLP regarded that as premature. But it successfully staged an overnight occupation, at which 511 people were arrested. The participants followed all the procedures and doctrines taught by the OC trainers regarding nonviolent resistance, and it ended peacefully. Because of the success of the student actions, people started to invest hope in the students as a leadership alternative to the OCLP, although the students had actually no concrete plan to work out a replacement.

After the People's Congress announced their ruling on Hong Kong political reform on August 31, 2014, the OCLP leaders were shocked and disappointed, as no room for further negotiation was in sight. In a rally held in Tamar Park, a number of speakers, including Benny Tai, expressed their extreme anger and frustration. Some former student leaders came out to confess their failures and proclaimed that "reunion-in-democracy" was dead. In a highly symbolic manner, the old master frame of the prodemocracy movement that had held for the past three decades was shattered. People were left without any schemata of interpretation to enable themselves to locate, perceive, identify, and make sense of their action in the future. In the absence of a stand-by execution plan foreseeing such an early rejection, OCLP and the pan-democrat politicians could not react to the crisis other than by issuing empty calls for scaled-up civil disobedience actions in all social sectors. At that moment, only the university students could respond to Beijing's August 31 decision with action, and that was with a class boycott. The student strikes were mainly conducted in Tamar Park, where teach-in activities filled out a week's schedule. The students then took a central role and caught all the limelight for it. OCLP were heavily condemned by many due to their wavering about the exact date of the occupation. They exposed themselves as totally unprepared for this drastic setback and, as a result, their leadership status quickly evaporated.[37]

By the end of the week of class boycotts, a rally was held on the Tim Mei Avenue next to the Civic Square[38] adjacent to the government building. Activists from HKFS and Scholarism broke into the Civic Square, an action that led to the arrest of student leaders, including Alex Chow and Joshua Wong. In the next two days, all streets and roads surrounding the government buildings and Legislative Council were occupied by thousands of protesters demanding the release of the arrested students. The actions were suddenly reframed spontaneously by the participants as supporting the students and calling for their release. Droves of people came to encircle the government building until the 28th of September, the day the occupation of Harcourt Road of Admiralty was triggered by the tear gas bombings. For this surprise attack and the series of contingencies, the original OCPL plan was abandoned just a few hours after Benny Tai hastily announced its beginning.

At the outbreak of the massive occupation, the participants seemed to have internalized the radical democrats' calls for nonviolent actions without a detailed, premeditated plan or dogmatic observance to well-rehearsed rules. Yet the yearlong teaching and publicizing of the principles of nonviolent resistance still took effect. In all three occupied sites, the principle of nonviolence was not compromised, even though it was interpreted and implemented very differently from what OCLP leaders perceived prior to the events. From this perspective, a clear continuity is seen between the initial OCLP plan and the Umbrella occupation after September 28th. In terms of organization, however, the original OCLP leadership completely crumbled, to be replaced by a new team of ad hoc leaders, with the students taking the central role. Many people celebrated the spontaneity and were awed by the self-restraint of the occupiers. Yet the effective decision-making mechanisms for the whole campaign broke down as the occupation dragged on. It was in such a vacuum that the right-wing localists came out to contest the ideological leadership of the whole movement and to suggest an alternative action frame.

Part C: Framing the 'Enemy Within'

As said before, the right-wing localists were unenthusiastic about the Occupy Central plan when it was first proposed by Benny Tai. For example, Wong Yeung-tat, the leader of Civic Passion, condemned the proposal as a set of "utterly futile" ideas. He faulted the OCLP as an attempt to marginalize the localists, discriminating them as if they were all rioters; he ridiculed the plan as one built upon "empty moral appeals."[39]

When the occupation was about to occur, however, the right-wing localists seized the opportunity. Some made themselves visible right at the spot. For instance, Civic Passion was at Admiralty with a booth of its own, then moved to Mongkok a few days later; others coordinated in their own ways to take advantage of the occupation.[40] They also made use of their own (mainly online) media channels, including *Passion Times* and *VJ Media*, to disseminate news and their own reports of the occupation. Wan Chin was also active in propagating his own analysis of the unfolding events through his own Facebook page.[41] Instead of coming out in person to take the leader's role for the whole campaign, the right-wing localists' intervention at this stage was mainly discursive, deploying a series of typical right-wing populist rhetorical devices and practices.[42] I am going to describe in the following sections the operation of the populist rhetorics and practices in four dimensions and analyze how localism could emerge after the Umbrella occupation as a full-fledged ideological force.

Framing the Sequence of Events:
Movement vs. Revolution

Although Mongkok occupiers came from all walks of life, it turned out to be the site in which right-wing localists were most active. The atmosphere there became tense after the raids by the police and the progovernment gangs and thugs that happened in the first week. Soon after those incidents, stickers and posters attacking HKFS and some of the well-known left-wing activists mysteriously appeared.[43] Rumors of attacks and espionage abounded. Waves of criticisms against the leftards, the OCLP picketers, and the HKFS organizers came from the right-wing localist media, accusing them of hijacking the occupation and attempting to disband the crowd.

Such accusations were associated closely with the localists' own narration of the sequence of events. As they said, the occupation right after the September 28th tear gas raids had nothing to do with the efforts made by Benny Tai and his group for the past two years. They claimed that the OCLP was already still-born as soon as OCLP and HKFS called for dispersing the crowd when rumors of plastic bullets were dispersed. What happened after the tear gas bombing was then a spontaneous and leaderless "Umbrella Revolution" that could run without organization.[44] The metaphor of revolution allows them to delink the occupation between past Hong Kong prodemocracy movements in general and the OC plan in particular. They celebrated the spontaneity of the occupation as "revolutionary" in the sense that no foreign powers (including the PRC and United States) could control the situation. For that matter, Wan Chin did not shy away from a making a parallel allegation against the OC Trio and the student leaders as puppets of the United States. As a matter of fact, soon after the occupation happened, Wan Chin started to claim himself to be the strategist of such a revolution. His daily, if not hourly, comments on the situation spread fast and wide on the Internet and attracted enthusiastic responses from his "disciples." He proclaimed that Hong Kong had entered a period of popular politics in which the people will take political matters into their own hands. His Facebook page soon became a commanding center of the right-wing localists' "imaged" war.

Recoding Class Politics: Elites vs. Grassroots

Like radical right-wing populists elsewhere in the world, Wan Chin and his followers consider society to be ultimately separated into two homogeneous and antagonistic groups, "the pure common people" and "the corrupt elite," and they argue that politics should be an expression of the general will of the people.[45] By simplifying the world in this manner, they can claim to speak for the pure common people against the corrupt elite. Such conceptual binarism allowed the populist adversarial framing to operate in the context of the Umbrella Movement and put in practice their anti-elitism by redrawing the map of confrontation. According to such a new framing, the contest no longer occurred just between the antigovernment masses and the state apparatuses; it was also a battle between the common people against the elites. The common people (appearing in the occupied sites as the ordinary occupiers), were celebrated as winning a spontaneous "revolution" that was, however, vulnerable to betrayal by the elites. The elites were colluding with each other to steal the fruit of the people's spontaneous revolution. Their trick was to pass themselves as the people's leaders, orchestrating the protests in various forms of the "main platform."

The anti-elitist cause soon found echoes among the occupiers and was concretized into actions against the main platform. But the words "main platform" had no precise meaning. Sometimes it referred to the group of ad hoc leaders that included the OC trio, the pan-democrats, the student bodies, etc.; sometimes it meant anyone who could get easy access to the biggest loudspeaker in the center of the Admiralty site. In any case, it was framed by the right-wing localists as symbolizing the elites' power. By reframing the occupation as a revolution against the elites, the objectives of the campaign would not be confined to requesting the government for concession but would include knocking the elites down from their leadership status, insulting them and depriving them of their credibility. In mid-October 2014, Wan Chin had indeed, through his Facebook page, called his followers to "deal a heavy blow" to the representatives of HKFS planning to come to Mongkok to hold a discussion forum there. From time to time, there were small squads of patrol teams wandering around, trying to shoot-down any leftards or student leaders speaking to their audience.

Throughout the occupation, there were numerous cases of clashes springing out of the controversies over the relocation of barricades, contraction of occupation zones for emergency traffic, and the like. The influence of these events was minor at the beginning, but when the occupation prolonged, incidents of protesters encircling the main speaker's platform located in the middle of the Admiralty occupation zone became frequent. Complaints about the exclusivity of the main platform (guarded mainly by the NGO activists and student leaders) created conflicts almost every night.

The ad hoc leadership of the occupation was clearly weak and fragile in organizational terms (see chapter 2). The doctrine of extreme spontaneity, as well as the vicious attacks on the main platform, did not allow for any kind of democratic mechanism to function. For the right-wing localists, however, blocking any attempts made by the elites to reach a compromise or "strategic withdrawal" was framed as safeguarding the fruit of the spontaneous revolution. The Umbrella occupation was thus soon trapped in a deadlock that made decision making impossible. Any decision made by the speakers on the platform that was based on a sampled survey of opinion or onsite discussion of small groups would be condemned by a substantial number of occupiers as undemocratic and unrepresentative. It rendered Umbrella occupiers incapable, by themselves and the belief they shared, to make decision for themselves or to act collectively. The only options left were either to continue to try everyone's patience until everything came to its exhaustion or to raise the level of bodily clashes with the policemen. On November 30th, HKFS and Scholarism yielded to the pressure to break the stalemate of the whole campaign. The ill-planned action of encircling the chief executive office ended with the worst violence since the beginning of the occupation.[46] HKFS's leadership took the blame, which resulted in a series of withdrawals from the HKFS campaign after the occupation ended.[47]

REMAPPING POLITICAL SPACE: ADMIRALTY VS. MONGKOK

The right-wing populist discursive logic of recoding political space was also found in how they strategically mapped the spatial dynamic of the different occupation sites. As soon as Mongkok was occupied on September 28, Wan Chin issued his geostrategic analysis through his Facebook page, in which he described Hong Kong island as the worst place to defend and Admiralty as a place suited only for the middle-class professionals; those people would have affinity with intellectual figures like Benny Tai. In contrast, Kowloon has roads and streets sprawling in different directions through which the grassroots people can easily pass. Therefore, Wan Chin deemed that the localist fighters should abandon Admiralty and take Mongkok as their strategic base.

Although groups of different political persuasions, including the far left Socialist Action and moderate left Age of Resistance, were also active in Mongkok throughout the occupation period, Civic Passion always promoted themselves as being in command of the whole Mongkok zone and insisted it was only through their antispying operation that OCLP and HKFS were kept from infiltrating Mongkok. It is of course true that Mongkok is populated by people with grassroots backgrounds. Yet the right-wing localists did not just want to include and organize more people of grassroots background to join. Rather, they wanted to make the most out of the cultural differences between the two places so that they could claim Mongkok as their own bastion in order to mark themselves off from the protesters in Admiralty. Mongkok was then repainted as distant from the elite's pseudo-resistance, representing the "truer" Hong Kong and serving as a cradle for the genuine revolutionaries.

Reframing the occupation in these populist terms was necessary for contesting the media images depicting Hong Kong protesters as always "civilized" and able to exercise self-restraint. The artful display found in Admiralty was considered by the right-wing localists as another way to perpetuate a middle class, Bohemian self-imagination, always the favorites of the Western media. The right wing, however, deemed that the Western gaze upon Hong Kong has been internalized as a liberal self-fantasy and that its consequences are disenabling. Because the elitist middle class is never serious about local political struggle, they only indulge themselves in artistic creativity and their self-fantasized moral appeals.

The imagined standoff between Admiralty and Mongkok strengthened a right-wing localist populist fantasy of an imagined culture war between the grassroots localist Hong Kongers and the cosmopolitan elites.

REINVENTING ACTION REPERTOIRE: CIVIL DISOBEDIENCE VS. SYMBOLIC MILITANCY

Undoubtedly, Mongkok was the place where the most violent clashes, both with the police and the progovernment thugs, occurred. Protesters of all political factions participated in these incidents, but the right-wing localists appeared to be getting the most out of the confrontations, as they were eager to lay claims on these events and made themselves look better when they occurred. For example, they always dressed to look more militant, first by wearing military outfits for war games and later by holding handmade wooden shields. To promote this self-styled militancy, some members of the City-State cult issued instructions for making the shields. Wan Chin also went in person to the Mongkok site to demonstrate how a shield could be made out of a suitcase; he even went on to perform certain stylistic, self-claimed religious rituals with his City-State cult members. One may see this as comical exhibitionism and be skeptical as to the value of these gadgets in combat and defense. Yet the symbolic values of such gadgets and performances were immense, for they served the purpose of defying the nonviolent doctrines upheld by Benny Tai's followers.

After the emergence of right-wing localists in 2011, militant resistance had been upheld as signaling how the legacies of "reunion-in-democracy" could be replaced. In that regard, Mongkok indeed became the stage on which militant resistance could be "performed." The function of these performances of symbolic militancy is not measured by how effective were in resisting the imposition of law and order by the government but by how they could exorcise the meekness and timidity of Hong Kong–styled protests. Countering the frame of "civic maturity," the right-wing localists could fully indulge themselves in the new self-image of belonging to a group of revolutionaries, who might not be totally convinced by the complex city-state theory but for whom an aesthetic resonance could easily be felt. In short, the symbolic militancy could provide signs around which new forms of identification (identity building) were made possible. (see also chapter 3)

The right-wing localists also had a strong devotion to keeping the militant spirit during the occupation; at times it ran with a kind of asceticism. They formed small squads to patrol the occupied site to make sure there were no leftard signs of "happy resistance," such as singing a song, which could contaminate the fighting spirit within the site. Therefore, while some of the leftist cultural activists were experimenting with the use of the occupied space to demonstrate how political resistance could be integrated with everyday life—making several attempts to screen films or organize table tennis games on the occupied road— the right-wing squad raided what they saw as "entertainment" activities.[48]

Conclusion: A Paradigm Shift?

Many political discussions after the Umbrella protest coined the term "paradigm shift" to describe the changes Hong Kong politics and oppositional movements had undergone. But the term "paradigm shift" means different things to different people. Some focus on the action repertoires, claiming that the Umbrella occupation has widened the range and options of actions taken by social campaigns by breaking the taboo of using militant action or even violence; others say that the new paradigm entails a new ideological outlook that breaks away from the old line of "reunion-in-democracy" and welcomes the era of not just localism but Hong Kong nationalism. This chapter's account of the context against which the Umbrella occupation occurred and the disputes involved within it can only offer a limited angle to answer these questions. What I can argue as a tentative conclusion is that the Umbrella Movement was basically not a battleground between old and new conceptions of identity; rather, the subject matter was, throughout the process, democratic reform. Having said that, I also think that no one can take the Umbrella Movement out of the bigger context of ideological contestation happening over the years and how these contestations affected the prodemocracy cause.

The Umbrella Movement was indeed overshadowed by an intense struggle for symbolic power, which might not help to organize the movement in a conventional sense. In other words, underneath the common quest for genuine direct election, a battle of anti-elitism was played out according to the populist logic that allowed its adherents to always play taboo breakers, going against political correctness. Disputes over framing and strategies went hand-in-hand with a subterranean campaign against the elites alleged to be gaining personal benefits by being part of the social movement industry or political establishment. The elites were reframed to be worse enemies than the regime in power instead of someone holding different judgments about tactics and action choices.[49] Such an anti-elitist battle deepened the "culture of distrust" in Hong Kong.

Calhoun, in his reflection of the Occupy Wall Street protests, has already highlighted the "populist" feature of occupation. He writes, "There is also fragility in the very project of representing the people by public gathering . . . the participation of a crowd encourages the sense of being a part of something bigger than oneself, of acting not just as a small minority of the population but as 'the people.' Yet this also encourages the illusion that one has found much wider support than perhaps one has."[50] Calhoun is still appreciative, however, of the populist mobilization for its potential to invoke "the people as the decisive locus of moral authority, because a populist message can keep a simple and straightforward focus on inequality and be able to unite people." I think the case of the Umbrella Movement in Hong Kong can offer us a counterexample to the optimism of treating occupation as a more effective action repertoire and a case for further debates about populism's implications for the causes of social solidarity and democracy.

Coda

After the Umbrella occupations came to a close by the end of 2014, militant resistance began to wane, despite sporadic confrontations with the police from time to time in the Mongkok district. The urban disturbance that happened on Chinese New Year Day 2016 did not draw massive support; an "uprising" of the people, fancied by the right-wing radicals, did not materialize. The incident marked a turning point at which the right-wing localists shifted their effort toward winning elections. Through the election campaigns and their results, we see a general "localism" rapidly developing in term of its popularity, especially among the young voters. Many young candidates emerged in the political scene for the first time claiming to be heirs of the Umbrella movement. They strive to attract votes by putting forward positions revolving around localism or self-determination.[51] Although these new localist forces can be in different positions of the spectrum ranging from left to right, they belonged to the same camp, refusing to pursue a political future for Hong Kong within the current framework of "one country, two systems." Altogether, six of these candidates won, with 19.1 percent of the total votes, although the main agitators of the right-wing localist current, such as Wan Chin and Wong Yuk-man, failed to be elected.

The elections helped the localists to consolidate their support by expressing it in concrete vote counts; localism has successfully become a prominent political ideology in Hong Kong. The competition for votes, however, also had its downside: speeding up internal splits and infighting.[52] The election campaigns were framed merely as a chance for the younger generation to succeed and replace the old one without a convincing articulation of the previous calls for militant action on the street. In short, localism can no longer offer a coherent collective action frame for oppositional politics. With the whole oppositional camp caught in a chaotic and fragmentary state, the government launched a counterattack, using dubious measures to keep some people from participating in the election and even removing some elected councilors from their seats. These councilors were charged with being insincere in supporting the Basic Law, as witnessed by their past deeds or their performance in the oath-taking ceremony. The National People's Congress came out to impose its own interpretation of the Basic Law; six of the elected representatives were unseated as a result. The government used every means to wipe out ideological challengers to its authority. Localists thus suffered a heavy loss.[53] To make matters worse, out of frustration and fatigue, public opinion started to swing back to the conservative and moderate mode in the 2017 chief executive election.[54] The radicals were isolated and widely condemned, even among the veteran democracy supporters. The low turnout in almost all kinds of political protest suggests also that the tide of radical social mobilization that began in 2014 might have died down for the time being.

Therefore, we are witnessing a "paradigm shift" of Hong Kong politics from that pertaining to a "liberal" society toward that of an authoritarian regime. The Umbrella Movement does not offer a "new paradigm of social movement organizing," as once envisioned by Benny Tai, nor an operable alternative anticipated by the right-wing localists. Therefore, the Umbrella occupation might be better seen as a manifestation of our crisis rather than as offering a practical model for the future. As Gramsci writes, "The crisis consists precisely in the fact that the old is dying and the new cannot be born; in this interregnum, a great variety of morbid symptoms appear."[55] No one is sure how long this interregnum will last.

NOTES

1. Arif Dirlik, "The Mouse That Roared: The Democratic Movement in Hong Kong," *Contemporary Chinese Political Economy and Strategic Relations: An International Journal* 2, no. 2 (2016): 665–81; Francis L. F. Lee and Joseph M. Chan, *Media, Social Mobilization and Mass Protests in Post-Colonial Hong Kong. The Power of A Critical Event* (London: Routledge, 2010); Brian C. H. Fong, "State-Society Conflicts under Hong Kong's Hybrid Regime. Governing Coalition Building and Civil Society Challenges," *Asian Survey* 53, no. 5 (2013): 854–82.

2. Master Frame is a mode of attribution and articulation across different collective actions and gives shape to a cycle of protest that lasts for a period of time. See David A. Snow and Robert Benford, "Master Frames and Cycles of Protest," in *Frontiers in Social Movement Theory*, ed. Aldon D. Morris and Carol M. Mueller (New Haven, CT: Yale University Press, 1992); William A. Gamson and David S. Meyer, "Framing Political Opportunity," in *Comparative Perspectives on Social Movements*, ed. Doug McAdam, John McCarthy, and Mayer Zald (New York: Cambridge University Press, 1996), 275–90.

3. W. Gamson, "Constructing Social Protest," in *Social Movements and Culture*, ed. H. Johnston and B. Klandermans (Minneapolis: University of Minnesota Press, 1995), 85–106; S. A. Hunt, Robert D. Benford and David A. Snow, "Identity Fields: Framing Processes and

the Social Construction of Movement Identities," in *New Social Movements: From Ideology to Identity*, ed. E. Larana, H. Johnston, and J. Gusfield (Philadelphia: Temple University Press, 1994), 185–208; G. Knight and J. Greenberg, "Talk of the Enemy: Adversarial Framing and Climate Change Discourse," *Social Movement Studies* 10, no. 4 (2011): 323–40.

4. Francis L. F. Lee and Joseph M. Chan, *Media and Protest Logics in the Digital Era* (New York: Oxford University Press, 2018), 148.

5. D. Meyer and S. Staggenborg, "Movements, Countermovements, and the Structure of Political Opportunity," *American Journal of Sociology* 101 (1996): 1628–60.

6. The then reformist Chinese prime minister, Zhao Zhiyang, once showed that he was interested in the "reunion-in-democracy" idea expressed in an open letter sent to him by young university student leaders. Prodemocracy activists groups were inspired by the promises and pledges the Chinese leaders made to allow Hong Kong to enjoy both autonomy and democracy under "one country, two systems." They organized political parties and run in elections to turn themselves into politicians or grassroot activists fighting for a full-fledged democratic system in Hong Kong.

7. For example, Szeto Wah had not commented on the idea of "reunion-in-democracy" advocated mainly by Meeting-Point throughout the Sino-British negotiation. Martin Lee was an advocate for the continuation of British rule in the same period but turned into a democrat leader after 1989. Both of them have become the most representative figures of moderate democrats, adopting the rhetoric of "reunion-in-democracy."

8. Alvin So, *Hong Kong's Embattled Democracy* (Baltimore: Johns Hopkins University Press, 1999); Ming Sing, "Mobilization for Political Change: The Prodemocracy Movement in Hong Kong (1980s–1994)," in *The Dynamics of Social Movement in Hong Kong*, ed. Tai-Lok Lui and Stephen Wing-kai Chiu (Hong Kong: Hong Kong University Press, 2000); Ming Sing, *Hong Kong's Tortuous Democratization: A Comparative Analysis* (London: Routledge, 2004).

9. For that matter, some people suggested they rename their cause "fighting against the communist rule by democracy." But no one ever called to reopen the disputes about reunification with China. This alternative naming gradually faded away as the democrats adopted a more moderate approach in their relationship with the Chinese government. After the handover, the meaning of "reunion-in-democracy" further shifted away from the more voluntary nationalistic motivation it had when it was first proposed toward a passive compliance with the fact of Chinese sovereignty in Hong Kong.

10. David A. Snow and Robert Benford, "Ideology, Frame Resonance, and Participant Mobilization," in *From Structure to Action: Comparing Social Movement Research Across Cultures*, ed. Bert Klandermans, Hanspeter Kriesi, and Sidney Tarrow (Greenwich, CT: JAI Press, 1988), 197–217.

11. Alvin So, "Social Conflict in Hong Kong after 1997: The Emergence of a Post-Modern Mode of Social Movement?" in *China's Hong Kong Transformed*, ed. Ming K. Chan (Hong Kong: City University Press, 2008).

12. On the contrary, the People's Congress in 2004 imposed further restrictions on direct elections for both the chief executive and legislative councilors.

13. Francis L. F. Lee and Joseph M. Chan, *Media, Social Mobilization and Mass Protests in Post-Colonial Hong Kong. The Power of A Critical Event* (London: Routledge, 2010).

14. Wing-sang Law, "Decolonization Deferred: A Historical Perspective on Hong Kong Identity," in *Citizenship, Identity and Social Movements in the New Hong Kong. Localism after the Umbrella Movement*, ed. Wai-man Lam and Luke Cooper (London: Routledge, 2018), 13–33.

15. Yun-chung Chen and Mirana M. Szeto, "The Forgotten Road of Progressive Localism: New Preservation Movement in Hong Kong," *Inter-Asia Cultural Studies* 16, no. 3 (2015): 436–53.

16. Betty Yung and Yuk-ming Leung, "Diverse Roles of Alternative Media in Hong Kong Civil Society: From Public Discourse Initiation to Social Activism," *Journal of Asian Public Policy* 7, no. 1 (2014): 83–101.

17. Doug McAdam, *The Political Process and the Development of Black Insurgency* (Chicago: University of Chicago Press, 1982).

18. In January 2012, a thousand demonstrators came to protest against a D&G shop in Tsimshatsui because the shop was rumored to have banned Hong Kong people from taking photos in front of it whereas tourists from Mainland China were allowed to do so.

19. Iam-chong Ip, "Politics of Belonging: A Study of the Campaign against Mainland Visitors in Hong Kong," *Inter-Asia Cultural Studies* 16, no. 3 (2015): 410–21; C. P. Chan, "Post–Umbrella Movement: Localism and Radicalness of the Hong Kong Student Movement," *Contemporary Chinese Political Economy and Strategic Relations: An International Journal* 2, no. 2 (2016): 885–908; Sebastian Veg, "The Rise of 'Localism' and Civic Identity in Post-Handover Hong Kong: Questioning the Chinese Nation-State," *China Quarterly* 230 (2017): 323–47.

20. Wan Chin, *Thesis on Hong Kong City-State* (Hong Kong: Enrich Publishing, 2011).

21. When Chin ran for the Legislative Council in 2016, however, he drastically modified his proposal to seek the continuation of the Basic Law after 2047 in order to sustain Hong Kong's status as a special administrative zone under Chinese sovereignty.

22. Hong Kong nationalism was proposed by a special issue of *Undergrad*, the student magazine of the Student Union of HKU, published in 2014. See also Justin P. Kwan, "The Rise of Civic Nationalism: Shifting Identities in Hong Kong and Taiwan," *Contemporary Chinese Political Economy and Strategic Relations: An International Journal* 2, no. 2 (2016): 941–73; Veg, "The Rise of 'Localism,'" 323–47.

23. In particular, Hong Kongers should resist the attempts to replace Cantonese with Putonghua and boycott the use of simplified Chinese characters instead of traditional Chinese characters. All these goals should be achieved through "ethnic struggles"; otherwise, Hong Kong will be devoured by the Mainland very soon.

24. They further identify three "identity fields" or categories of actor, namely protagonists, antagonists, and audience. See Scott A. Hunt, Robert D. Benford, and David A. Snow, "Identity Fields: Framing Processes and the Social Construction of Movement Identities," in *New Social Movements: From Ideology to Identity*, ed. E. Larana, H. Johnston, and J. Gusfield (Philadelphia: Temple University Press, 1994), 185–208.

25. Benford and Snow see "adversarial framing" as a kind of "diagnostic framing." See Robert D. Benford and David A. Snow, "Framing Processes and Social Movements: An Overview and Assessment," *Annual Review of Sociology* 26 (2000): 611–39.

26. Carl Schmitt, *The Concept of the Political*, trans. George D. Schwab (Chicago: University of Chicago Press, 1996).

27. Wan Chin, *Thesis on Hong Kong City-State*.

28. Wan Chin, *Records of the Calamities Made by the Leftards* (Hong Kong: Arcadia Press, 2015).

29. The three campaigns include the following: campaign against the National Education Curriculum (2012); campaign against the denial of a TV license for HKTV (2013); and campaign against the North East New Territories (NENT) New Development Planning (2014). The stories were often seen as minor infighting among the campaigners and were seldom considered as newsworthy for mainstream media. They were, however, widespread over the Internet through the Facebook pages of famous online key opinion leaders and the new online media.

30. Lee and Chan, *Media and Protest Logics*, 58.

31. Sebastian Veg, "Legalistic and Utopian. Hong Kong's Umbrella Movement," *New Left Review* 92 (March–April 2015): 55–73.

32. David A. Snow et al., "Frame Alignment Processes, Micromobilization, and Movement Participation," *American Sociological Review* 51, no. 4 (1986): 464–81.

33. The whole idea of "Holding OC in check" was supported by radical democrats such as Stephen Shiu Yeuk-yuen, the key sponsor of the online broadcasting media Hong Kong People Reporter. Other radical democrats, such as legislator Leung Kwok-Hung of LSD, Albert Chan of People Power, and even the fringe far left group Socialist Action expressed more or less the same view.

34. For example, in their online radio programs, they kept on discussing the concept of "mobile occupation," which are unled and unplanned spontaneous actions such as pretending to pick up a large number of lost coins on the street.

35. Joshua Wong, "Scholarism on the March," *New Left Review* 92 (2015): 43–52.

36. They were also put off by the exclusive measures proposed by the OCLP leaders, for example, that participants had to sign a statement declaring their degree of involvement and the suggestion that restrictions be imposed against underage youngsters' participation unless the parent's approval was available in written form.

37. According to a survey conducted by Joseph M. Chan and Francis L. F. Lee, around 14.2 percent of the interviewees consider supporting calls made by HKFS (and 13.2 percent for Scholarism) as very important for their participation in Umbrella occupation, whereas only 6.6 percent consider supporting the calls made by the OC trio as very important. See Lee and Chan, *Media and Protest Logics*, 226.

38. Civic Square refers to the small place in front of the government building, the place named after the activists during the 2012 Anti-National Education Curriculum Campaign. After a series of big overnight demonstrations in 2014, the government built a high fence around it, prohibiting people's entrance.

39. He criticized Occupy Central for making extensive use of the mass media, gathering political celebrities and wasting energy on designing an election reform proposal that as yet had content. He teased Occupy Central as only a plan to "steal the lime-light."

40. Wan Chin's cult (Hong Kong Resurgence) once occupied Canton Road at Tsimshatsui for a week. The place is seen by the right-wing localists as a sacred site because it was where the first anti-Mainlander protest (the D&G ban) broke out. Most of the speakers there repeated the messages of blocking the leftards from disbanding the occupying crowd. Only a few people joined the occupation at this site. After a week, the site was abandoned.

41. During the first week of occupation, the posts on his Facebook page had attracted up to 2,100 likes and nearly a thousand shares—numbers that had doubled or even tripled the previous average—although the number seems to be insignificant in comparison with what the pages of HKFS or Scholarism were getting at that time.

42. Ruth Wodak, *The Politics of Fear. What Right-Wing Populist Discourses Mean* (Los Angeles: Sage, 2015).

43. Pictured posters attacking Yip Po-lam, Chan King Fai, and Lam Fai, the three activists of the 2007 campaign for preserving Queen Piers, appeared in almost every corner of Mongkok. These activists had been accused before by the right-wing localists as leftards sabotaging other antigovernment protests. But they were actually not playing any key role in the Umbrella protests. Lam Fai was not even in Hong Kong at that moment.

44. For this reason, they strongly reject the term "Umbrella Movement." See *Passion Times*, ed., Records of the Failed Umbrella Revolution (Hong Kong: Passiontimes, 2016).

45. Cas Mudde and C. R. Kaltwasser, *Populism in Europe and the Americas. Threat or Corrective for Democracy?* (Cambridge: Cambridge University Press, 2012); Cas Mudde, "The Populist Zeitgeist," *Government and Opposition* 39, no. 4 (2004): 542–63.

46. The actions resulted in twenty people being arrested. More than one hundred people were wounded, some seriously; thirty-one of them were admitted to the hospital.

47. In 2015, HKFS lost four member unions in toto, as the student unions of HKU, PolyU, BaptistU, and CityU completed the withdrawal processes through referendums in their respective campuses.

48. The right-wing asceticism, however, had not influenced how things ran in the Admiralty site, where one could find a big makeshift study room built for the high school occupiers.

49. M. Edelman, *Constructing the Political Spectacle* (Chicago: University of Chicago Press, 1988).

50. Craig Calhoun, "Occupy Wall Street in Perspective," *British Journal of Sociology* 64, no. 1 (2013): 26–38.

51. Civic Passion and Youngspiration won three seats altogether in the 2016 Legislative Council election. Both of these two parties carried a strong anti-Mainland-immigrant agenda. Another alliance advocating the "democratic self-determination" of Hong Kong also won three seats. The alliance consisted of Demosistō, the young political party transformed from Scholarism, Eddy Chu, a former progressive localist, and Lau Siu-Lai, an independent social activist. They adhered to the more left-wing traditions of social activism endorsing a kind of localism without xenophobic orientation.

52. The infighting among the right-wing localists—Civic Passion, Youngspiration, and the cults of Wong Yuk-man and Wan Chin—have almost shattered the whole camp.

53. Among the six "disqualified" Councilors, four come from the broadly defined localist camp.

54. Although most Hong Kong citizens do not have a vote in the election, John Tsang, a moderate bureaucrat, launched a campaign to gain popularity as if everybody had a vote. He has attracted huge public support in comparison to Carrie Lam. Many moderate democrats enthusiastically threw their support behind Tsang and thus annoyed the radicals, who believed that supporting a candidate of the establishment camp betrayed the prodemocracy cause. For that matter, Tsang's supporters had a bitter dispute with the radicals, who were condemned harshly by the former.

55. Antonio Gramsci, *Selections from the Prison Notebooks*, ed. and trans. Quintin Hoare and Geoffrey Nowell-Smith (London: Lawrence & Wishart, 1971), 276.

5

MEDIASCAPE AND MOVEMENT

The Dynamics of Political Communication,
Public and Counterpublic

Francis L. F. Lee

In their seminal discussion of media and movements as interacting systems, Gamson and Wolfsfeld noted that one major challenge facing social movements is to gain visibility and standing in the news media,[1] which are crucial to the capability of a movement to garner public attention and support. Yet there is a fundamental imbalance in the media-movement relationship: the news media have plenty of choices of news stories and sources, whereas social movements are much more reliant on the media for the oxygen of publicity. Meanwhile, many scholars argue that the mainstream media are embedded in the dominant political-economic structure and hence are primarily agents of social control. They tend to delegitimize social movements by either ignoring them or portraying them as dangerous and deviant.[2]

Two decades later, the media-movement nexus is complicated by substantial changes in the media landscape. Up to the 1990s, the "news media system" consisted primarily of a limited set of resourceful organizations specializing in the production of public affairs content. Alternative media existed but had limited reach.[3] There was no effective platform for social groups to communicate directly with the public. The scenario changed with the emergence of digital media, which reduced the cost of content distribution and facilitated the growth of alternative media.[4] Digital media also became the tools for citizens to communicate and coordinate among themselves, leading to new forms or "logics" of protest actions.[5]

The contemporary mediascape is constituted by the combination of mainstream media institutions, alternative media, and digital media platforms. The former two refer to content-producing institutions, whereas the latter are spaces for communication and content distribution that may have their own operational logic. The three are intertwined. Mainstream media have their online presence. The contents of both mainstream and alternative media are often reliant on social media for distribution. Online contents and phenomena can feedback into the mainstream media. Together they form a holistic mediascape offering a range of mediation opportunities[6] for social movements. What remains unchanged is the concern over whether and how social movements could garner public attention and support through communication.

Based on the above premises, this chapter reviews the relationship between the media and the Umbrella Movement. It argues that the mainstream media, aided by digital media outlets and platforms, play the important role of the public monitor in times of major social conflicts, even though the Hong Kong media do so in an environment where partial censorship exists. The impact of digital media in large-scale protest movements is similarly multifaceted and contradictory. Digital media empower social protests by promoting oppositional discourses, facilitating mobilization, and contributing to the emergence of connective action, but they also introduce and exacerbate forces of decentralization that present challenges to movement leaders. Meanwhile, during and after the Umbrella Movement, one can also see how the state has become more proactive in online political communication, thus trying to undermine the oppositional character of the Internet in Hong Kong.

The following begins by reviewing the configurations of the mainstream media and the development of digital political communication before the Umbrella Movement. These are the bases on which the roles and impact of media and communication during the occupation are analyzed. The chapter then discusses post–Umbrella Movement developments. The concluding section summarizes the analysis and briefly compares the case of Hong Kong to other societies.

Mainstream Media in Hong Kong before the Umbrella Movement

Although the conceptualization of the mediascape in this chapter emphasizes its holistic character, it would still be useful to discuss the mainstream media and digital media (together with online alternative media) separately for clarity. The most important mainstream news media in Hong Kong before the Umbrella Movement included two free-to-air TV stations, several multichannel pay TV services, three radio broadcasters, and eighteen daily newspapers. Under "one country, two systems," the Hong Kong media have remained free from direct government control. The primary means for the state to tame the Hong Kong media has been to co-opt owners. By the mid-2000s, most media organizations in Hong Kong were owned by businesspeople with heavy commercial interests in the Mainland. Many of them also held formal political titles, such as being members of the Political Consultative Committees at the city, provincial, or national level. For instance, five of the sixteen Hong Kong–based members in the 12th session of the Chinese People's Political Consultative Committee starting in 2012 are owners of or are closely related to media organizations in the city.[7] In other words, media ownership in Hong Kong is largely concentrated into the hands of a group of businesspeople sharing the same basic interests of pleasing or at least not provoking China.

As a result of ownership changes and other strategies employed by the state (e.g., the issuing of occasional informal warnings),[8] media self-censorship became a serious concern. In a survey of journalists conducted by the Chinese University of Hong Kong in 2006, 29.3 percent of the respondents regarded media self-censorship as serious. In the corresponding survey in 2011, 39.0 percent regarded the problem as serious. The problem of self-censorship has been worsening over the years in the eyes of professional journalists.

Not all practices of self-censorship were equally prevalent. In the 2011 survey, 22.1 percent and 35.6 percent of the respondents stated that the media frequently toned down negative news about the Hong Kong government and the Chinese government respectively, whereas only 11.3 percent and 18.4 percent stated that the media frequently omitted negative news about the Hong Kong government and the Chinese government respectively. These varying figures suggest that the media would not practice self-censorship too unscrupulously. The media were more likely to self-censor when handling news about China as opposed to news about Hong Kong, and they tended to employ methods that are relatively less conspicuous (e.g., toning down instead of omitting negative news).

These variations suggest the existence of constraints on the extent to which the Hong Kong media could succumb to political pressure. The constraints are the result of several counteracting forces. First, most Hong Kong media organizations are commercial entities. A loss of credibility could damage the media outlets financially. Besides, to the extent that critical and prodemocracy views have a "market," there would be incentives for some media owners to try to capture it. *Apple Daily* is an obvious case. Since its publication in 1995, it has positioned itself as a prodemocracy newspaper, often adopting a highly critical stance toward the Chinese and Hong Kong government on political and social issues.[9] Commercial interests also partly accounted for the prominence of radio phone-in shows in Hong Kong since the late 1990s. Between 1997 and 2011, many of the most influential talk radio programs were hosted by outspoken prodemocracy persona. Talk radio contents were often reported by the mainstream media as "news," contributing to the vibrancy of public discourse at the time.[10]

It follows that the mainstream media system in Hong Kong was not totally homogeneous. Although conservative media outlets outnumbered daring ones, the presence of even only a few relatively outspoken outlets could extend the space of operation for all. Besides media outlets driven by commercial interests, the public broadcaster Radio Television Hong Kong (RTHK) also provided public affairs contents that are often critical toward the power holders. Media outlets such as *Apple Daily* and RTHK served as test balloons pushing the boundaries of acceptable discourses. Their presence alleviates the political pressure on other media outlets because the latter would not be seen as the main "troublemakers." The test balloons also created another kind of pressure for the others: when a story is already broken by someone, it would become difficult for the others to totally ignore it.

More broadly speaking, the information environment in Hong Kong remained open. Information from media around the world were easily accessible. This was another fundamental reason why the Hong Kong media could pay a heavy price in credibility if they totally ignored certain news due to political considerations. The chance is that a large portion of citizens would know about the events through other means. Outright omission could become clear and indisputable signs of self-censorship.

Last but not least, Hong Kong journalists retained a strong sense of professionalism. They continued to believe in the ideal of a media system independent from political and economic power. They valued autonomy and the watchdog role of the press.[11] Admittedly, journalists were also salaried workers. Actual operational autonomy was limited by the hierarchical nature of newsrooms, news production routines, and general lack of resources. That Hong Kong journalists have low pay and have to face harsh working conditions also worsened the situation, as many would leave the field after only a few years. This led to an inexperienced journalistic corps and an enlarged "cultural capital gap" between the frontline journalists and the news managers, which further limited the autonomy of the frontline journalists.[12] Nevertheless, journalistic professionalism remained a force constraining the extent to which media organizations could self-censor. As previous research has illustrated, media self-censorship in Hong Kong could better be understood as an "organizational product" achieved through strategic allocation of human resources and informal strategies aiming at creating tacit understandings of what to do and what not to do.[13] The point is that it was difficult for media owners and top-level managers to nakedly enforce self-censorship. On the flip side, it was possible for experienced and mindful journalists to resist suspected attempts of self-censorship.

As a result of the complexities of the external forces impinging on the media and the complexities of newsroom operations, media performances can be uneven and contradictory. The Hong Kong mainstream media may have been generally and increasingly docile, but they could still serve some of their normative roles. This would be apparent in the performance and impact of the mainstream media during the Umbrella Movement.

The Growth of Internet-Based Political Communication and Alternative Media

Hong Kong has long had one of the highest Internet penetration rates in East Asia. In 2006, 60.8 percent of Hong Kong citizens were Internet users, and the figure stood at 74.8 percent by 2014.[14] According to government statistics, 78.7 percent of Hong Kong households had personal computers connected to the Internet in summer 2014.[15] Hong Kong citizens have also been avid users of social media. According to news reports, by 2014 there were 4.4 million users of Facebook, by far the most popular social media site in the city.

It is therefore unsurprising that digital and social media could play an important role in the political communication process in the city. In a survey conducted by the Chinese University of Hong Kong in March 2013, 23.6 percent of the respondents acknowledged that they obtained news and public affairs information via social media sites at least "sometimes." About one in ten (9.5 percent) expressed their personal views about public affairs via social media at least "sometimes," and 5.9 percent acknowledged that they had some connections with political party members, social activists, or public affairs commentators via social media.

An important development in the online arena in Hong Kong highly pertinent to social movement mobilization was the growth of online alternative media. Here, alternative media refer to media outlets that challenge the concentration of the power to define reality in the mainstream media.[16] Alternative media are typically independent structurally and financially from the dominant political-economic institutions, they adopt ideological stances critical of the existing power structure, and they often dismiss conventional journalistic norms in favor of advocacy.[17] In Hong Kong, the rise of online alternative media was closely related to social protests. The first wave of online alternative media appeared after the historic 2003 July 1 protest, which succeeded in forcing the government to postpone national security legislation.[18] The social energy generated by the protest was partly channeled into a range of online radio stations and the public affairs commentary website *Inmedia*.

While most of the online alternative radio stations did not survive for long due to financial reasons, a second wave of online alternative media, mainly in the form of alternative news-cum-commentary websites, emerged in 2012. Prominent examples included, among others, the House News (which was later closed down and re-emerged as the Stand News) and Passion Times (which had close connections with the radical political group Civic Passion). In a July 2014 population survey, 16.5 percent of the respondents claimed that they visited House News occasionally or frequently, while 5.8 percent visited Inmedia occasionally or frequently.[19] These figures are not huge. Alternative media, almost by definition, are unlikely to capture the mainstream mass audience. But these frequent consumers of alternative media are not small in absolute numbers. They could constitute a core group of the most politically aware citizens with the highest generalized protest potential.

Online alternative media can be considered as contributing to the formation of a counter–public sphere in which oppositional discourses and ideologies are articulated and communicated. The "counter-public" character of online alternative media is evidenced by the fact that citizens perceiving the problem of media self-censorship as more serious were more likely to consume alternative media.[20] Besides, online alternative media played a role in communicating and distributing oppositional knowledge: online alternative media consumption was significantly related to the ability to recognize prominent social activists and the ability to talk about the concept of civil disobedience.[21] Notably, consumption of mainstream media did not contribute to such oppositional knowledge. In other words, online alternative media did have a unique role in the transmission of oppositional political knowledge in Hong Kong.

More broadly, through a case study of Inmedia, communication researchers Yung and Leung outlined five major functions of alternative media. First, online alternative media provide alternative information and viewpoints that are largely absent or downplayed in the mainstream media. Second, they provide the space for like-minded individuals to discuss public affairs and articulate their views. Third, alternative media serve as a platform for civil society groups and movement activists to communicate with each other, their supporters, and the public. Fourth, alternative media generate social activism among users. Fifth, alternative media have the potential to initiate public discourses and "propose" items onto the news agenda.[22]

The last function identified by Yung and Leung pointed toward the connections between online alternative media and the mainstream mass media. On the one hand, alternative media typically have limited resources and few staff members. They are reliant on the mainstream media for the "raw materials" they can comment on, repackage, criticize, and satirize. On the other hand, discussions in the online alternative media could occasionally feed back into the mainstream media. A case in point is how Inmedia helped promote discussions of Occupy Central in early 2013. As the original proponent of Occupy Central, Benny Tai, acknowledged, his newspaper article outlining the idea of an occupation campaign published in January 2013 did not garner too much public attention until Inmedia published a follow-up interview with him. When the interview generated heated debates online, the mainstream press paid attention and further reported on the idea.

The contents of the online alternative media are usually consumed through social media platforms, especially Facebook. Political communication via social media in Hong Kong, at least before the Umbrella Movement, exhibited a general "prodemocracy bias." Empirical studies have shown significant relationships between political use of social media in Hong Kong and protest participation.[23] Notably, netizens are not necessarily persuaded to participate in protests by movement groups or alternative media sites. Rather, the Internet and social media are the platforms through which citizens can "self-mobilize" by persuading each other to participate in collective actions.[24] Self-mobilization via the Internet would also be a prominent phenomenon in the Umbrella Movement, as will be discussed in the next section.

But just as the mainstream media system is not completely homogeneous, one should not ignore the presence of pro-establishment forces in the digital arena. From around 2012, there was the emergence of a number of notable progovernment Facebook public pages. An example is Silent Majority for Hong Kong, created by the informal group bearing the same name. The group was established in 2013 to oppose Occupy Central. Another example is Speak Out Hong Kong, established by a foundation founded by a close ally of Chief Executive of the SAR Government C. Y. Leung. The number of "fans" attracted by these two pages are comparable to the public pages of many mainstream media and major online alternative media. Even before the Umbrella Movement, the pro-establishment forces have already started to build their own social media presence to counteract the influence of the prodemocracy alternative media.

Roles and Impact of the Integrated Mediascape in the Umbrella Movement

The above discussions set the stage for us to make sense of the role and impact of the media in the Umbrella Movement. When the mainstream media is concerned, the present author has developed the notion of the partially censored public monitor to capture the contradictory impact of the mainstream media.[25] The concept highlights the point that the mainstream media did exercise a certain extent of self-censorship and exhibit a degree of progovernment bias when covering the movement. Conservative newspapers, for instance, framed the occupation as a conspiracy plotted by foreign powers, as a nuisance to the everyday life of ordinary people, and as a violation of the rule of law. Meanwhile, representative surveys conducted during the occupation campaign showed that exposure to television news in general was negatively related to support for the occupation movement and positively related to attitudes toward the police after a range of other attitudinal and demographic factors were controlled.

Consistent with the aforementioned point that the mainstream media system is not completely homogeneous, however, not all consumption of mainstream media outlets is associated with negative views toward the movement. Survey analysis has shown that reliance on the dominant free-to-air broadcaster Television Broadcasting (TVB) and the popular newspaper *Oriental Daily* was related to more negative attitudes toward the Umbrella Movement, whereas reliance on the paid television service NOW TV and the prodemocracy *Apple Daily* was associated with more positive attitudes toward the movement.[26] These patterns probably signify selective exposure rather than media effects, but they do highlight the point that there were channels and outlets favored by pro-movement citizens. Table 5.1 shows the findings derived from an onsite survey conducted in early October in the Admiralty occupied area.[27] When asked to evaluate the credibility of five mainstream media outlets, the protest participants rated the pay television service Cable TV, *Apple Daily*, and *Ming Pao* very positively, whereas TVB and *Singtao Daily* were rated very negatively.

More important, the "censorship" of the mainstream media was incomplete due to the complex set of factors discussed previously. The overall result is that the media still played an important role in informing the public and monitoring the actions of the power holders. The capability of the mainstream media to play these roles was also tied to how digital media widened the reach of mainstream media contents.

TABLE 5.1 Umbrella Movement participants' perceptions of credibility of mainstream media outlets

	CREDIBLE/VERY CREDIBLE	NOT CREDIBLE/VERY NOT CREDIBLE
TVB	4.9	76.7
Cable TV	50.5	5.2
Apple Daily	63.9	3.3
Ming Pao	37.5	9.8
Singtao Daily	9.3	30.1

Note. The original answers were registered in a five-point Likert scale. Entries are percentages giving the stated answers. N = 969.

Two cases most conspicuously illustrate the public monitor role of the media. The first is related to how the police's firing of tear gas on September 28 contributed to the quick scaling up and transformation of the occupation. In the original plan of Occupy Central for Love and Peace (OCLP), the occupation was not expected to last for more than a few days. OCLP urged occupiers to abide by the rule of nonviolence and not to resist when the police evicted the occupation. OCLP originally proposed to take action on October 1. The schedule of the action was altered by the dynamics kick-started by the student protests in the week of September 22. The original "script" of the action was then destroyed by the police in the late afternoon of September 28. The firing of tear gas into the protesting crowd created images that shocked the citizenry. The images were transmitted through live broadcast television to people who were glued to the TV set to follow the happenings of the day. The images generated "mediated instant grievances" and led more people to participate in the protests. The aforementioned survey of the Umbrella Movement participants conducted in early October in the Admiralty occupation area found that more than half of the respondents (55.8 percent) said they decided to join the movement only on September 28.[28]

For this chapter, what is remarkable about the events of September 28 is that on the one hand, there were signs of media self-censorship when the media followed the events throughout the day. A television news reporter told the author that she/he was asked by editors within the newsroom not to use the word "police baton" when conducting live coverage of police-protester conflicts. But on the other hand, the police's firing of tear gas backfired because of the spectacular live broadcast images resulting from the action. Barring the extreme action of stopping the live broadcast, there was no way for television stations to censor live images. In terms of consequences, the mainstream media played its watchdog role exposing the police's disproportionate use of violence.

The second, more complicated case occurred in the early morning hours of October 15 and is dubbed the "dark corner incident" in local discourse. The event involved seven police officers carrying a protester to a "dark corner" near the occupation area and beating the protester as he was lying on the ground. The event occurred after police-protester skirmishes earlier at night. The excessive police violence was captured by a TVB reporting crew, and a story was aired on the twenty-four-hour news channel of TVB after midnight. It was then "re-edited" in the morning around 6 a.m., with a specific statement from the original voice-over deleted. This re-edit led to outcries of self-censorship among citizens. More than one hundred journalists within TVB signed an open letter expressing disagreement with the editorial decision. The station manager insisted that the revision was based on concerns about the report's objectivity. In any case, the "revision" did not stop the circulation of the original version, as the latter was quickly uploaded onto YouTube and went viral on social media.

Notably, many mainstream newspapers covered the dark corner incident by toning down or "excusing" the police violence, such as through blaming the protester for provoking the police or by emphasizing that the protester was a member of a prodemocracy political party (i.e., not an ordinary citizen-protester). Such coverage explains why, as mentioned earlier, regular consumption of mainstream media during the movement was associated with a more negative attitude toward the movement and more positive attitude toward the police and the government.

The dark corner incident, however, did lead to an immediate and general decline in public trust toward the police. Opinion polls showed that public evaluation of the police declined significantly and immediately on October 15.[29] Once again, in terms of consequences, the dark corner incident illustrated the public monitor function of the media. Paradoxically, the news images were captured by TVB, the dominant free TV station most heavily criticized by the Umbrella Movement participants as conservative and self-censoring. There was indeed a highly suspicious self-censorship attempt. But the original story was aired nonetheless due to the operational autonomy of the frontline reporters and mid-level personnel in the newsroom, the contingency of the event happening late at night, and the nonstop news cycle created by the twenty-four-hour news channel. The event illustrated the inevitable incompleteness of censorship. The spread of the "uncensored" story on YouTube and social media also highlighted how digital media could strengthen the public monitor function of the mainstream media.

While both cases recounted above involved the mainstream media publicizing the highly questionable conduct of the power holders, leading to observable shifts in public opinion, the influence of the mainstream media as a public monitor was not necessarily achieved through what the media showed to the public. The mere presence of the public monitor could compel political actors to adjust or shift their strategies. In fact, after the dark corner incident, the Hong Kong government and police ostensibly changed toward a strategy of attrition and adopted a more passive approach to handle the movement.[30] There were few police-protester conflicts between mid-October and late November, until the protesters started to escalate their actions. Of course, there were likely to be numerous factors and considerations behind the government's strategic shift. But it should be fair to say that the presence of the media monitor was one of the factors the government could not ignore.

Meanwhile, the online counter–public sphere constituted by online alternative media and social media communications contributed to the formation of the

Umbrella Movement. For the public, online alternative media and social media were key sources of pro-movement information and discourses. Survey analysis has found that reliance on Facebook for public affairs information among the general public was significantly related to a more positive attitude toward the Umbrella Movement, a more negative attitude toward the government, and more negative attitude toward the police.[31] A study of university students during the Umbrella Movement also found that sharing political information via social media and connections with political actors via social media were consistently related to a more positive attitude toward the occupation and higher levels of various kinds of participation in the movement.[32]

Digital media were crucial in facilitating not only participation but also citizen self-mobilization. Lee and Chan's analysis of the July 1 protest series found that most participants in the protests were not connected to social and political groups. They were drawn into the protests through a horizontal process of social mobilization occurring among citizens themselves, and digital media constituted part of the platforms for such self-mobilization.[33] The same applies to the Umbrella Movement. Only 8.9 percent of the respondents in the October protest onsite survey claimed that they were participating in the movement with the social groups or organizations they belonged to, and only 2.2 percent participated with the social sector they belonged to. In contrast, 80.8 percent of the respondents participated with their friends, 42.3 percent participated with their classmates, and 18.8 percent participated with their family. Many participants actively called upon others to join the movement; more than 81.6 percent of the respondents stated that they had done so. Inviting others to join the movement, meanwhile, is positively related to a full range of online political communication activities.

The significance of digital media to the Umbrella Movement went beyond its role in transmitting pro-movement messages and facilitating citizen self-mobilization. Similar to other occupation movements around the world, the Umbrella Movement was marked by the production of what Castells called a "space of autonomy" constituted by cyberspace *and* urban space.[34] Beyond the collective action of occupying the streets, numerous forms of personalized and small-group-based actions were conducted both online and offline. Certain onsite actions, such as confronting the police and counterprotesters, required real-time coordination, which was in turn partly reliant on digital communication through mobile technologies. More generally speaking, digital and social media provided the platforms for people to construct their own distinctive ways of participating in the movement.[35]

Findings relevant to the latter point came from a protest onsite survey conducted in November in both the Admiralty and Mongkok occupied areas.

The survey asked the respondents if they had participated in a range of digital media activities. About 70 percent of the respondents had changed their profile pictures to show support for the movement. More than half had published commentaries about the movement. More than 40 percent had set up mobile chat groups to discuss the Umbrella Movement. More than half had explained to foreign friends about the situation in Hong Kong, and more than 40 percent had explained to Mainland friends about the situation in Hong Kong.

Some of the digital media activities the movement supporters engaged in were highly significant to the dynamics of the movement itself. The most obvious example is how movement participants dealt with rumors online. In the first two weeks of the occupation, there were numerous rumors spread in the online arena, ranging from claims that the People's Liberation Army was ready to be dispatched, to faked stories about how traffic congestions caused by the occupation had led to tragic consequences to individual citizens. As a response, movement participants engaged in collective rumor dispelling. Several Facebook pages were set up, and individual participants could share the information from those sites with others. The onsite survey found that more than 90 percent of the participants in both occupied areas encountered movement-related rumors, and more than half encountered rumors frequently. About 80 percent had tried to refute rumors online, whereas about 30 percent did so frequently.

In an extended occupation campaign, not everyone was available to stay in the occupied areas for long periods of time. Digital media allowed people to stay in touch and remain a participant even when they were not physically present in the occupied areas. Digital media (as well as mainstream media) facilitated a form of "monitorial participation": people could constantly monitor the situation of the occupied areas and take action when needed. At the same time, participating in various digital media activities was indeed positively related to the depth of participation among the protesters: those who participated in various digital media activities more frequently also tended to stay in the occupied areas for longer periods of time, be more active in frontline actions in the occupied areas (e.g., confronting the counterprotesters), be more active in various supportive activities such as donating resources to the movement, and be more likely to have persuaded friends to participate in the movement.

Nevertheless, digital media participation also brought challenges to the Umbrella Movement. As table 5.2 shows, based on the protest onsite survey conducted in November, how time spent in the occupied area and degree of digital participation correlated with willingness to listen to a range of entities on matters of movement direction and strategies.[36] The findings show that the most deeply involved participants were actually less willing to listen to a range of groups, including the main organizers of the occupation campaign, on questions

TABLE 5.2 Correlations between involvement in the movement and willingness to listen to specific groups on matters of movement strategies and directions

	TIME SPENT IN THE OCCUPIED AREA	DIGITAL PARTICIPATION
Willing to listen to		
Hong Kong Federation of Students	−.09*	.05
Scholarism	−.08*	.05
Occupy Central for Love and Peace	−.15***	−.03
Parties or groups that one supported	−.12**	.06
Friends	−.08	.15***
Public opinion as reflected in polls	−.06	.11**
Newspaper editorials	−.10*	.07
Online promovement commentaries	−.10*	.14***

Notes. Willingness to listen to the various entities was captured by a five-point Likert scale ranging from very unwilling to very willing. Time spent in the occupied area is an index composed of three items regarding whether the respondents had stayed overnight in the occupied area, how many days they had spent in the occupied area, and on average how long each visit to the occupied area was. Digital participation is an index composed of fifteen items related to a range of online activities related to the Umbrella Movement. Entries are Pearson correlation coefficients. Ns range from 522 to 555. *** $p < .001$; ** $p < .01$; * $p < .05$.

of movement strategies and direction. Digital participation, meanwhile, relates positively only to willingness to listen to friends and "public opinion" as reflected in polls or online commentaries.

In addition, an analysis of more than 140 Facebook public pages about the Umbrella Movement created during the occupation period found that the public pages were only loosely connected to each other, and the pages of the three main organizing groups—the OCLP, Scholarism, and the Hong Kong Federation of Students—were by no means clearly at the center of the network constituted by the pages. The Umbrella Movement exhibited a substantial degree of decentralization.

On the whole, digital activities during the occupation had helped connect the participants with each other more than with the main organizers. While the possibility of carrying out small-group-based actions and digital media activities allow more people to participate in the campaign in their own specific ways, it also contributed to people's feeling that they were autonomous actors independent from the movement leaders.

It should be acknowledged that digital media activities are not the only or prime cause of decentralization. Decentralization and internal conflicts within the movement had their organizational, cultural, and spatial bases. Discussions of these bases of internal conflicts are out of the scope of this chapter. Suffice it to say that digital media did contribute to the trend of decentralization during the movement by facilitating the formation of a fragmented communicative space and exacerbating existing tensions.

Although scholars have noted that the lack of a strong central leadership is not necessarily a problem for a large-scale "networked social movement,"[37] the Umbrella Movement did have a concrete programmatic demand of institutionalizing genuine popular elections. Hence the movement had the need to engage in negotiation with the government. The forces of decentralization made it difficult for the leaders to "represent" the whole movement. It arguably contributed to the strategic impasse paralyzing the Umbrella Movement in its later stage. Although the strategic impasse definitely had other causes, the prevalence of digital media activities did not make deliberation within the movement easier.

Changes after the Umbrella Movement

A critical event can alter people's perceptions of reality and political actors' goals and strategies. The 2003 July 1 protest brought about the rise of online alternative media, as mentioned earlier. It led the Chinese government to pinpoint "one newspaper, one magazine, and two microphones" as major mobilizers behind the protest. In 2004, talk radio suffered a serious blow as three prominent hosts resigned in quick succession due to political pressure.[38] Did the Umbrella Movement have similar impact on the media scene?

It is difficult to draw causal connections between the Umbrella Movement and the happenings afterwards. But certain developments in the media scene do deserve attention. When the mainstream media are concerned, while the majority of media organizations remain in the hands of pro-China businesspeople, Chinese capitalists have started entering the market and exercising direct control of the local media. The trend did not begin after the Umbrella Movement. In year 2000, Chinese businessman Wang Jing became the major shareholder of Asia Television Ltd. In early 2014, another Mainland businessman, Ku Zhuoheng, bought the daily newspaper *Sing Pao*. However, both ATV and *Sing Pao* were peripheral players in the media market facing financial difficulties at the time of purchase. More eyebrow-raising was the news in 2015 that Mainland media tycoon Li Ruigang would join as a major investor in Young Lion's Holdings Ltd., which owns 26 percent of TVB's shares and is the largest single shareholder of the broadcaster. In December 2015, Jack Ma, owner of China's e-commerce giant Alibaba, purchased *South China Morning Post*. With these purchases, Chinese capitalists are starting to take control of the more influential media outlets. According to the Hong Kong Journalists Association, by mid-2017, 35 percent of all mainstream news outlets in Hong Kong had Mainland Chinese stakes.[39]

The changes in ownership might not have visible immediate impact on press freedom in the city, partly because the actual operations of the media organizations cannot be changed radically in a short time. If there was a "political mission" behind such purchases, the power holders should also understand that immediate changes would lead to substantial resistance. Ownership structure is more like a "basic setup" that ensures the efficacy of political-economic influence *when the latter is needed.*

With or without changes in ownership, however, the performance of certain mainstream media organizations seemingly deteriorated further. The situation is clearest in the case of TVB. Most of the journalists who cosigned the open letter criticizing the station during the Umbrella Movement had left the organization. Citizens continued to perceive TVB news as exhibiting a heavy pro-establishment bias. In one of the most inexplicable cases, in the evening before the voting day of the 2016 LegCo election, a few prodemocracy candidates announced they would forfeit the election in order not to take away votes from other prodemocracy candidates. Such an important story was totally ignored by TVB news in the evening. It seems that TVB was willing to employ more conspicuous methods of self-censorship. It is now an open question of whether, in some major media outlets, the intraorganizational dynamics of self-censorship as described by earlier media studies in Hong Kong has changed toward a more open and explicit form.

It is therefore not surprising that TVB's credibility continued to decline. According to a series of surveys conducted by the Chinese University of Hong Kong over the years, the broadcaster's credibility scores declined from 7.30 on a 0-to-10 scale in 2009 to 5.88 in 2016, the lowest score among all broadcasting organizations. The credibility of many mainstream media outlets also declined between 2013 and 2016, but there are several exceptions. The prodemocracy *Apple Daily*, because of its sensationalism and mass-market orientation, had never had high levels of credibility. But its credibility score did rise between 2013 and 2016. Also gaining in credibility were the two pay television services Cable TV and NOW TV. The latter might be partly the result of a "contrast effect" with TVB, that is, as TVB is seen as seriously self-censoring, citizens may see Cable TV and NOW TV as offering news that is more professional and occasionally critical.[40]

Therefore, while we may argue that political pressure on the Hong Kong mainstream media had continued to increase, the complexity of the media system did not disappear entirely. The persisting complexity of the Hong Kong media system is probably epitomized by the new online news organization HK01. Starting its operation in early 2016, HK01 is owned by controversial businessman Yu Pinhai, who has close connections with officials and businesspeople in the Mainland. Without a clearly sustainable business model at its start, HK01 nonetheless hired hundreds of journalists. Most commentators believed that the capital came from the mainland. But many journalists working in the organization remain the typical liberal and professional-oriented journalist in Hong Kong. Hence the daily news content of the outlet may not exhibit clear pro-establishment biases. The outlet was even active in investigative journalism, breaking a few stories that uncovered official wrongdoings. Yet the editorials of the outlet could at times be conspicuously progovernment, leading many people in the industry to regard the outlet as "schizophrenic."

Depending on how one judges its background, HK01 can also be taken as signifying the establishment's attempt to gain stronger foothold in the online arena. At the time of the writing of this chapter, the majority of the most prominent online news sites in Hong Kong (including those of conventional mainstream media and online alternative media) are prodemocracy outlets. But a small number of progovernment outlets have also established themselves in the online arena. An example is Bastille.com, which was established in 2013 under the progovernment Sing Tao News Corporation. In terms of online traffic, according to data from Alexa.com, Bastille.com would actually rank second among all media organizations in Hong Kong in year 2016, behind *Apple Daily*'s website only.[41]

The same situation can be discerned on Facebook. By March 2017, Silent Majority for Hong Kong, HKG Pao, and Speak Out HK—three major progovernment Facebook public pages—were liked by 159,144, 79,400, and 300,995 people respectively. These figures are much lower than the 2,061,223 likes on *Apple Daily*'s main Facebook page or the 419,749 on Passion Times' Facebook page, but they are comparable to the number of likes on the pages of Ming Pao Instant News (302,632) and The Stand News (197,656).

Sheer numbers of likes on the pages do not tell how active the pages are and how capable they are in attracting people's attention. Table 5.3 summarizes the results derived from the search engine QSearch. Using keywords, the search engine could identify the Facebook pages that had attracted the largest amount of cumulative engagement (based on number of likes, comments, and shares) on specific topics. In three of the most heated political controversies in Hong Kong in late 2016 and early 2017, the same five Facebook pages occupied the top five positions, and three of the five were progovernment pages.

The data need to be qualified. The engagement scores do not tell the number of unique users. The scores refer to cumulative engagement. Hence high levels of total engagement scores could be the result of the progovernment pages actively pushing large number of posts. But even with these qualifications, the table does show that the progovernment Facebook pages are nowadays very active in addressing the hot political issues of the day and are capable of generating high degrees of "engagement" among social media users.

TABLE 5.3   Facebook pages with the highest levels of engagement in several controversies

	KEYWORD: "NPC INTERPRETING THE BASIC LAW"	KEYWORD: "IMPERIAL PALACE"	KEYWORD: "SEVEN POLICEMEN"
	TIME PERIOD: OCT 12–DEC 31, 2016	TIME PERIOD: DEC 23–JAN 22, 2017	TIME PERIOD: FEB 14–27, 2017
1	*Apple Daily*	**Speak Out HK**	*Apple Daily*
2	**HKG Pao**	Apple Daily	Stand News
3	**Silent Majority for HK**	Stand News	**Speak Out HK**
4	**Speak Out HK**	**Silent Majority for HK**	**Silent Majority for HK**
5	Stand News	**HKG Pao**	**HKG Pao**

Notes. The results came from keyword searches conducted on QSearch—a system allowing people to conduct keyword search for posts on Facebook public pages—in June 2017. Levels of engagement refer to the total amount of likes, shares, and comments attracted by the posts. The controversies are: (1) the National People's Congress interpreted the Basic Law in order to disqualify proindependence legislators in Hong Kong, (2) the plan to build an Imperial Palace Museum in Hong Kong, and (3) the court verdict on the case in which seven policemen beat a protester during the Umbrella Movement. Bolded ones are progovernment Facebook pages.

The implication of the above findings is that political communication via social media is by no means one-sidedly critical toward the government. The progovernment forces have already established their own information enclave. Even if the progovernment websites and pages may not be able to influence the attitudes of Facebook users at large, they may at least provide a communicative space for reinforcing the views of the progovernment citizens.

In fact, an analysis of survey data in 2015 during the debates surrounding the political reform proposal found that using Facebook as a source of political information was related to more negative attitude toward the government's proposal only among the prodemocracy and "centrist" citizens. Among proestablishment citizens, using Facebook as a source of political information did not relate significantly to attitudes toward the government's proposals.[42] The finding that Facebook use could lead the centrists to view the government's proposal more negatively suggests the overall prevalence of critical content on social media; but the finding that Facebook use does not affect the pro-establishment citizens' attitudes suggests that the latter were largely "insulated" from the critical online contents.

Conclusion

This chapter reviewed the relationship between the media and Umbrella Movement through a discussion of the evolution of the media landscape in Hong Kong. Much discussion of the relationship between media and social movements began with a rough distinction between the mainstream mass media and digital media. While the former is often treated as exhibiting a general bias against social movements because of its embeddedness in the dominant power structure, the latter is seen as providing the platforms for the rise of online alternative media and for social movements to construct counter–public spheres for the articulation, transmission, and promotion of oppositional discourses.

The reality, of course, is much more complicated. The mainstream media in Hong Kong were indeed under heavy political pressure. Self-censorship was believed to be prevalent. They did tend to cover the Umbrella Movement negatively, portraying the movement as a nuisance to people's everyday life and a violation of the rule of law. But this chapter emphasized that the mainstream media also played the role of the public monitor during the Umbrella Movement. There is a limited yet non-negligible degree of internal diversity within the mainstream media system. Most frontline journalists uphold the liberal ideal of professionalism, and media censorship and bias in Hong Kong are not absolute. The media can still play part of its normative role of informing the public and monitoring the power holders.

The notion of the partially censored public monitor should be applicable to varying extents to other countries as long as media censorship is not extreme. In the case of the Arab Spring, for instance, many national media of the authoritarian Arab countries had totally refrained from reporting on the ongoing protests. But even in the Arab Spring, some activists believed that the presence of the television network Al Jazeera had provoked the Egyptian government to resort to military suppression.[43] That is, the presence of the media monitor did influence the strategies of political actors.

Another core premise behind the discussion of this chapter is that mainstream media institutions, alternative media outlets, and digital media platforms are not separate entities unrelated to or merely competing with each other. Rather, they are intertwined to form an integrated media system. The public monitor function of the mainstream media is aided by digital media as the latter widen the circulation of mainstream media contents and, at times, serve as repository of news coverage that people can refer to when the mainstream media attempt to be self-censor. Putting it the other way around, the mainstream media remain crucial for political communication via alternative media institutions and social media platforms. The mainstream media have human and technological resources that are unmatched by alternative media institutions and social movement groups. They remain a key source of raw materials for alternative media and ordinary citizens to comment on.

In recent theorizations and research on various occupation movements around the world, digital media have often been treated as playing an essential role facilitating coordination among networked actors, which contributed to the rise of new forms of "networked social movements"[44] or "connective actions."[45] On the one hand, digital media did play similar roles in the Umbrella Movement in Hong Kong. Many Umbrella Movement participants were active in a wide range of digital media activities. Such activities allowed people to construct their own ways and manage their own degree of participation in the movement. Digital media were also important in real-time coordination among activists in the occupied areas. Our analysis, however, also pointed toward how digital media might have contributed to the decentralizing tendency of the movement and therefore made it more difficult for the movement to develop a coherent and effective strategic response to the power holders.

When Castells published *Networks of Outrage and Hope* on the back of the "success" of Arab Spring, commentators and academics were generally optimistic about the capability of digital media to aid the search for social and political change. In Bennett and Segerberg's theorization of connective action, digital communication is portrayed as capable of replacing conventional social movement organizations in giving rise to large-scale protest campaigns. There were questions, however, about the capability of digital-media-based protest campaigns to become sustainable and to achieve tangible outcomes. A few years later, such problems became ever more apparent. In a widely publicized talk, Arab Spring activist Wael Ghonim questioned the overall impact of social media on politics. Nowadays, well-established themes about the problems of social media include the tendency for people to stay within their own echo chambers and listen to only like-minded views, the power of the mysterious social media algorithm in determining what people read and do not read, the extreme difficulty for people to navigate the "data smog" created by an overabundance of materials, the pervasiveness of fake news and rumors, and the shortening of the news cycles as well as people's attention cycle in an ever-accelerating media environment.

It is beyond the scope of this chapter to discuss in detail these general problems of social-media-based political communications. Suffice it to note that since the Umbrella Movement, the limitations of digital and social media for aiding social change in Hong Kong have also become increasingly clear. While digital media had been and will continue to serve as the platforms for social movements and civic groups to communicate to their supporters, there is a sense that the online alternative media only keep preaching to the choir. The growing presence of the progovernment forces in the online arena further limited the possible influence of the prodemocracy alternative media. The overall impact of online communication on public opinion seems to be a case of increasing polarization instead of movement toward a single direction.

In fact, divisions and polarization occur even within the prodemocracy or anti-establishment camp. Online alternative media could be distinguished between the "localists" and the "leftists." Both sides have their adherents, and in the online arena, the criticisms leveled by the supporters of the two camps at each other can be as fierce as, or occasionally even fiercer than, the criticisms they leveled at the pro-establishment parties. In other words, there is no singular counter–public sphere in the online arena. Instead, there seems to be the emergence of counter–public sphericules. This has had an adverse impact on the capability of the prodemocracy camp to put forward sustained and powerful challenges to the established order.

Moreover, the Hong Kong case also highlights the role of the state in taming the Internet. In recent years, some scholars have started to theorize about the authoritarian states' increasingly sophisticated approach to control the Internet.[46] A few empirical studies have shown that in the context of certain authoritarian states, social media consumption can actually be related to proregime ideologies and beliefs.[47] Although Hong Kong is not a typical authoritarian system, how the government, armed with levels of resources that cannot be matched by civil society and social movement groups, intervenes into the online public opinion landscape and thus potentially alters the impact of social media communication is something that deserves close attention in the future.

For social movement activists and supporters, the challenge would reside in how to go beyond communicating with one's sympathizers and actually persuade the broader public to support one's cause. The media—mainstream media, alternative media, and digital media platforms—do provide some opportunities for the purposes. Yet the aforementioned limitations also mean that successful organizing and communication may require not only skillful handling of the media, but also the maintenance of interpersonal networks and the building of mutual trust in the "real world."

NOTES

1. William A. Gamson and Gadi Wolfsfeld, "Movements and Media As Interacting Systems," *Annals of the American Academy of Political and Social Science* 528, no. 1 (1993): 114–25.

2. Joseph Man Chan and Chin-Chuan Lee, "Journalistic Paradigms on Civil Protests: A Case Study of Hong Kong," in *The News Media in National and International Conflict*, ed. Andrew Arno and Wimal Dissanayake. (Boulder, CO: Westview, 1984), 183–202; Melvin Small, *Covering Dissent: The Media and the Anti-Vietnam War Movement* (New Brunswick, NJ: Rutgers University Press, 1994).

3. John Downing, *Radical Media: Rebellious Communication and Social Movements* (Thousand Oaks, CA: Sage, 2001).

4. Susan Forde, *Challenging the News: The Journalism of Alternative and Community Media* (New York: Palgrave McMillan, 2011).

5. W. Lance Bennett and Alexandra Segerberg, *The Logic of Connective Action: Digital Media and the Personalization of Contentious Politics* (New York: Cambridge University Press, 2013).

6. Bart Cammaerts, "Protest Logics and the Mediation Opportunity Structure," *European Journal of Communication* 27, no. 2 (2012): 117–34.

7. These five members are: (1) Victor Li, elder son of tycoon Li Ka-shing, who is group co–managing director of CK Hutchinson Holdings, which owns Metro Radio (his younger brother Richard Li owns NOW TV, a paid television service in Hong Kong, and the influential financial newspaper *Hong Kong Economic Journal*), (2) Peter Woo, head of the Woo family, which owns Wharf Holdings, which in turn owns Cable TV, another paid television service, (3) Charles Ho, chairperson of Sing Tao News Corporations, which runs the daily newspapers *Sing Tao Daily* and *Headline Daily*, (4) Chan Wing-kei, formerly CEO of free television broadcaster Asia Television Ltd., and (5) Liu Changle, CEO of Phoenix TV, a television broadcaster stationed in Hong Kong though targeting mainly Mainland audiences.

8. See Francis L. F. Lee, "Press Freedom and Political Change in Hong Kong," in *The Routledge Handbook of Chinese Media*, ed. Gary D. Rawnsley and Ming-Yeh T. Rawnsley (London: Routledge, 2015), 131–44.

9. Francis L. F. Lee and Angel M. Y. Lin, "Newspaper Editorial Discourse and the Politics of Self-Censorship in Hong Kong," *Discourse & Society* 17, no. 3 (2006): 331–58.

10. Francis L. F. Lee, *Talk Radio, the Mainstream Press, and Public Opinion in Hong Kong* (Hong Kong: Hong Kong University Press, 2014).

11. Joseph Man Chan, Francis L. F. Lee, and Clement Y. K. So, "Journalists in Hong Kong: A Decade after the Transfer of Sovereignty," in *The Global Journalist in the 21st Century*, ed. David H. Weaver and Lars Willnat (New York: Routledge, 2012), 22–35.

12. Allan K. L. Au, "Institutional Logics as Constitutive Censorship: The Case in Hong Kong Broadcast News Media" (PhD diss., The Chinese University of Hong Kong, 2016).

13. Francis L. F. Lee and Joseph Man Chan, "The Organizational Production of Self-Censorship in the Hong Kong Media," *International Journal of Press/Politics* 14, no. 1 (2009): 112–33.

14. The figures were derived from the website http://www.internetlivestats.com/internet-users/china-hong-kong-sar/.

15. See http://www.statistics.gov.hk/pub/B11302592016XXXXB0100.pdf, accessed on October 15, 2018.

16. Nick Couldry and James Curran, eds., *Contesting Media Power: Alternative Media in a Networked World* (Lanham, MD: Rowman & Littlefield, 2003).

17. Forde, *Challenging the News*.

18. Dennis K. K. Leung, "Alternative Internet Radio, Press Freedom and Contentious Politics in Hong Kong, 2004–2014," *Javnost-The Public* 22, no. 2 (2015): 196–212.

19. Francis L. F. Lee, "Opinion Media: From Talk Radio to Internet Alternative Media," in *Routledge Handbook of Hong Kong Studies*, ed. Tai-Lok Lui and Stephen W. K. Chiu (London: Routledge, forthcoming).

20. Dennis K. K. Leung and Francis L. F. Lee, "Cultivating an Online Counter-Public: Examining Usage and Political Impact of Internet Alternative Media," *International Journal of Press/Politics* 19, no. 3 (2014): 340–59.

21. Francis L. F. Lee, "Internet Alternative Media Use and Oppositional Knowledge," *International Journal of Public Opinion Research* 27, no. 3 (2015): 318–40.

22. Betty Yung and Lisa Yuk-Ming Leung, "Diverse Roles of Alternative Media in Hong Kong Civil Society: From Public Discourse Initiation to Social Activism," *Journal of Asian Public Policy* 7, no. 1 (2014): 83–101.

23. Gary K. Y. Tang and Francis L. F. Lee, "Facebook Use and Political Participation: The Impact of Exposure to Shared Political Information, Connections with Public Political Actors, and Network Structural Heterogeneity," *Social Science Computer Review* 31, no. 6 (2013): 763–73.

24. Francis L. F. Lee and Joseph Man Chan, *Media, Social Mobilization, and Mass Protests in Post-Colonial Hong Kong* (London: Routledge, 2011).

25. Francis L. F. Lee, "News Media as the Public Monitor in a Large-Scale Protest Campaign: The Case of Hong Kong's Umbrella Movement" (in Chinese), *Communication & Society* 38 (2016): 165–232.

26. Paul S. N. Lee, Clement Y. K. So, and Louis Leung, "Social Media and Umbrella Movement: Insurgent Public Sphere in Formation," *Chinese Journal of Communication* 8, no. 4 (2015): 356–75.

27. For the method of the survey, please see Francis L. F. Lee and Joseph M. Chan, *Media and Protest Logics in the Digital Era: The Umbrella Movement in Hong Kong* (New York: Oxford University Press, 2018).

28. Gary K. Y. Tang, "Mobilization of Images: Effects of TV Screen and Mediated Instant Grievances in the Umbrella Movement," *Chinese Journal of Communication* 8, no. 4 (2015): 338–55.

29. Lee, "News Media as the Public Monitor in a Large-Scale Protest Campaign."

30. Samson Yuen and Edmund W. Cheng, "Neither Repression Nor Concession? A Regime's Attrition against Mass Protests," *Political Studies* 65, no. 3 (2017): 611–30.

31. Lee, So, and Leung, "Social Media and Umbrella Movement."

32. Francis L. F. Lee, Hsuan-Ting Chen, and Michael Chan, "Social Media Use and University Students' Participation in a Large-Scale Protest Campaign: The Case of Hong Kong's Umbrella Movement," *Telematics and Informatics* 34, no. 2 (2017): 457–69.

33. Lee and Chan, *Media, Social Mobilization, and Mass Protests in Post-Colonial Hong Kong.*

34. Manuel Castells, *Networks of Outrage and Hope* (Cambridge: Polity, 2012).

35. Francis L. F. Lee and Joseph Man Chan, "Digital Media Activities and Mode of Participation in a Protest Campaign: The Case of the Umbrella Movement," *Information, Communication & Society* 19, no. 1 (2016): 4–22.

36. Time spent in the occupied area is a variable composed of the number of days the respondents spent in the occupied area, the amount of time they spent each day, and whether they had stayed overnight in the occupied areas. Digital participation is a measure composed of whether the respondents had engaged in fifteen digital activities related to the movement, such as changing profile pictures on social media to show support, helping dispel rumor online, forwarding movement-related news and commentaries, etc. For more details of the surveys and the items, see Lee and Chan, *Media and Protest Logics in the Digital Era.*

37. Castells, *Networks of Outrage and Hope.*

38. Lee, *Talk Radio, the Mainstream Press, and Public Opinion in Hong Kong.*

39. "Two Systems under Siege: Beijing Turns the Screws on Hong Kong Media, Annual Report of the Hong Kong Journalists Association, 2017," last modified July 2017, https://www.hkja.org.hk/wp-content/uploads/2018/04/Annual_report_2017-1.pdf.

40. Clement Y. K. So, "Media Credibility in Hong Kong See New Low" (in Chinese), *Ming Pao*, September 8, 2016.

41. Clement Y. K. So and Alice Y. L. Li, "Some Facts about Number of Visitors to News Sites in Hong Kong" (in Chinese), *Ming Pao*, November 3, 2016.

42. Francis L. F. Lee et al., eds., "Conditional Impact of Facebook as an Information Source on Political Opinions: The Case of Political Reform in Hong Kong," *Asian Journal of Political Science*, forthcoming.

43. Philip N. Howard and Muzammil M. Hussain, *Democracy's Fourth Wave? Digital Media and the Arab Spring* (New York: Oxford University Press, 2013).

44. Castells, *Networks of Outrage and Hope.*

45. Bennett and Segerberg, *The Logic of Connective Action.*

46. Rebecca MacKinnon, "China's 'Networked Authoritarianism,'" *Journal of Democracy* 22, no. 2 (2011): 32–46.

47. See, for example, Ki Deuk Hyun and Jinhee Kim, "The Role of New Media in Sustaining the Status Quo: Online Political Expression, Nationalism, and System Support in China," *Information, Communication & Society* 18, no. 7 (2015): 766–81.

6

WHERE HAVE ALL THE WORKERS GONE?

Reflections on the Role of Trade Unions during the Umbrella Movement

Chris K. C. Chan

Labor and working-class organizations played a significant role in democratic movements around the world. Taking the example of the United Kingdom, the first industrialized country in the world, workers struggled for economic and political rights simultaneously in the first half of the nineteenth century. On the one hand, the working-class and the lower middle-class radicals actively participated in the Charter Movement, which was for universal suffrage. On the other hand, the rights to strike and organize, working hour regulations, improvement of the working conditions, and the Poor Law amendment were also on the top of the labor movement agenda.[1] In the "third wave democracy" since 1970s, labor mobilization has continued to be an essential part of democratization in Southern Europe, South America, Africa, Eastern Europe, and East Asia.[2] In South Korea, for example, the democratic trade union movement contributed substantially to the end of authoritarian rule in 1988 and the stepping down of the right-wing president in 2016, although in both cases it was students who initiated the protests.[3]

Hong Kong's experience seems to have diverged from this general pattern, as trade unions played only marginal roles in the Umbrella Movement, the most historically significant democratic movement in the history of Hong Kong. This marginality was even more puzzling if we consider that surveys found a disproportionate representation of lower-class participants. According to a survey conducted by Samson Yuen and Edmund Cheng, most of the participants in the Umbrella Movement identified themselves as coming from the lower middle class or lower class/grassroots. About 30 percent of the participants were students and nearly 60 percent were managers, professionals, and clerks. Fifty-five percent of the participants had a bachelor's degree or above; 85 percent were aged thirty-nine or lower, more than 70 percent aged between eighteen and thirty-nine.[4] Among student participants, our own research[5] also found that those with neither parent having tertiary education were much more likely to participate in the movement than those with at least one parent having tertiary education. Students from lower-class backgrounds who graduated from public secondary schools, lived in rented public housing with monthly household income lower than HK$30,000, and did not have a parent with a tertiary education were more likely to participate in the movement.

The grassroots profile of participants in the Umbrella Movement reflects the widespread socioeconomic grievances experienced by the general public and the students, their anxiety about future mobility, and the increase in socioeconomic inequality in the post-1997 period. In this context, one would expect democratic trade unions in Hong Kong to follow in the footsteps of their counterparts in other newly industrialized countries (NICs) and play a key role in the Umbrella Movement. As will be demonstrated in this chapter, however, trade unions and grassroots organizations played only a supportive role. The author argues that the failure of trade unions to call a general strike and their alliance with grassroots organizations that had a limited capacity to mobilize workers' participation have significantly weakened trade unions' political influence during the movement and led to their marginalization in the first post–Umbrella Movement Legislative Council (LegCo) election and afterwards. The limitations of the democratic trade unions to mobilize their members during the Umbrella Movement in turn are due to structural, institutional, and ideological factors, namely political division in trade unionism, weak workplace organizing power, and the liberal ideology of the political elites in Hong Kong. Although this chapter focuses more on the Hong Kong Confederation of Trade Unions (HKCTU), the main trade union center in the prodemocracy camp, our analysis also covers grassroots organizations such as Neighbourhood and Worker's Service Centre (NWSC) as they are also part of the democratic labor movement broadly.

Labor and Unionism in Hong Kong: A Historical Background

Political Unionism: Left and Right

As early as the 1920s, labor movements in Hong Kong were characterized by intervention from political forces that supported either the Chinese Communist

Party (CCP) or Chinese Nationalist Party (KMT). In 1948, the Hong Kong Federation of Trade Unions (HKFTU) was formed by pro-CCP trade unions. In the same year, pro-KMT forces founded the Hong Kong and Kowloon Trade Union Council (HKTUC).

The riots in 1967 changed the fate of labor movement in Hong Kong. Spurred on by pro-CCP forces, the conflict in a plastic flower factory quickly went from a labor conflict to an anticolonial movement. Public opinion turned against the HKFTU after the "leftists" planted bombs in government and police buildings. In the 1970s, the HKFTU became a service provider and was seldom involved in industrial action. On the other hand, the HKTUC was co-opted by employers and government and was unable to play a central role in the labor movement. During this period, labor nongovernmental organizations (NGOs) emerged, assisting the development of an independent labor movement. One of the most important labor NGOs was the Hong Kong Christian Industrial Committee (HKCIC).

The 1980s saw labor turn to politics again. As Hong Kong's future was discussed in the Sino-British negotiations, the Hong Kong government launched an unprecedented public consultation on political reform. Conflict between the HKCIC and the HKFTU was aroused over the HKFTU's support for Beijing and the HKCIC's advocacy for direct elections. Their conflict deepened after the HKCIC and independent trade unions in their network participated in the support of the student democratic movement in Beijing in 1989, in which its organizer Lee Cheuk Yan was detained in Beijing. In 1990, HKCTU was established with a call for democracy, with the HKCIC director Lau Chin-shek as the founding president and Lee as the chief executive. Lee has been general secretary since 1995. Both Lau and Lee were regarded as popular and charismatic leaders in both the labor and democratic movements. They were the standing committee members of Hong Kong People's Alliance for the Support of Democratic Movement in China. Lau was the founding member of the Democratic Party, and Lee was the core member of the political organization, the Frontier. Under their leadership, the HKCTU had been firmly established as part of the prodemocratic force by 1997. M. Chan pointed out that "the CTU, with its social movement allies and the prodemocracy political parties emerged during the past decade as a potent force counterbalancing the FTU. Indeed, the China factor helped to realign the Hong Kong union scene into a new configuration of FTU vs. CTU, contending over democratisation and labour rights."[6]

The Rise of Social Movement Unionism

The traditional approach to theorizing trade unions has put trade unions into two categories: political unionism (trade unions with a mission to change the social order) and economic unionism (trade union focuses on improvement of wage and working condition through collective bargaining).[7] The term social movement unionism (SMU) was developed out of the need to account for perceived changes in the labor movement in the Global South since the 1980s. These labor movements were thought to be different from traditional trade unionism in their goals and alliances, as well as their organization. The Korean Confederation of Trade Unions (KCTU) in South Korea, the Congress of South African Trade Unions (COSATU) in South Africa, and the Central Única dos Trabalhadores (CUT), or Unified Workers' Central in Brazil are typical examples of SMUs. For instance, in South Africa and South Korea, trade unions allied with antiapartheid and prodemocracy movements respectively, and played important roles in wider social movements.[8] To understand these developments, labor theorists developed the model of SMU that, according to Suzuki, generally comprises the following elements: broad goals of social justice to challenge state and corporations, coalitions with social and community movements, and alternative ways of union organizations unconstrained by workplace-based issues.[9]

In Hong Kong, while the HKFTU and the HKTUC are typical examples of political unionism, the formation and development of the HKCTU has strong elements of SMU. First of all, the HKCTU was organized by the social movement organization the HKCIC and has carried on the tradition of the HKCIC to work closely with community and grassroots organizations. Second, since the 1980s, the HKCIC, HKCTU, and their leaders have been the essential part of the democratic movement in Hong Kong. Third, the HKCTU has also been active in international labor solidarity, especially the support of workers' struggles in Mainland China. The cooperation of HKCTU with civil society groups and the international labor movement has been strengthened in the twenty-first century, under the framework of the antineoliberalism movement.

The year 2003 was a milestone in Hong Kong's democratic and social movement. It became a historical event when more than half a million people joined the march on July 1st, 2003, to oppose the enactment of a national security bill. Fewer people but still a huge number joined demonstration on the same day in 2004 to demand for "democracy and people's livelihood." HKCTU took a key role in organizing the struggle, joining more than thirty local prodemocracy and human rights groups to form the Civil Human Rights Front, which organized the two demonstrations. The spokesman in July 1st, 2003, was an assistant to HKCTU's president, while the assembly commander was HKCTU general secretary. HKCTU rank-and-file members formed a significant part of the picket.

In 2005, the World Trade Organization (WTO) held its ministerial conference in Hong Kong. HKCTU was the leading organization in the Hong Kong

People's Alliance, which organized a big protest with ten thousand participants from more than a hundred countries. This protest was said to have a critical impact on social movements in Hong Kong as the South Korean protesters had brought a militant but creative approach to protests to Hong Kong and inspired the new generation of activists. The media in Hong Kong had widely reported the protesters' views on the negative impact of free trade and neoliberalism on peoples' livelihood. While NGOs usually take a leading role in the antiglobalization campaign in the Western countries, in Hong Kong, HKCTU, a trade union, led the protest.

The HKCTU has also successfully led the minimum wage campaign. It has lobbied for a legal minimum wage since late 1990s. In 2003, taking the "United Students Against Sweatshops," a student organization in America, as an example, the HKCTU started to build linkage between university students and workers to demand minimum wages within the campus. It set up "grassroots concern groups" with student unions in universities to lobby the university management for better working conditions for cleaning workers and security guards. As a further step, in 2006 the "People's Alliance for the Minimum Wage" was formed with participation from many community and grassroots organizations. The alliance finally pressured the government to introduce a minimum wage policy in 2011.

Another successful example of a student and workers alliance was during a dockworkers strike in May 2013. The strike of five hundred subcontracted dockworkers lasted for forty days in the Hong Kong International Terminal (HIT). The striking workers had to work twenty-four-hour shifts, on a salary even lower than wage levels before 1997. The strike, which was organized by the affiliate of the HKCTU, led to a pay rise of 9.8 percent for more than 4,500 workers and gained significant public support, including solidarity action by civil society groups, HKFS, and university students. The strike fund set up by the union raised more than HK$8 million (around $1.03 million US) from the public. The strike attracted global attention and for the first time the local media used the term "SMU" when referring to the strike and the HKCTU. The above examples have demonstrated the social movement dimension of the HKCTU. In social and labor right movements such as the anti-WTO protest, minimum wage campaign, and dockworkers strike, the HKCTU took on a leadership role with support from many civil society groups. In the civil rights campaigns, such as the anti–National Security Law mobilization, the HKCTU joined hands with political parties and human rights groups to play the organizing role. Comparing with these previous events, the HKCTU, its affiliates, and civil society partners, such as the NWSC and Hong Kong Women Workers Association (HKWWA), have played only a supportive role in the Umbrella Movement.[10] As a matter of fact, the protest was a political movement led by intellectuals and students. Although students and young professionals from lower middle-class, working-class, or grassroots families had more actively participated in the movement, most of the participants were not mobilized by political parties, trade unions, or community organizations. In the next section, we will elaborate how democratic trade unions and grassroots organizations participated in the occupy movement and interacted with student organizations, political parties, and other civil society groups.

The Role of Trade Union and Civil Society Groups during the Umbrella Movement

When the three leaders of Occupy Central (OC) formed a secretariat to coordinate the preparation for the Occupy movement in mid-2013, they decided to invite individuals, rather than organizations, to join the secretariat. Lee Cheuk Yan was one of the important members in the secretariat to coordinate the mobilization of trade unions and the grassroots. Kwok Siu-kit, the then vice chairman of HKCTU, was assigned to lead the marshals, as the HKCTU is experienced in dealing with the police in large-scale demonstration. Within the HKCTU, discussions were organized in the first half of 2014 and it core members were mobilized to join the marshals' team of the OC secretariat.

Without support from the OC, the Hong Kong Federation of Students (HKFS) organized a mini-occupy on the July 1, 2014, at which five hundred participants were arrested. The HKFS had contacted a number of progressive politicians, including Lee Cheuk Yan, to support their action, and they appreciated Lee's contribution. The exercise of mini-occupy had encouraged the students to build a broader alliance. When the HKFS planned to organize class boycotts in early September, they contacted many potential supporters in the civil society, and the organizers of the HKCTU were invited to share their experience in organizing large-scale protests and their views on the next step of the movement.

On September 22, HKFS called for a student strike. The students moved to a park outside the governmental headquarters to hold an assembly. During the week of the strike, representatives from trade unions and grassroots organizations carried out different forms of support activities for students. The Dockworkers Union, who received great support from HKFS and students in their strike in 2013, was one of the most active grassroots groups in the support of students. On September 26, the students occupied the "Civil Square," and the leaders of HKFS and Scholarism were detained by the police. Thousands of citizens surrounded the square in support of the students. The arrest of the student leaders caused a leadership crisis for all the demonstrators. Before

Alex Chow and Lester Sum, the general secretary and deputy general secretary of the HKFS, and Joshua Wong, the convener of Scholarism, charged into the Civil Square, Nathan Law, the standing committee member of the HKFS, was assigned to stay outside and take up the leadership. While he was giving a speech, however, a group of plainclothes police suddenly moved to arrest Law. Many trade union and civil society group members who were assisting the students attempted to protect Law, but after a stalemate, Law gave up and was taken away by the police.

In the early morning of September 27, some members of NGOs contacted Lee Cheuk Yan and sought his help in contacting OC and asking it to consider starting the Occupy Central action, which was originally planned to take place on October 1, earlier. HKCTU and seventeen grassroots organizations formed the Civil Society Alliance for the Support of Students and Universal Disobedience (the Alliance), which aimed to provide practical support to HKFS and the students. With the help of the Alliance, HKFS declared that demonstrations would continue and an assembly would be organized for the evening of September 27. On the night of September 27, thousands of protesters continued to stay outside the government headquarters after the assembly ended. The OC then decided to announce the commencement of the Occupy Central action after meeting with the HKFS leaders.

September 28 was the starting date of the Umbrella Movement, which had gotten out of control for the OC secretariat and its leaders. When asked by the media during the preparation of the class boycott in September, Chow mentioned that strikes were a possible tactic for struggle, but few people believed that a political strike could happen in Hong Kong. Surprisingly, on September 28, when Chow was still in the police station, the HKFS, the HKCTU, and its largest affiliate, the Hong Kong Professional Teachers' Union (HKPTU), called for a general strike on September 29. We do not know how many workers actually participated in the general strike, but the best example promoted by the HKCTU was that two hundred members of the Swire Beverages (Hong Kong) Employees General Union staged a two-day strike. The student leaders were released on September 29 and called for a meeting with the Alliance to seek further support. The members of the Alliance agreed to support the HKFS by organizing marshals and other supportive actions. The Alliance had functioned until the end of the Occupy Movement. The core members and organizers of the HKCTU were arrested by the police on the last day of the Occupy movement.

With the eighteen organization members in the Alliance, the HKCTU and the NWSC were two of the major groups that consistently provided manpower to support the operation of the occupy zone in Admiralty. While the leadership of the HKFS and OC were not always well-coordinated during the Occupy

Movement due to their different political orientations, both the HKCTU and the NWSC provided support to both sides. Their support to the HKFS was through the Alliance, and to the OC via the OC secretariat. Kwok Siu-kit, the vice chairman of the HKCTU, told us in an interview that when the Umbrella Movement broke out after September 28, 2014, the situation was different from OC's original plan. When three main occupation areas in Admiralty, Mongkok and Causeway Bay emerged spontaneously, Kwok said the plan that "ten picket teams for coordinating ten districts" was no longer an option. Even so, the HKCTU had provided equipment and manpower to coordinate the main stage outside government headquarters in Admiralty, and such support lasted till the end of the occupation in Admiralty.

Since September 29, the HKCTU had a booth set up just beside the main stage of the occupy zone in Admiralty, with staff and volunteers working twenty-four-hour shifts. The idea of setting up the main stage and holding regular assemblies was first suggested by members of the HKCTU to the HKFS leaders. The marshals who were assigned to maintain the order of the main stage during the evening assembly were retired union members of the HKCTU. The members of the NWSC also led a team of volunteers to collect the opinions of occupants by focus-group discussion and reflect them to the Alliance, and then through the Alliance to the student leaders. As a matter of fact, the HKFS, Scholarism, and OC had built up the image of leadership in the Occupy Movement by having their leaders speak almost every evening on the main stage of Admiralty. Members from the prodemocracy political parties and the Alliance also gave speeches in the assemblies from time to time, but they were playing a secondary role to the three major leading groups.

In Mongkok, the situation was more complicated, with the far-right groups, such as Civic Passion, reportedly attacking the leftist groups. Under the umbrella of the Alliance, a team of volunteers had monitored the situation in Mongkok and reported to the student leaders and other relevant parties. Mak Tak Ching, the former organizer of the HKCTU, who was elected a District Board member representing the Labor Party in 2015, was one of the core members in the team. The League of Social Democrats (LSD), another member organization of the Alliance that has a strong stance of supporting the interests of the working class and the grassroots, set up a booth in Mongkok. To avoid direct attack from and confrontation with the rightist groups, the LSD did not use its name directly in the booth. Instead, other like-minded groups or individuals used the platform to promote their ideas. The Age of Resistance was a group that worked closely with LSD and was a member organization of the Alliance. Its core member, Lau Siu-lai, was one of the main speakers in the public forum organized in the LSD booth. Lau, a lecturer in a community college, rose as a popular speaker in Mongkok and transformed the forum into "Democracy Groundwork" in the later stages of the Occupy Movement.

The occupy zone in Causeway Bay was smaller and more peaceful compared to Mongkok and Admiralty. It was coordinated by the Land Justice League. The league was also a member of Alliance, but their coordination in Causeway Bay was as early as the start of the occupation on the evening of September 28. The group joined the Alliance several days later to show solidarity with the trade unions and civil society groups. Eddie Chu was one of the core members of the league who had contributed significantly in advising the students in general and supporting the Causeway Bay occupation zone in particular. With the help of another core member of the league, a daily newsletter was published by the Alliance. The newsletters were printed and circulated in the three occupation zones in some days, but its major function was to summarize reports in the media and inform the key participants in the movement.

Although both the Age of Resistance and the Land Justice League were members of the Alliance and their representatives attended the meetings of the Alliance, their relations with the HKCTU and the NWSC were loose. These two groups represented the newly formed civil society groups led by young elite activists with creative strategies to promote their ideas (online and offline), while the HKCTU and the NWSC were traditional workplace and community groups with emphasis more on grassroots participation. Compared with the HKCTU and the NWSC staff, the Age of Resistance and the Land Justice League also had better communication with the student leaders thanks to the similarity in age, social movement experience, and lifestyle. Even though the HKCTU and the NWSC staff made a serious effort to mobilize and coordinate their rank-and-file members to support the movement, apart from the two-day strike at Swire Beverage, most of the participation from trade union members were on an individual or volunteer basis rather than as a group coming together to join the occupation. Many of them worked as marshals in shifts, and some of them spoke in the evening assembly to show support on the behalf of their unions. For the NWSC, their staff also tried to carry out an opinion survey among the occupants and reported the result to the assembly to facilitate the communication among the leaders and participants.

As suggested by the student leaders, a five-party coordination body was formed on September 30, including the HKFS, Scholarism, OC, the prodemocracy political parties, and the Alliance. Although it was not a final decision-making party, as the real power rested with the HKFS and OC, this coordination body, with Lee Cheuk Yan as an informal convener, had functioned as a platform to coordinate strategies for the occupation. Compared with the other four parties, the influence of the Alliance in the coordination body was weak. It was formed after September 27 and did not have a strong political foundation. Instead, it was a loose network with eighteen member organizations from a wide range of the political spectrum. Within the Alliance, it was difficult to compromise and reach a common position. For example, some of the groups did not prepare for taking up political leadership, while others were more ready to do so. The five-party coordination body was founded as a platform to exchange information and compromise ideas while the decision-making power rested with the HKFS and OC. Several days after the five-party body was formed, an informal discussion on the possibility of making this platform into a real decision-making mechanism was initiated, and members of the Alliance were consulted. Some members highly supported this idea, as they believed it would centralize and strengthen the leadership of the movement. Others were worried about this development since their organizations, being identified as pressure groups or NGOs, were not in a position to take up political leadership. Discussion was suspended because it was difficult to reach a consensus. Its participation in the coordination body was invited by the leaders of the HKFS, but the cooperation between the HKFS and the Alliance was also not satisfactory for both sides. For trade unionists and the civil society groups, the students did not respect grassroots organizations enough as key partners in the movement. A representative from the HKFS regularly sat in the meeting of the Alliance, but it was hard to persuade more student core members to join the meeting. Key student leaders complained that meeting with the Alliance was time-consuming, as they always had important decisions to make among themselves or with the OCs apart from talking with the media.

Compared to the relatively successful models of the SMU in other countries, such as South Korea, South Africa, and Poland, the students and intellectuals in Hong Kong have committed much less to the labor and grassroots movements, while the organizing power of the democratic trade unions in Hong Kong was also significantly weak. The practice of SMU in Hong Kong has been constrained by structural (political division of trade unions), institutional (weak organizing power), and ideological (liberal tradition) factors. In the next session, we will explain this in detail.

Limitations of SMU in Hong Kong

It has been argued that the independent trade union movement in Hong Kong shares many characteristics of SMU with its strong connection with the social movement, prodemocratic parties, and international civil society. Different from political trade unionism, which subordinates itself to a political party, and the economic trade unions, whose major concerns are workers' wages and working conditions, SMU has a broader social and political agenda.[11] Social injustice, political rights, and full citizenship are among the core demands of the SMU. In this sense, the HKCTU shares many similarities with the KCTU in South Korea, COSATU in South Africa, and CUT in Brazil as examples of SMUs. Therefore, the HKCTU was able to place itself within the center of many important events in the city. From the Hong Kong people's support to the Tiananmen Square Democratic Movement in 1989, the demonstration against the National Security Law in 2003, and the global protest against the WTO in 2005, the leaders, organizers, and core members of the HKCTU all played significant roles. The union was also able to mobilize strong public support for workers' rights and workers' struggle by building alliances with students and civil society groups, as we could see in the cases of the minimum wage campaign and dockworkers strike.

Compared with democratic trade unionism in Brazil, South Africa, and South Korea, however, the workplace organizing base and the capacity of the HKCTU to mobilize its members are much weaker. Even in the case of iconic dockworkers strike, only 500 of the 4,500 workers were mobilized to join the strike. Organizers in HKCTU were pessimistic about calling members of the HKFTU or nonunion members to join in the strike. Their efforts were focused on maintaining support from the media and the public to pressure the corporations and the government.[12] In other words, without strong workplace organizations, the HKCTU has to rely on the power of society by using media strategies and alliances with democratic parties and civil society groups to advocate both labor rights and political rights.

The term SMU has been used by scholars in different ways. Based on her study of successful trade union mobilization to support undocumented workers in Los Angeles in 2006, Engeman argues that the practice of SMU should take a "balance of union organizational and [social] movement dimensions."[13] Engeman criticized some of the labor scholars for focusing solely on the movement dimension of SMU (i.e. "adopting social change goals" and "allying with other community organizations").[14] In her study, she finds that the union organizational dimension also has an important influence on the dynamics of SMU.[15] This finding can also apply to Hong Kong, where the HKCTU has a strong social movement connection but weak union organizational power. While the HKCTU gained public support—through its alliance with civil society, in its campaigns for labor and civil rights as demonstrated in examples of anti–National Security Law protest, minimum wage movement, and dockworkers strike—it failed to mobilize its rank-and-file members in confronting the political crisis between Hong Kong and Beijing. The student leaders were sensitive and understood the extreme inequality in power between Hong Kong and Beijing and therefore sought trade unions' support to prepare and call for a general strike. After the HKCTU and HKPTU failed to play this role, student leaders took an instrumental attitude to win the protest and no longer considered the trade unions a key partner in the movement. But what accounts for the weak mobilization capacity of the democratic trade unions during the Umbrella Movement?

Structural Factor: Strong Competition from Pro-establishment Unionism

As mentioned before, organized labor in Hong Kong has been highly politically divisive.[16] Before the 1990s, the major division was between the pro-CCP leftist trade union, the HKFTU, and the pro-KMT rightist trade union, the HKTUC. This division has been replaced by a new rivalry after 1997: the prodemocratic social movement union, the HKCTU, and the pro-establishment union, the HKFTU.[17] According to the Labor Department, HKCTU has 81 affiliated trade unions and 139,056 members,[18] while HKFTU has 189 affiliated trade unions and 415,145 members, or 63.7 percent of the total declared union membership in the city.[19]

The sharp confrontations between the HKCTU and the HKFTU could be witnessed in all of the major political, social, and economic issues. During the privatization debate on the shopping arcades and parking lots in public housing estates from 2004 to 2005, the HKCTU was critical of the privatization plan, while the HKFTU supported it. Though both the HKFTU and the HKCTU voted for the motion "Demanding the Suspension of Privatisation" in the Legislative Council on June 1, 2005,[20] a pro-privatization "Investors' Alliance" was formed in 2004, and Hong Kong Securities and Futures Employees Union, one of HKFTU's member unions, joined the alliance and described the anti-privatization movement as "a chaos created by bad politicians."[21] The anti-express-rail movement in 2009 and 2010 was another example of confrontations. When HKFTU mobilized members to support the construction of the Guangzhou–Shenzhen–Hong Kong Express Rail Link in the name of "creating jobs," HKCTU union leaders publicly questioned the numbers of jobs created and the need to build such a rail by demolishing others' home villages.[22] HKFTU was also against HKCTU's more militant attitudes in the 2007 steel fixers strike[23] and 2013 dockworkers strike,[24] while the HKCTU viewed the HKFTU as misrepresenting workers' interests in the negotiations with the employers.

The Umbrella Movement was no exception in terms of trade union division. The pro-Beijing union had been criticizing Occupy Central from the very beginning, and their mass countermobilization was symbolized by the formation of the "Alliance for Peace and Democracy" (APD) in July 2014. Chau-pei Ng, the chairperson of HKFTU, was one of its founders, and HKFTU members unions supported the Alliance by coordinating petitions against Occupy Central before and during the Umbrella Movement.[25] The petition was conducted in the name of restoring law and order and to "reopen the roads for the people." During the interviews with the leaders of the Federation of Hong Kong Trade Unions in Tourism, Eating Establishment Employees General Union, and Hong Kong Department Stores & Commercial Staff General Union, they admitted that their union members and volunteers, attracted by the HKFTU's routine social services (such as interest classes, recreational activities, tourist tours, discounted shops), were mobilized to maintain the petition stations on the streets. They also said that long-developed relations with the members were necessary to attract their help. Other union leaders suggested that the widespread use of smartphones was useful for spreading information in their industries. It was reported that the OPD's petition received 1.83 million signatures against Occupy Central in November 2014.[26]

Besides petitions, more vigorous actions were also conducted. Assemblies and rallies were organized by the HKFTU during the occupation.[27] In October 2014, representatives of the Taxi Drivers and Operators Association marched to the occupied area in Admiralty and urged the police to clear the protesters.[28] They brought pliers and broke some of the occupiers' barricades. It should be noted that the HKFTU was reluctant to organize militant actions in its own name. In an interview, the taxi union leader did not admit that their "barricade breaking" action was organized by the union or union members. Instead he used the term "the industry" several times. The duration of mobilization may vary among different unions, but the main objectives for mobilization were more or less the same. All interviewed HKFTU member union leaders emphasized the damage done by Occupy Central to their members' livelihoods, the need to follow the law, and the importance of Chinese national identity.

Institutional Factor: Weak Workplace Organizing Power

It is true that a lot of manpower and resources were put forward by the HKCTU to support the Occupy Movement, but its capacity to mobilize its rank-and-file members in the protest was significantly weak if we compare the HKCTU with its counterpart in Korea, the KCTU. In Korea, many political movements were also initiated by students, but the trade unions had provided essential backup by general strike and large-scale mobilization of their members.[29] In Hong Kong, however, although many of the young participants in the Occupy Movement came from lower middle-class or grassroots background, they were not mobilized by the trade unions or other social groups. Social class was not a salient identity during the protest and participants were easily drawn to the far-right "localist" groups' militancy.

In Taiwan, labor also took a supportive role in the democratic movement of the 1980s, which was much weaker than in Korea. Since the Democratic Progressive Party won the presidential election in 2000, some of the democratic trade unions have lost their role in challenging the authorities. Compared to Taiwan today, the advantage of HKCTU is its strong connections with social movements and broad concerns about social justice. But in terms of institutional and workplace organizing power, Taiwanese trade unions, especially in public sector and large corporations, are still comparatively stronger than their Hong Kong counterparts. Therefore, while the failure of the HKCTU leaders to mobilize their members to support the Umbrella Movement was mostly due to weak workplace organizing power, the low capacity of Taiwanese trade unions to support students in the Sunflower Movement was also because many of these trade unions have turned to economic unionism.

The atmosphere and external conditions for a general strike on September 29 were present, but there was no powerful organizing base to make the general strike happen. The call for a strike by the HKPTU and the HKCTU had a symbolic meaning since they are the biggest independent union and independent union confederation respectively. The HKPTU, which has more than eighty thousand members, is the largest affiliate of the HKCTU and its members take up more than half of the HKCTU membership.[30] Yet their political mobilization capacity is limited. On the one hand, the HKPTU emphasizes its professional image, rather than class solidarity, and its operation relies on providing welfare to its members. Its main income is from the revenue of discounted supermarkets, not membership dues. On the other hand, since the establishment of the HKCTU, it has faced financial challenge. In order to compete with the HKFTU in membership and union coverage, it has to raise funds externally, including seeking support from international trade unions, which were attacked by the pro-Beijing press during the Umbrella Movement. Its operation relies on organizers who are college graduates and who have experience in social movement participation. This gives rise to a model of SMU that is able to connect with the broader social movement and organize the most vulnerable workers by offering legal advice and assistance during the labor disputes.[31] But many of the new members who sought the HKCTU's help during labor disputes have no incentive to renew their membership once the disputes were resolved. There are several reasons for this. First, the right to collective bargaining is not legally protected. Second, the HKCTU is unable to offer much benefit to its members like the HKFTU does. Third, most of these members work in the informal sectors or small and medium-sized enterprises (SMEs), the workplace organizations of which are difficult to consolidate.

The HKCTU has more than ninety affiliates, but just a few of these subordinate trade unions, such as the HKPTU, Cathay Pacific Airways Flight Attendants Union, and a few civil servant trade unions, have their own office and staff. All the other affiliated unions don't have financial capacity to rent an office or employ a full-time staff. The average union fee in Hong Kong is around one hundred to two hundred Hong Kong dollars per year. Most of the HKCTU's core affiliates have a thousand members or fewer. The secretariat of the HKCTU, with around twenty full-time organizers, has to take care of the organizing work of most of its affiliates apart from the administration of the confederation itself. Also, the secretariat of the HKCTU has to work hard to raise external funding to employ its full-time staff. This includes individual donations, international trade union, local and international charity foundations, as well as the HKSAR government. It also runs workers retraining programs that are subsidized by Employees Retraining Board (ERB). The affiliates of the HKFTU, however, usually have their own offices and staff. The HKFTU plays a central coordination role and has regional offices in many parts of the city to offer community-based service to its members.

Ideological Factor: Liberal Tradition of Democratic Activists

The leaders of the democratic movement in Hong Kong in the past three decades, being highly influenced by the ideology of liberalism, have presented themselves as a middle-class professional and social elite. They are attorneys, scholars, doctors, social workers, and so on who use their professional knowledge to promote social change. Surely some of them are rooted in community organizing, but few would be aware that Hong Kong needs a large-scale strike to fight for democracy. Without the foundation of grassroots and workplace organizing, such strike is unlikely to occur even if the political leaders call for a strike. The intellectuals and young students of South Korea in the 1980s had a different choice of strategy. After the suppression of the Gwangju Uprising in the 1980s, the activism went underground. The students chose to work in big corporations and developed independent trade union or workers' networks.[32] In 1987, before the military government held the Olympic Games to showcase their economic achievements, many former student leaders led workers to the streets and initiated a general strike. Hundreds of independent and democratic trade unions were established afterwards. The period between 1980 and 1987 has built an important foundation for the democratic movement and socioeconomic development in South Korea. In Hong Kong, however, the old "left" (e.g., HKFTU) has been absorbed into the authoritarian regime, and the youth movement in Hong Kong since the 1980s has been embedded in a strong liberal tradition.

One of the examples that demonstrates the liberal tradition of the prodemocratic activists in Hong Kong was the 1999 debate on the minimum wage. In the light of the wave of wage cuts after the Asian financial crisis in 1998, Lee Cheuk Yan raised a motion for minimum wage legislation in the LegCo. The Democratic Party, the main prodemocratic force at that time, was divided, with its mainstream faction opposing this motion. It should be noted that the leadership and core members of the Democratic Party were mostly lawyers, social workers, and teachers who had been student movement leaders in 1970s or 1980s. Similarly, the leaders of the other major prodemocratic political group, the Frontier, demanded pay cuts for civil servants, which was strongly opposed by the unions.[33] In 2005, when the community groups staged a campaign against the government's plan to privatize the shopping malls, wet markets, and parking lots in the public estates, they did not get much support from the prodemocratic LegCo members. In fact, the Democratic Party voted for the privatization. All these developments showed that labor rights and trade union organizing were never a key concern of the mainstream prodemocratic activists in Hong Kong who believed in the tradition of market liberalism. A handful of the activists, for example Lee Cheuk Yan, who was a graduate of the University of Hong Kong in late 1970s, did choose to join labor organizations such as the HKCIC and HKCTU as organizers. But it was a marginal phenomenon and there were two main limitations compared to the Korean intellectual involvement in labor movement, which was strongly influenced by Marxism. First, Hong Kong activists are isolated from the workplace, as they work as paid staff members in trade unions, while their Korean counterparts choose to work in factories or for large corporations as workers or staff members. Second, Hong Kong democratic trade unions or labor NGOs can only employ a small number of full-time organizers, while hundreds of student activists in Korea were able to organize workers in their own workplace. Similar to Hong Kong, in Taiwan the tradition of Marxism in labor movements was much weaker than in Korea, and working in labor NGOs or trade unions as full-time organizers was also the major career choice for prolabor intellectuals.

Conclusion

This chapter has evaluated the labor, trade unions, and grassroots organizations' contributions to the Umbrella Movement in Hong Kong. Although most of the participants in the Umbrella Movement were students, young professionals, or white-collar workers, from families of lower middle-class or grassroots background, most of them were not mobilized by trade unions, political parties, or community organizations. The democratic trade unions and their allies played a significant supportive role in the Umbrella Movement, but not a mobilizing role.

This phenomenon can only be understood within the history of the trade union movement in Hong Kong. The labor movement in Hong Kong was highly divided politically by "left vs right" as the two major trade union centers, the HKFTU and the HKTUC, had subordinated themselves to political parties in authoritarian Chinese political regimes. The rise of the HKCTU and the decline of pro-KMT HKTUC since the 1990s have created a new pattern of trade union division (authoritarian unionism vs. SMU). The strength of the SMU model in Hong Kong lies in its strong network with political parties and social groups, but its weakness lies in workplace organizing and mobilization. Requested by the students, a general strike was called by the HKCTU during the Umbrella Movement, but it was far from successful.

With strong social and democratic movement connections and rich experiences in organizing mass protests, the HKCTU put great effort to participate in the Umbrella Movement, including building up a students and workers alliance. But after the Umbrella Movement, in the LegCo election held in September 2016, the leaders of trade unions, political parties, and community organizations with an image of representing the interests of the working class and the grassroots, suffered a serious setback. The Labour Party's legislators dropped from four to one, while both the NWSC and Hong Kong Association for Democracy and People's Livelihood lost in the geographical constituency. To account for this new development, the author offers reflections on three levels.

Structurally, the strong competition from the HKFTU in the anti-Occupy mobilization has constrained the HKCTU from taking a leading role in the movement and representing the working class. Institutionally, the vulnerable workplace organizing base of the HKCTU is the major weakness accounting for the lower mobilizing power of the trade union. Ideologically, the liberal bias among Hong Kong's political elites means that they pay relatively less attention to the labor and workplace organizing, leaving HKCTU without a strong political ally and enough workplace organizers. The old "left" (e.g. HKFTU) has been absorbed into the authoritarian regime, and the youth movement in Hong Kong is embedded in a strong liberal tradition.

These constraints left the democratic labor movement in Hong Kong with numerous challenges after the Umbrella Movement. Apart from the loss of the Labour Party and other prolabor political groups in the LegCo election, we also witnessed the increasing alienation between the HKCTU and the student movements, which are now under the influence of "localism." On the eve of May Day 2016, the major student unions from nine universities, which had previously been on friendly terms with the HKCTU, released a joint statement declaring their withdrawal from the Solidarity March hosted by the HKCTU. In their eyes, union struggles are "simply a matter of rituals," "claiming to safeguard workers' rights and interests, pleading the communist-run Hong Kong Government to pity and improve Hong Kong people's situation, yet no improvement on labor rights has been achieved in Hong Kong."[34] Although the HKCTU and grassroots organizations do not always support the mainstream democratic parties, especially on the issues of social policies and labor rights, as mentioned above, the new generation of "localist" activists regarded them a part of the pan-democratic camp which was conservative and old-fashioned. This challenge calls for a new effort to empower workers in the workplace and a new strategy to build up a workers-student alliance in the civil society. In 2016, Carol Ng from Hong Kong Cabin Crew Federation was elected as the first woman president of HKCTU. The election of Miss Ng was a breakthrough in the history of HKCTU. Compared to her predecessors, Ng is younger and able to appeal to her members and the public through social media. The unions in her industry are also much better organized. Cathay Pacific Airway Flight Attendants Union, for example, is one of the rare successful cases where workers' power forced management to conduct regular collective bargaining with the union even though the right to collective bargaining is absent in Hong Kong. In 2017, HKCTU mobilized some of its affiliated unions to join students groups in eight tertiary institutions to establish the Student Labour Action Coalition. One of the coalition's core members, Nga Man Wong, ran for Student Union president at Hong Kong Baptist University as the only candidate. Unfortunately the voter turnout was too low for her to be elected due to the countercampaign from the right-wing localist groups, but it was the first attempt from the progressive left to take back the leadership of the university student unions after the Umbrella Movement.

NOTES

This research was supported by a special grant from Department of Applied Social Sciences, City University of Hong Kong (2015–2017). The author is grateful for the research assistance from Mr. Julian Yeung.

1. See http://www.unionhistory.info/ for the history of the labor movement in Britain.

2. Ruth Berins Collier, *Paths Toward Democracy: The Working Class and Elites in Western Europe and South America* (New York: Cambridge University Press, 1999).

3. Hagen Koo, *Korean Workers: The Culture and Politics of Class Formation* (Ithaca, NY: Cornell University Press, 2001).

4. This is one of the most reliable sources of data about the social background of the participants in the Umbrella Movement. Samson Yuen and Edmund Cheng conducted a seven-day survey with 1,681 random and valid samples at the occupied sites at Admiralty, Mongkok, and Causeway Bay between October 20 and 26, 2014. The survey had a response rate of 97 percent. See Samson Yuen, "The Umbrella Movement: Who, Why and

What Next?" (paper presented in the workshop on "Hong Kong's Social Transformation in the Context of Taiwan-Hong Kong Comparison," Institute of Sociology, Academia Sinica, Taiwan, November 21, 2014); Edmund W. Cheng and Wai-Yin Chan, "Explaining Spontaneous Occupation: Antecedents, Contingencies and Spaces in the Umbrella Movement," *Social Movement Studies* 16, no. 2 (2017): 222–39. White-collar work such as managers, professionals, and clerks had been regarded as middle class in Hong Kong. In this survey, most respondents identified them as from the lower middle class or grassroots; it might indicate the changing quality of jobs and the subjective experience of downward mobility in society.

5. A survey targeting the Hong Kong college students' participation in the Umbrella Movement was conducted from November 2015 to February 2017. Students from nine tertiary institutions (Hong Kong Baptist University, City University of Hong Kong, University of Hong Kong, Chinese University of Hong Kong, Hong Kong Community College, Hong Kong Polytechnic University, Hong Kong Shue Yan University, Hong Kong University of Sciences and Technology, and Lingnan University) joined the survey and 850 questionnaires have been successfully collected.

6. Ming K. Chan, "Hong Kong Workers Towards 1997: Unionisation, Labour Activism and Political Participation under the China Factor," *Australian Journal of Politics and History* 47, no. 1 (2001): 65.

7. Andrew Brown et al., eds., *Organising Labour in Globalising Asia* (New York: Routledge, 2001).

8. Kim Moody, *Workers in a Lean World: Unions in the International Economy* (London: Verso, 1997).

9. Akira Suzuki, *Cross-national Comparisons of Social Movement Unionism: Diversities of Labour Movement Revitalization in Japan, Korea, and the United States* (Oxford: Peter Lang, 2016), 6.

10. During the protest, an eye-catching media report about the HKCTU was not about the participation of trade union or workers in the movement, but about "scandal" that HKCTU had received funding from the United States. As mentioned above, the HKCTU has a long history of collaborating with international trade unions and obtaining financial support from some of them, including the American Center of Labor Solidarity, which is a part of the AFL-CIO, the trade union center in the United States. The Pro-CCP media in Hong Kong had portrayed the HKCTU and its general secretary as one of the hidden initiators of the Occupy Movement backed by the foreign forces. This report had been widely quoted by the Chinese media in the Mainland. This image, however, did not match the perception of the occupy participants in the HKCTU and its leaders. The democratic trade union had played a supportive rather than leading role throughout the movement.

11. Peter Waterman, *Globalisation, Social Movements & The New Internationalisms* (London: Mansell Publishing Limited, 1998).

12. Chris K. C. Chan, Sophia S. Y. Chan, and Lynn Tang, "Reflecting on Social Movement Unionism in Hong Kong: A Case Study of the 2013 Dockworkers' Strike," *Journal of Contemporary Asia* (2018), doi: 10.1080/00472336.2018.1448429.

13. Cassandra Engeman, "Social Movement Unionism in Practice: Organizational Dimensions of Union Mobilization in the Los Angeles Immigrant Rights Marches," *Work Employment & Society* 29, no. 3 (2014): 456.

14. Engeman, "Social Movement Unionism in Practice," 444.

15. Engeman, "Social Movement Unionism in Practice."

16. Data for this section was collected and compiled by the author's research assistant, Mr. Julian Yeung.

17. For the concept of authoritarian unionism, see Robert Lambert, "Labor Movement Renewal in the Era of Globalisation: Union Responses in the South," in *Global Unions? Theory and Strategies of Organised Labour in the Global Political Economy*, ed. Jeffrey Harrod et al. (New York: Routledge, 2002), 185–203.

18. This number was lower than the HKCTU's own figure of 180,000 total union members. The major difference was the HKCTU also counted the membership of the Federation of Hong Kong and Kowloon Labour Unions (HKFLU), which joined the HKCTU as a union federation. The government statistics only counted members of HKCTU's affiliates who were registered as trade unions. Although affiliated with the HKCTU, the political stand of HKFLU was closer to the HKFTU. Therefore, it was reasonable to exclude HKFLU when comparing membership and organizing power of HKCTU and HKFTU.

19. "Annual Statistical Report of Trade Unions in Hong Kong 2015," Hong Kong Labour Department, accessed 29 December 29, 2016, http://www.labour.gov.hk/tc/pub lic/pdf/rtu/ASR2015.pdf.

20. "Council Meeting—Voting Result on 1 June 2005," Hong Kong Legislative Council, accessed December 29, 2016, http://www.legco.gov.hk/yr04-05/english/counmtg/voting/v0506013.htm.

21. "Jin ri liao wu wan ren fan zheng ke you hang" (50,000 people expected to join today's antipolitician rally) (in Chinese). *Oriental Daily*, January 1, 2005.

22. "Chen ba gen: wei kai gong chai jia yuan en tuo," (Chan Ba-gun: It is wrong to have jobs by demolishing others' homes) (in Chinese) *Apple Daily*, January 14, 2010.

23. Man-hon Poon et al., eds., *Tuan jie bu zhe wan: xiang gang du li gong yun xun suo 40 nian* (In solidarity: The forty-year history of independent labor movement in Hong Kong) (in Chinese) (Hong Kong: Step Forward, 2012).

24. "Wai pan ruan ying jian shi tu zhu ge ji po" (Sub-contractors tried to divide and defeat their enemies) (in Chinese), *Apple Daily*, April 3, 2013.

25. "Da lian meng ni shou ji 80 wan ge qian ming bao pu xuan fan zhan zhong shang hui gong hui lian shou" (Businessmen and unions plan to collect 800,000 people to sign a petition against Occupy Central) (in Chinese), *Sing Tao Daily*, July 4, 2014.

26. "Da lian meng: ji 183 wan ren qian ming cu huan lu yu min" (Alliance for Peace and Democracy: 1.83 million signatures obtained to call for opening the roads) (in Chinese), *Oriental Daily*, November 4, 2014.

27. "Gong lian qian ren shen su you sheng ji wu hua hong" (Thousand people from FTU worried about their livelihoods and bonus) (in Chinese), *Ming Pao Daily News*, November 4, 2014.

28. "Bai kou zhao dang li qi chai lu zhang fan zhan zhong 3 lu ga ji bao chong tu ju 22 ren" (Hundred masked men with knives broke the barricade, Anti-Occupy Central team attacked from three directions, twenty-two arrested) (in Chinese), *Ming Pao Daily News*, October 14, 2014.

29. One of the examples was the protest in 2016 that led to the stepping down of President Park Geun-hye. See http://www.zoominkorea.org/south-koreans-to-launch-general-strike-and-national-civil-disobedience-for-parks-ouster/.

30. Chan, Chan, and Tang, "Reflecting on Social Movement Unionism in Hong Kong."

31. This is similar to the SMU in the United States in which the full-time organizers have also played an important role as found by Voss and Sherman. The difference is that in the United States, the SMU was transformed from business unionism and so has a stronger membership base, but the HKCTU was established by a NGO, the HKCIC, and so its workplace base is weak. See Kim Voss and Rachael Sherman, "Breaking the Iron Law of Oligarchy: Union Revitalization in the American Labor Movement," *American Journal of Sociology* 106, no. 2 (2000): 303–49.

32. See Koo, *Korean Workers.*

33. Ming Sing, "Weak Labor Movements and Opposition Parties: Hong Kong and Singapore," *Journal of Contemporary Asia* 34, no. 4 (2004): 449–64.

34. For the analysis on the political challenge of the HKCTU after the UM, see the author's commentary article at http://en.hkctu.org.hk/mainland-china/position-and-analysis/torn-between-authoritarian-rule-and-right-wing-populism.

7

HOW STUDENTS TOOK LEADERSHIP OF THE UMBRELLA MOVEMENT

Marginalization of Prodemocracy Parties

Ming Sing

In 2014, the eye-catching Umbrella Movement (UM) sought genuine democracy in Hong Kong, astounded the world and gripped global attention. Many people around the world applauded the movement, as tens of thousands of people had the bravery to challenge the Chinese government in a straightforward manner regarding democracy.

During this movement, the opposition parties were sidelined by student leaders in initiating and shepherding the Umbrella Movement, despite the parties' having consistently obtained more than 50 percent of votes in legislative elections. Equally noteworthy is that the prodemocracy parties have been the major leaders of Hong Kong's democracy movements since the early 1990s. Ultimate decision-making power had been vested in the student leaders throughout the Umbrella Movement. Among the occupiers, about twice as many considered the student leaders the heads of the movement as those who considered the political parties for the same role.[1] The marginalization of the prodemocracy parties occurred even though all the prodemocracy parties have publicly supported the Umbrella Movement.

Considering the mammoth frustration of the prodemocracy public with Beijing's reneging on its promises to allow Hong Kong to democratize after waiting for three decades, the pressure on all the prodemocracy parties to join the Occupy Movement has been enormous. But the prodemocracy parties, especially the relatively larger ones, have played only a supporting rather than a leading role and have taken moderate measures to buttress the Umbrella Movement. The Democratic Party (DP), the largest prodemocracy party with the greatest number of legislators for the greatest length of time since 1997, had already expressed its willingness to join Occupy Central if Beijing failed to deliver universal suffrage for Hong Kong before the outbreak of the Umbrella Movement.[2] The DP had been under particularly heavy pressure to join the movement to demonstrate its commitment to Hong Kong's democratization after its back-door negotiation with Beijing over Hong Kong's democratization in 2010 brought no democratic breakthrough and, instead, brought pervasive criticisms of it as having betrayed Hong Kong. Its former chairperson, Albert Ho, claimed in 2013 that the party could initiate a de facto referendum in concert with Occupy Central to champion democracy. In 2014, more than a hundred DP members were ready to join Occupy Central. DP also organized workshops and trainings on nonviolent resistance.[3]

The Civic Party, another major prodemocracy party, displayed support for Occupy Central early on relative to other prodemocracy parties. Its leaders agreed that Occupy Central, as an act of civil disobedience, would be the last resort for universal suffrage.[4] The party supported the organizer of the Occupy Central movement, Occupying Central with Love and Peace (OCLP), and their events, such as organizing Deliberation Day 2—a deliberative forum integral to the OCLP campaign—and advocating an electronic referendum on June 22, 2014.[5]

The third largest prodemocracy party, the Labor Party, was also receptive to Occupy Central.[6] The party joined OCLP Deliberation Day and put forth suggestions for improving the OCLP organization, mobilization, and connection with pan-democratic parties.[7] The relatively smaller prodemocracy parties, including People Power, League of Social Democrats, and Neighborhood and Worker's Service Center (NWSC), also pledged to join Occupy Central.

Most of those parties performed one or more important functions, such as (1) acting as marshals to maintain security for the movement's participants, (2) offering infrastructural resources such as tents and speakers, (3) joining an informal alliance called the "Five Parties Platform" to guide the Umbrella Movement, (4) holding forums for public education and maintaining participants' spirits, (5) issuing statements buttressing the Umbrella Movement, and (6) boosting morale for the movement and the student leaders by waiting for the police's mass arrests during the last day of the occupation.[8]

In addition to the aforementioned functions, some more important activities were also undertaken by the pan-democratic parties. For instance, after the police's use of tear gas against movement participants, the leader of the Labor Party and the Confederation of Trade Unions, the largest prodemocracy labor alliance, called for Hong Kong–wide labor strikes. The largest prodemocracy teachers' alliance, the HKPTU, echoed this action by advocating for teachers to launch a class boycott for a week. The members of Swire Beverage Union and the Hong Kong Social Workers' General Union responded positively by limiting their work. That said, the labor strikes lasted for just a few days and very limited in scale, generating little political pressure.[9]

Though prodemocracy parties supported the Umbrella Movement and provided logistical support, the prodemocracy parties disagreed with student leaders' insistence on widening and prolonging the area of occupation and with their use of physical confrontation to mobilize crowds to surround government buildings to secure government concessions. This chapter will address two related research questions:

1. Why have the prodemocracy parties been marginalized or sidelined by student leaders in shepherding the Umbrella Movement, considering that those parties have been the major champions of Hong Kong's democracy movement in the last few decades rather than students?
2. While there was partial cooperation between two student bodies and the prodemocracy parties during the movement for greater democratization, why have they experienced severe conflicts in different stages of the Umbrella Movement?

Two Logics of Action: Political Parties and Social Movements

To explain the conflicts between the prodemocracy parties and the student leaders, it is useful to turn to McAdam and Tarrow's research on social movements, including their discovery of an "inherent tension between the logic of movement activism and the logic of electoral politics."[10] McAdam and Tarrow found that to survive and prosper in electoral politics, political parties need to compromise, act as a centrist force, and form coalitions. Without the need to survive and prosper in elections, civil society groups, which contain student bodies, tend to be more committed to principles and less willing to compromise than political parties. Civil society groups are also more likely to adopt narrow and, at times, militant positions than parties.

The above discrepancy in logics of actions has been echoed by research on democratization in Asia and elsewhere. For instance, a study of twenty democratic transitions in European and Latin American countries identifies a cleavage between civil society and political society in the arena of actions. This study finds that clashes over tactics between civil society organizations and political parties were prevalent[11] and that parties were more likely than civil society organizations to use negotiations, compromises, and interest-based actions, while the latter tended to adopt more militant protests and principle-based actions to fight for democratization.[12] Given the above divergent operational logics, conflicts between civil society organizations and political parties in movements are rife.[13] Moreover, civil society groups sometimes endeavor to monitor political parties, which can induce greater tensions.

Evaluating the relationship between student bodies and prodemocracy parties in Hong Kong in light of the aforementioned logics of actions will explain their limited cooperation and the clashes between them during the Umbrella Movement. The evaluation will clarify the subsequent sidelining of the prodemocracy parties during the Umbrella Movement and the movement's outcome.

To better comprehend the conflicts between the student leaders and the prodemocracy parties, it is imperative to understand how Hong Kong citizens, especially the youth, had grown increasingly discontented with those parties long before the Umbrella Movement. Surveys show that those parties have suffered a decline since 1998, a year after the reversion of Hong Kong's sovereignty to China.[14] Their decline in mass support underlays their loss of leadership during the Umbrella Movement of 2014. The subsequent section will thus first elaborate on how Beijing has used institutional and noninstitutional engineering to weaken the capacity of the prodemocracy parties to address public desires. This drastically truncated capacity has disappointed many progressives, including students. The disappointment has been manifested in the limited cooperation and repeated conflicts between student leaders and those parties before and during the Umbrella Movement. The student leaders who spearheaded the Umbrella Movement were eager to attain progress in democratization had begun agitating for riskier and more militant measures when the movement got stuck in a morass with little headway. One drastic measure undertaken by the student leaders was summoning the public to surround the government's buildings. This measure, however, ended in a state-led bloody crackdown and the cessation of the Umbrella Movement. The exclusion of the prodemocracy parties from the circle of leadership of the Umbrella Movement prevented them from effectively aborting the drastic measure of surrounding the buildings, despite their tacit opposition to it. Finally, the chapter concludes with a discussion of the post–Umbrella Movement tensions between student leaders and the prodemocracy parties due to their divergent logics of action.

Institutional Marginalization of the Legislature

Similar to some hybrid regimes, Hong Kong's post-handover legislature was designed to ensure that the government would be able to secure a majority to support its policies.[15] Only half of Hong Kong's legislature is constituted by popular elections and geographical constituencies, while the other half is constituted by occupation-based, functional constituencies with a franchise encompassing less than 5 percent of Hong Kong's population. The limited enfranchisement and the "winner-take-all" method for generating functional, occupation-based constituencies, plus the proportional representation electoral system for producing the directly elected members have made it impossible for the pan-democratic parties to occupy a majority of the seats in the legislature.[16]

Among the occupation-based or functional constituencies, most of them represent progovernment and antidemocratic business or professional interests. After the reversion of sovereignty to China, the legislature's monitoring power has been truncated further based on the Basic Law, that is, the mini-constitution for Hong Kong engineered by Beijing. Since mid-1997, when the Basic Law became operative, any motion introduced by individual members of the legislature has required "separate voting" of simple majority support in each of the functional and geographical constituencies for successful passage. Subsequently, the "separate voting" endows the business and professional groups with an effective veto over motions in the legislature. Consequently, there are many motions relating to both livelihood issues and constitutional reforms that are rejected under the Beijing-engineered "separate voting" arrangement, which would have been passed under the pre-handover simple majority rules.[17] The prominent rejection of those motions has contributed to the irrelevance of the political parties and the public's discontent with the prodemocracy parties.

Concomitantly, legislators' power to launch private members' bills has also been attenuated since the handover by Article 74 of the Basic Law. This article tightens the requirement for the passage of private members' bills by demanding that only bills unrelated to "public expenditure or political structure or operation of the government may be introduced" by legislator(s). Accordingly, the number of such bills passed in the legislature plunged after the handover. Legislators have seldom been able to use private member bills to press the government since the handover. With the rise of the Asian financial crisis in 1997, the public's concern over socioeconomic issues has escalated. The state-led installation of separate voting in the legislature and the huge obstruction to the passage of private members' bills have debilitated the prodemocracy parties and, subsequently, disenchanted some voters with the incapacity of those parties. In July 2014, two months before the outbreak of the Umbrella Movement, only 28.3 percent of the public agreed that the parties could effectively monitor the government to reduce bad governance.[18]

Beijing has thus effectively emasculated the prodemocracy parties via a weakened legislature. The following government measures in the electoral arena have further eroded the seat share, influence, and popularity of the prodemocracy parties.

CCP Suppressed Party Development

The Chinese Communist Party (CCP) has invested an enormous amount of time and resources in fostering pro-Beijing parties of the Democratic Alliance for the Betterment of Hong Kong (DAB) and the Hong Kong Federation of Trade Unions (HKFTU) in Hong Kong. In addition, the Liaison Office, Beijing's de facto representative in Hong Kong, sent candidates from pro-Beijing parties to various districts to secure voters' support. The Liaison Office coordinated with DAB, FTU, and other united front organizations to work out electoral campaign tactics.[19] Since 2003, Beijing has multiplied its efforts to promote pro-Beijing parties' patron-client networks by organizing more recreational activities, welfare services, subsidiaries for local activities, and the provision of cheap or free grassroots services.[20] Given the limited power of the District Councils, the constituency services were more pivotal in shaping the outcome of District Council elections than political beliefs. Huge donations from China's conglomerates and other surreptitious sources for the pro-Beijing parties have significantly eclipsed those for their prodemocracy counterparts, greatly boosting the edge of pro-Beijing parties over their counterparts in terms of their capability to deliver constituency and welfare services at the district level. This vast difference in capacity has enabled the pro-Beijing parties to enjoy an increasing seat share in the District Councils over time; recently, the pro-Beijing parties controlled 76 percent of the seats in the District Councils.[21] The continuous surge in the vote and seat share of the pro-Beijing parties in the District Councils has magnified their support base at the grassroots level, which considerably improves their strategic electoral coordination for the Legislative Council elections.[22]

Finally, the government's imposition of a proportional representative system for legislative elections after the handover has induced multipartyism, fragmented prodemocracy parties, and caused the blossoming of smaller prodemocracy parties.[23] The electoral competition among the prodemocracy parties seriously undermines the solidarity among the pan-democrats.[24]

Beijing's aforementioned maneuvering with regard to legislative and electoral arrangements since the handover has directly injured the influence and mass support for the pan-democratic parties and fostered the growth of the pro-Beijing parties. Beijing has also indirectly weakened the pan-democrats' influence by undercutting the size of their memberships. The proportion of the population in Hong Kong that is affiliated with any political party has been meager when compared with either relatively new or well-established democracies. In 2013, only 0.74 percent of Hong Kong's electorate was affiliated with any local party.[25]

Many people worry that joining the DP would affect their job and ability to enter Mainland China.[26] Thus many DP supporters prefer to be volunteers instead of party members. In addition, another former chairperson of the DP said the DP had instituted a complicated process of applying for party membership to preclude penetration by the Chinese Communist Party.[27] The cumbersome procedure has also severely negatively affected the size of its membership.

For the Civic Party, another large prodemocracy party in the legislature, lawyers, doctors, and academics have been its leaders. The party leaders have openly discussed the enormous difficulty of recruiting professionals as members who are willing to run for election in a hybrid regime, engaging in an uphill struggle for democratization. This failure results in the party's poor networking at the grassroots and community levels, which turns bottom-up mobilization into a herculean task.

In addition to their meager size, the low capacity of the prodemocracy parties in mass mobilization has been fomented by their own de-emphasis of and divergent stance on mobilization. The preoccupation of the majority of the public with livelihood issues and economic matters, rather than political affairs, has disposed the major prodemocracy parties toward de-emphasizing bottom-up mass mobilization for democratization.

Growing Discontent with Political Parties

There were increasing signs that the governance crisis was approaching a breaking point in Hong Kong by 2014, arising from the widespread and recognized difficulty related to upward social mobility, the perceived intensification of crony capitalism, the decline in freedoms, and Beijing's thwarting of democracy.[28] Disenchanted with the prodemocracy parties' mild, nondisruptive tactics and their incapacity to compel the Beijing and Hong Kong governments to launch reforms, more younger people since the early 2010s have tended to believe in the efficacy of confrontational and disruptive tactics to realize reforms. In 2012, already 24.7 percent of the public, or 1.48 million citizens, agreed or strongly agreed with the statement "that only the use of radical means can make the government respond to demands," according to a representative Hong Kong–wide survey sample.[29] The survey defined "radical means" as blockading streets and physical conflicts. Many young people, who were most victimized by the dim prospect of economic opportunities and democratization, could be deemed "progressives," or people supporting or using more confrontational and disruptive means to achieve democratic reform. Indeed, as will unfold in the following analysis, the majority of the Umbrella Movement occupiers and supporters were from the younger generation; they were more willing to support disruptive and confrontational measures than moderate tactics such as the highly predictable peaceful gatherings and mass rallies adopted by the prodemocracy parties. That said, alongside the more militant public there have been moderates, the mainstream public, who have embraced more peaceful movement tactics and prioritized social and economic issues over democratization.

Surveys conducted since 1997 have revealed that the majority of the public is most concerned with economic and livelihood issues such as education, transportation, and housing. Seldom could we find more than 10 percent of the public putting political affairs, including democratic reform, as their top concern. Even in 2014, the year the Umbrella Movement occurred, when political awareness and discontent presumably rose to a relatively high level compared with other years, only 17.9 percent of citizens regarded political affairs as most important, a figure that was dwarfed by the 55 percent that accorded livelihood issues the highest concern.[30] Additionally, in 2012, 75.3 percent of the public did not agree on the necessity of using radical means to make the government responsive to public demands.[31]

Why have the majority of the public been moderates, relegating democratic reform to a relatively low priority? Beijing's recurring aversion and robust objection to democratization in Hong Kong has fostered among many citizens a strong sense of powerlessness with regard to the implementation of democratic reforms. The continual refusals by the HKSAR Chief Executives to review the pace of democratization since 1997 has strengthened this sense of powerlessness.

In addition, while economic crises have triggered democratization in many former authoritarian countries, prolonged economic crises have been unfamiliar for most Hong Kong people, who have gotten used to continuous economic growth over the past few decades. Though the economic troubles stemming from the post-handover economic crisis were considerable for many, the crisis was too brief for the public to discard the enduring successful recipe of economic development in which political stability was accentuated to buttress the economic growth and concomitant progress in living standards.

Last but not least, the massive injection of China's capital into the local media, the Beijing government's employment of the Mainland's huge market opportunities as economic bait, and the political absorption of many media tycoons into China's political organs have fostered an increasingly pro-Beijing and antidemocracy media culture; Hong Kong's media has practiced pervasive self-censorship since the handover of Hong Kong. As a result, Hong Kong has suffered a precipitous decline in press freedom based on a number of authoritative international and local benchmarks. For instance, predicated on the evaluation of "Reporters without Borders," Hong Kong's press freedom fell from eighteenth in 2002 to sixty-first in 2014, which was worse than many semiauthoritarian societies in the world.[32]

Amid the above divided public priorities, the majority of prodemocracy parties, especially the DP, have positioned themselves as moderate parties in order to capture the votes of the mostly moderate public. The DP is especially worth mentioning, as it has been the largest prodemocracy party with the greatest number of legislators for most of the time since 1997. A major strategist of the DP underscored that the party has attempted to capture the votes of both the middle and working classes to survive and thrive. The moderate and centrist stance of the DP was manifested by its focusing on the provision of constituency services and livelihood issues for moderate and middle-aged voters rather than on mobilizing the public to achieve greater democracy. To appeal to the middle and working classes, the DP and some other prodemocracy parties stressed the quality of and preparation for legislative debates.[33]

But with the installation of the separate voting and proportional representation systems within Hong Kong's hybrid regime and the all-out mobilization by Beijing to suppress the prodemocracy parties, those parties have been largely emasculated if not outright disabled with regard to shaping policies or legislation. The public has thus witnessed in detail how the conventional legislative debates preferred by the majority of prodemocratic parties have become pointless in shaping the overriding majority of government policies. Consequently, the moderate prodemocracy parties are continuously scorned by the younger and politically disaffected generation for staging ritualistic political shows in the legislature or media to maintain their interests in the political establishment.

The public has also seen that the prodemocracy party leaders have accorded an overriding priority to party building and legislative politics rather than promotion of civil society and bottom-up mass mobilization. Subsequently, a former chairperson of the DP conceded that the DP's decades-long nondisruptive and nonviolent strategies have alienated both youths and militant supporters.[34] The inefficacious tactics of the moderate prodemocracy parties have also frustrated many civil society organizations, including student movement bodies, which felt embittered by the parties' inability to push for reforms.[35] Worse still, some civil society bodies have had escalating tensions with the parties due to their jockeying for leadership positions in the movements. Many civil society organizations have attempted to empower the public to run the movements, which collided with the parties' goal of self-aggrandizement by finishing the tasks more swiftly and increasing their power in society. In short, the moderate tactics and centrist stance of the relatively large prodemocracy parties have chipped away at their moral legitimacy to lead movements in the eyes of the progressive public and civil society groups.

The preoccupation of prodemocracy parties with electoral and legislative politics and their disaffection with civil society bodies have partly contributed to either their absence or low-profile participation in many social movements since the mid-2000s. The parties have failed to lead a myriad of preservationist, localist, antidevelopmentalist, and political movements since the mid-2000s, including the Queen's Pier and Star Ferry, and the anti-express rail campaign. Those movements were mostly steered by young activists using disruptive tactics such as occupying roads and public buildings to champion their goals. There were some specific causes of the failure of prodemocracy parties to lead those movements.

For instance, with regard to the campaign against the building of the express railway connecting Hong Kong and Mainland China, both the Democratic Party and the Civic Party agreed in principle in 2007 to the building of the railway in Hong Kong on the assumption that the project would be a boon for Hong Kong's economy. They were forced to change their stance when crony capitalism, land injustices, and financial and environmental costs were exposed by civil society organizations that initiated the campaign against its installation in 2009. After this campaign, those parties were criticized by progressives for having ignored the political and economic hazards of subjugating Hong Kong to greater economic dependence on China. In addition, nearly all the prodemocracy parties ignored the rise of the preservationist and new urban movements seeking democratic planning for Hong Kong when they first arose between 2003 and 2007 to preserve Lee Tung Street.[36] Their ignorance of such issues reflects the detachment of the parties from new civil society groups and their insensitivity to the rise of postmaterialistic values among the younger generation.

Regarding the localist movements, anti-Mainland sentiments sprouted and spread in Hong Kong as many Mainland mothers gave birth in Hong Kong's hospitals, making it difficult for local mothers to find hospital beds. Baby powder was in acutely short supply as cross-border traders snapped it up to satisfy the needs of Mainland mothers. Moreover, over 70 percent of the graduate students achieving research degrees in the local universities were from the Mainland and they received scholarships from the HKSAR government. These students could possibly stay and compete in Hong Kong's job market after graduation.[37] Despite the outbreak of localist movements and the rising public concern for prioritizing the Hong Kong people's interest in public policies since 2011, only four prodemocracy party legislators agreed to the legislative motion giving priority to upholding Hongkongers' interest in policy making. Other legislators from those parties refused to endorse it, worrying in part that the motion would discriminate against Mainlanders and might result in the loss of potential votes during elections.

Still another event has deepened progressives' discontent with the majority of prodemocracy parties. The League of Social Democrats (LSD), a new radical party in Hong Kong, together with the Civic Party, promoted the use of a "de facto referendum" as a proactive tactic to push for democratization in 2010. These parties advocated that five of the twenty-three prodemocracy legislators— one from each of Hong Kong's five geographical constituencies—should resign simultaneously so that the public could express their desire for Hong Kong's democratization by voting for prodemocracy members during the by-elections. The two parties argued that the campaign would result in enormous domestic and international pressure on Beijing to accelerate Hong Kong's democratization if the by-elections received pervasive and favorable public support.[38]

But only nine out of the twenty-three legislators of the prodemocracy parties supported the campaign. The other prodemocracy parties, including the DP, the Hong Kong Association for Democracy and People's Livelihood (ADPL) and the Neighborhood and Worker's Service Center refrained from supporting the campaign. The reasons they gave were: (1) the perceived lack of mass support for the campaign, as reflected in opinion polls, (2) the perceived absence of public resolve to fight strenuously for democracy, (3) the need to spend more than 10 million Hong Kong dollars to run the campaign, (4) the hazard of losing the required minimum number of legislators' votes to veto problematic legislative motions if the by-elections did not fare well, and (5) the risk of failing to compel the government to democratize since the government had refused to recognize the result of the by-elections as a genuine referendum.[39] In short, those parties were worried the campaign would backfire on prodemocracy parties and result in decreased voter support during elections and the loss of some seats in the legislature.

The campaign encountered substantive resistance when the pro-Beijing parties declined to compete for legislative seats that left vacant because of the resignation of the five legislators. Their refusal to compete could dampen the public incentive to vote because of the absence of real competition, and they could discredit the entire campaign if the turnout rate was small.

Instead of passively watching the lack of political competition in the by-elections and the possible failure of the de facto referendum campaign, five former student leaders of the HKFS decided to run for the by-elections in 2010 soon after their term as office bearers in the HKFS expired. Those student leaders endeavored to forge political competition, to boost the total voter turnout rate, and to increase the political pressure on Beijing to democratize. The student leaders stated clearly that they were participating proactively to strive for democratization and the abolition of functional constituencies.[40] Finally, the total voter turnout rate, plagued by the boycott of the pro-Beijing parties and the absence of collective mass mobilization by any of the prodemocracy parties, could only reach a dismally low level of 17.1 percent. The low turnout failed to result in much pressure on Beijing to respond to the demand for democratization. On the other hand, after several rounds of back-door and secret negotiations between Beijing's representatives and several prodemocracy parties in Hong Kong, the DP, ADPL, and others passed a constitutional reform package in the legislature in 2010 that fell far short of achieving any major breakthrough in democratization.

For many progressives, especially the younger generation, the prodemocracy parties have exhausted the political dividend of "suspicion or fear of the Chinese Communist Party" to rally their support. For the progressives, other than shouting slogans demanding democracy, freedoms, and rule of law and holding some highly predictable, peaceful gatherings, the prodemocracy parties have failed to provide policy guidelines to cope with the sharply escalating Sino–Hong Kong tensions ensuing from the deepened Sino–Hong Kong integration. The widely perceived failure of those parties to lead effectively and proactively for various causes by robust mass mobilization has inexorably eroded their credibility in shepherding the democracy movement.

Radicalization of the Movement

With the pervasive perception of dwindling freedoms in Hong Kong, and Beijing's repeated reneging of constitutional promises to implement democracy, Hong Kong's supporters of democracy had increasingly turned to more confrontational tactics to push for democratization before the Umbrella Movement, ranging from occupying roads, hurling things at the de facto organ of Beijing in Hong Kong, and engaging in physical scuffles with the police. The escalation in confrontations, however, has coincided with Xi Jinping's installation in office; he is an ultraconservative and uncompromising leader in a posttotalitarian regime. Xi has reinforced Beijing's resolve to impose more overt threats to Hong Kong's democratization, freedoms, and rule of law.

In June 2014, Beijing promulgated the white paper on "One country, Two systems." The white paper asserted that Beijing has the right to control the nomination of candidates running for the post of Hong Kong's Chief Executive. Confronted with Beijing's clear reneging of its promises to implement universal suffrage in Hong Kong, three Hong Kong leaders advocated for the Occupy Central with Love and Peace (OCLP), a civil disobedience campaign, to force Beijing to concede to universal suffrage in 2013.

At the historic juncture of 2013 and 2014, HKFS and Scholarism, student bodies representing universities and secondary schools respectively, were driven by the logic of movement activism. They were more insistent on achieving progress on democratization and were less willing to compromise than were the political parties. The two bodies were prepared to adopt much more proactive, confrontational, and disruptive tactics such as occupying public spaces and blocking government buildings, and they stood out as audacious and committed champions of democracy. Several factors underpinned why the leaders of the student bodies became the leaders of the Umbrella Movement, besides the aforementioned fact that the governance crisis had come close to a breaking point in Hong Kong by late 2014.

First, the student bodies had boldly taken the step of occupying the central business district on July 2, 2014, where more than five hundred persons were arrested, including more than a hundred student activists and their leaders. Rather than resorting to the conventional, nondisruptive rallies or peaceful gatherings adopted by the prodemocracy parties, the student leaders' use of a highly disruptive tactic echoed with the yearning of the more militant segment of the public. Student leaders' pioneering roles and sacrifices reinforced their image as daring and dedicated shepherds for the struggle for democracy. By contrast, only three leaders of the prodemocracy political parties joined this initial occupation.

Second, other than conventional verbal denunciations, the prodemocracy parties failed to effectively pressure Beijing over the latter's announcement of a pseudo-democratic proposal made on August 31, 2014. By contrast, the students' orchestration of a five-day boycott of classes, the unanticipated student leaders' sudden charging of the government's headquarters on September 26, 2014, their subsequent arrests, and the police's firing of eighty-seven canisters of tear gas that triggered the Umbrella Movement further consolidated the image of the student leaders as valiant and determined shepherds for democracy. By contrast, none of the leaders of the prodemocracy parties had joined the students in charging the headquarters. The supporters of the Umbrella Movement particularly preferred student representatives as leaders because the occupiers were younger, more educated, and more supportive of those political parties that were slightly more willing to confront China than the average public, such as the Civic Party, the League of Social Democrats, and People's Power.[41]

Third, the student leaders unwaveringly preferred the use of civic nominations to produce the candidates running for the chief executive between 2013 and 2014. Their preference underscores their respect for the power of individuals rather than for party-based nominations or the complex Election Committee that could be easily manipulated by Beijing. Their insistence on civic nominations contrasted starkly with some of the prodemocracy parties' compromised models of using party-based nominations or a broadly representative Election Committee to nominate the candidates for chief executive. Finally, an electronic referendum held in June 2014 affirmed that among the top three models preferred by 800,000 voters, all of them contained the option of civil nominations, which were supported approximately by 50 percent of all voters.[42] This result shows that a sizeable chunk of the potential supporters of the civil disobedience movement were supportive of the more egalitarian nomination process than of a compromised model for the nomination of Hong Kong's top leader. The aforementioned elements buttressed the authority of the student leaders in marshalling the Umbrella Movement.

For many Hongkongers, Beijing's stark reneging on democracy has bluntly affirmed the failure of the prodemocracy parties in their three-decade-long democratic campaign. The fervent and impatient supporters for democracy yearned for new, disruptive, and more powerful tactics to be undertaken by some fearless new leaders in the crusade for democracy to maximize the chance of success. With the blessing of the majority of the occupiers, the student leaders were given the leadership roles for the Umbrella Movement, but they had to rely upon the prodemocracy parties' logistic support and mass mobilization to run the huge movement. Therefore, despite the student leaders' discontent with the prodemocracy parties' ineffective strategies, the former worked with the parties during the Umbrella Movement. Their limited cooperation, however, has been tainted by serious conflicts, which were underpinned by two conflicting logics: the logic of movement activism and that of electoral politics.

Conflicts between the Student Leaders and Parties

Under the sway of the logic of electoral politics, political parties usually consider the feasibility, costs, and benefits of political actions and are willing to compromise for electoral survival. Civil society groups, embracing the logic of movement activism, tend to be committed to ideal principles, are less willing to compromise than are parties, and are more likely to adopt militant strategies than are parties.

Based on my interviews with seventeen leaders from the two leading student bodies, 88 percent of the interviewees expressed the idea that trying to achieve progress on democratization was their major reason for joining the Umbrella Movement. Many of these student leaders demonstrated great resolve to achieve democratization; more than 90 percent of these student leaders abandoned their schooling and work to join the movement. Moreover, 58.8 percent of these student leaders were prepared to suffer physical assault and persecution, and 41.2 percent of them were ready even for imprisonment. In contrast, many prodemocracy party leaders expressed within the first month of the occupation the need to withdraw, partly because of the perceived diminished feasibility of achieving democratization and partly to reduce street inconvenience and mitigate the risk of electoral catastrophe. Their contrasting logics also illuminate the following conflicts between the parties and the student bodies.

Soon after the start of the Umbrella Movement, many civil society organizations joined the occupation alongside the two key student bodies, the pan-democratic parties, and the OCLP. Some of the civil society organizations aspired to form an alliance among the above five groups, which was dubbed the Five-Party Platform, to collectively decide on actions for effectively handling the unfolding challenges during the Umbrella Movement. Some core members of the HKFS, however, expressed distrust of the prodemocracy parties during their discussion to establish a power-sharing Five-Party Platform. Such distrust was understandable given their conflicting logics toward movements and the long-term ineffectual repertoires of the prodemocracy parties in the democracy movement. Moreover, the pan-democratic parties failed to reach consensus on the decision-making or voting procedures in case of conflicts over issues within the alliance.[43] The failure to concur on voting rights created a stalemate that prevented the loose platform from becoming a real collective decision-making unit. Consequently, the power to make major decisions was vested in the two popular student bodies, especially the HKFS. Another major conflict concerns the timing of the withdrawal from the occupied sites.

Dissensus over the Timing of the Withdrawal

In October 2014, the HKFS and Scholarism rejected withdrawal during the occupation on the grounds that they would not be able to persuade the occupiers to withdraw.[44] Later, two student leaders stated that they were not considering withdrawal as the government did not comply with the protesters' demand for the resignation of the unpopular chief executive and the removal of Beijing's pseudo-democratic platform.[45] Still another argument against withdrawal was that the occupation was not simply a bargain with the government but also a social experiment for realizing democracy in daily lives and a rebellion against crony capitalism.[46]

Impacted by the logic of movement activism, student leaders not only vehemently rejected withdrawal but also escalated their confrontation by calling on protesters to surround the government's headquarters in late November 2014 after making no headway with their two-month-long occupation. Based on my interviews with nineteen members of the HKFS and Scholarism, slightly more than 60 percent of the interviewees supported the escalation. Since the movement had reached a stalemate, the student groups used the escalation to manifest their resolve to secure concessions from Beijing. Their support for the escalation also mirrored their unpreparedness to end the movement without any progress on democratization. With the benefit of hindsight, the student leaders acknowledged that they overestimated their support for their risky escalation.

What were the consequences of the loose alliance and the sidelining of the prodemocracy parties? Noticeably, mass support for the Umbrella Movement never exceeded 40 percent, as registered in four consecutive monthly surveys conducted between September and December 2014, which spanned the entire period of the occupation.[47] Moreover, by early November 2014, 73 percent of Hong Kong's public agreed with the withdrawal of the occupiers; street inconvenience was cited by 47.6 percent of the public as the reason they favored withdrawal.[48] By November 30, 2014, as the Umbrella Movement had lasted for more than sixty-two days, further occupation would embarrass Beijing and the HKSAR government internationally. The embarrassment would be enormously enlarged if the protesters were able to block the entry to the government's headquarters, which would have hampered the delivery of public services. As the occupation continued, public frustration with the street inconvenience mounted and further decreased support for the Umbrella Movement. The declining support for the movement, the protesters' charging the government's headquarters on November 30, and some protesters' use of helmets, shields, and rods were perfect justifications for the police to forcefully crack down on the movement participants. The police's clampdown caused many serious injuries to movement supporters, ushering in a demoralizing defeat of the student leaders and the eventual termination of the movement.[49]

Though the prodemocracy parties were aware of the student-led escalation on November 30, 2014, the marginalization of the prodemocracy parties in the loose alliance had rendered it impossible for the parties to halt students' escalation. To dissuade the student leaders from further endangering the safety of participants and to protect themselves from being accused of supporting the students' militant escalation, twenty-three out of twenty-seven legislators from the prodemocracy parties publicly disavowed the students' escalation.[50] Next, despite the partial support of the prodemocracy parties for the Umbrella Movement, Scholarism's distrust of the pan-democratic parties continued undiminished after the Umbrella Movement.

Post–Umbrella Movement Tension

The student leaders of Scholarism, influenced by the logic of movement activism, detested a possible compromise between Beijing and the prodemocracy parties that might constrain democratization. In 2015, Scholarism suspected that the Democratic Party (DP) would compromise on a political package with Beijing. While the DP denounced the suspicion as unfounded, Scholarism urged citizens to monitor the political parties.[51] A week later, Scholarism warned the parties unequivocally that if any pan-democratic legislator supported Beijing's pseudo-democratic framework announced in August 2014, it would be tantamount to a betrayal of the Umbrella Movement.[52] Soon after that, Scholarism and the HKFS allied with several civil groups, issuing a joint statement opposing any secret talks between Beijing and the pan-democratic parties and urging the parties to veto any pseudo-democratic package fashioned by Beijing.[53]

The tension among the different prodemocracy parties and civil society organizations also persisted during the legislative election in late 2016. Some student leaders who championed the Umbrella Movement founded a new political party and challenged the mild stances and tactics of the existing prodemocracy parties.

The significance of the legislative election held in 2016 was monumental. Its electoral outcomes mirrored the degree of the public's acceptance of various stances and tactics after Beijing's clampdown on the Umbrella Movement. The electoral outcome also indicated whether supporters of the Umbrella Movement continued to support prodemocracy forces, which would impact the thrust of the democracy movement.

The entire prodemocracy camp was splintered into three camps during the election: the prodemocracy parties established before 2012, the self-determinists, and the nativists. Amid the grave public fragmentation over their stances toward the Umbrella Movement, the overall proportion of seats of the entire prodemocracy camp in the legislature increased in 2016 (41.43 percent) vis-à-vis 2008 (38.33 percent). Concomitantly, the seat share of the prodemocracy parties set up before 2012 slightly decreased, while the newly formed party of self-determinists, which included the core student leaders who led the Umbrella Movement, obtained four seats during the fiercely contested election.

The self-determinist activists who won seats in the election included a student leader of the Umbrella Movement who belonged to the new Demosistō party formed in 2016, which included many student leaders of the Umbrella Movement. The Demosistō tried to differentiate itself from the existing prodemocracy parties by striving for democratic self-determination and autonomy from the CCP's control via direct actions, popular referendums, and nonviolent means.[54] Though the party does not agree on the independence of Hong Kong, it plans to hold a referendum by 2026 to decide on Hong Kong's future after 2047.[55] By contrast, the existing prodemocracy parties did not mention popular referendums to decide Hong Kong's future. This rupture within the existing prodemocracy camp represents the persistence of the underlying tensions between the mild, prodemocracy parties buttressed by the middle-aged and relatively older members of the public and the more proactive, confrontational, and disruptive new party backed up by younger citizens.

Did the Umbrella Movement shape voting behaviors during the election? The transformative effect of the Umbrella Movement can be gleaned from the survey data of a Hong Kong–wide representative sample conducted immediately after the election by the author.[56] The survey found that the level of mass support for the movement was positively correlated with the votes for both the self-determinists and existing prodemocracy parties. The positive correlations indicate that those supporting the Umbrella Movement have been more likely to vote for the prodemocracy camp, notwithstanding the setback of the Umbrella Movement to achieve any progress on democratization.

Conclusion: An Uneasy Partnership

This chapter explores why the prodemocracy parties were sidelined by student leaders during the Umbrella Movement. It also investigates the conflicts between the leaders of student bodies and the prodemocracy parties, which affected the trajectory of the Umbrella Movement. One factor accounting for the sidelining of the prodemocracy parties was that Beijing had largely enervated the prodemocracy parties' capacity in the legislature to shape policies via institutional and noninstitutional components of the nonsovereign, hybrid regime of Hong Kong. The debilitation made the parties irrelevant in addressing public needs and thereby eroded the public's trust in the parties and contributed to their decline, as has been found in many Western democracies. Beijing's engineering alone, however, cannot fully explain the decline of those parties. The parties' conscious choices with regard to positioning and tactics, amid an increasingly divided public, were also relevant to their decline.

In the face of the vigorous and recurring opposition from Beijing regarding Hong Kong's democratization, an increasingly pro-Beijing mass media, and the absence of prolonged economic crisis, the mainstream public felt powerless to achieve democratization. Despite the public's nominal support for democracy in Hong Kong, they have often accorded democratic reform a lower priority than economic and livelihood issues. The public has been moderate, rejecting the use of disruptive tactics during movements for fear of upsetting their stability and prosperity. The public's priorities have incentivized the major prodemocracy parties to undertake moderate and yet ineffectual tactics in championing democratization for the three decades before the Umbrella Movement.[57] The incapability of those parties' leaders to shape policies under the hybrid regime has frustrated even the political moderates, sapping their trust in such parties. The parties' decline is worsened when the younger public is taken into account.

The institutional constraints imposed by Beijing on Hong Kong's hybrid regime have largely undermined the power of the prodemocracy parties to be responsive to the public's social, economic, and political needs since the handover. Hong Kong's younger citizens, similar to those of Western democracies, experience a higher level of postmaterialism and have greater access to political information via social media.[58] These elements have raised their awareness and rejection of the declines in freedom, the rising Sino–Hong Kong tensions, the reduced chance of upward mobility, the worsening income inequality, and Beijing's interference with "One country, Two systems." Such awareness and rejection has sparked the younger generation's greater discontent with the prodemocracy parties for failing to offer an actionable framework for responding to Hongkongers' craving for genuine democracy, better governance, and the preservation of Hong Kong's core values.

Even though the prodemocracy parties played a supporting role during the Umbrella Movement, in the eyes of some progressives the parties were only forced to play a low-profile role to avert the loss of votes.[59] The prodemocracy parties' repeated urging of student leaders to end the occupation also triggered ill feelings and widened distrust among some student leaders. Their intense discontent with the parties and the Beijing and HKSAR governments has finally turned some of them into progressive citizens who are determined supporters of the Umbrella Movement and democratic reform. Among those determined supporters were the student leaders whose bravery and determination both before and during the Umbrella Movement outshined the uninspiring prodemocracy parties' leaders, enabling the students to be regarded as leaders during the Umbrella Movement.

To account for the conflicts between the student body leaders and those of the prodemocracy parties, the logic of movement activism and the logic of electoral politics, which guide the actions of the student bodies and prodemocracy parties respectively, have been adduced. Swayed by the logic of movement activism, student leaders were resolute in securing concessions from Beijing for democratization, refusing to budge and persisting with the occupation. The students' tactics contrasted sharply with those of the party leaders, who mostly preferred to halt the prolonged occupation in order to shorten the street inconvenience and diminish the risk of voters' backlash in impending elections.

A predominant proportion of the occupiers during the Umbrella Movement were progressive citizens who were more supportive of the more daring and confrontational actions of the student bodies rather than of the prodemocracy parties and more disinclined to withdraw before securing concessions on democratization. Since the student leaders had a stronger power base than the parties, and since no concessions were secured on democratization, the student leaders rebuffed the notion of withdrawal and left their supporters in the occupied sites. The student leaders' firm stance rejecting an earlier withdrawal set them apart from the prodemocracy parties and sowed the seeds of the former's eventual bungled escalation on November 30, 2014, and their subsequent eviction. That said, the Umbrella Movement has produced a transformative effect in that those who supported the Umbrella Movement attitudinally have also been more willing to vote for different parties in the prodemocracy camp during 2016 legislative election.

Before the Umbrella Movement, the tensions between prodemocratic civil society and the political parties in Hong Kong stemming from the two conflicting logics of actions had already weakened the democracy movement. Divisions over tactics, positioning, and interests have split civil society and political parties not only in Hong Kong but also in Africa, Europe, East Asia, and Latin America. In Hong Kong, their conflicts depleted the power of prodemocracy alliances between 1986 and 2000 in terms of the scale of mass mobilization.[60] The conflicts between the student bodies and the prodemocracy parties during the Umbrella Movement have manifested another stage of the structurally ingrained conflicts between the two types of organizations.

Notwithstanding the tensions between civil society bodies and political parties, as found in Argentina, Spain, Thailand, Indonesia, Malaysia, Taiwan, and South Korea, these groups have collaborated in pushing for democratization. Their cooperation would likely occur when undemocratic regimes are domineering and eclipse the power of prodemocracy parties and civil society bodies. Under those repressive settings, prodemocracy parties and civil society bodies have been incentivized to collaborate to survive and to advance democratization. In Hong Kong, besieged by the daunting prospect of rising repression under the largest posttotalitarian regime on earth, the question is whether the leaders of the new and old prodemocracy parties as well as the civil society bodies can revitalize the democratic movement by establishing a new and close-knit alliance. It is a question that will surely impact the dynamics and outcomes of future democratic struggles.

NOTES

1. Chi Kwok and Ngan Keung Chan, "Legitimacy and Forced Democratization in Social Movements: A Case Study of UM in Hong Kong," *China Perspectives* 3 (2017) (in press).

2. "Civic Party Welcomes Democratic Party Joining Occupy Central" (in Chinese), *Apple Daily*, March 2, 2013.

3. "Albert Ho Agrees to Act Concert with Occupy Central by Resignation Which Can Trigger a De Facto Referendum" (in Chinese), *Inmediahk*, March 7, 2013. Available at https://goo.gl/KUbQNG; "Democratic Party Said They Are Ready for Occupy Central" (in Chinese), *Apple Daily*, July 9, 2014; "Democratic Party Was 'Sniped' in Oath-taking Event for Occupy Central" (in Chinese), *Inmediahk*, February 5, 2014. Available at: https://goo.gl/XfVJCP.

4. "Benny Tai's Proposal Received Wide Responses: Democratic Party Supports Occupy Central for Universal Suffrage" (in Chinese), *Apple Daily*, February 19, 2013.

5. "Civic Party's Deliberation Day 2" (in Chinese), press release, last modified November 16, 2013, https://goo.gl/UDLkGo, and "Hold Firm to join 6.22 Referendum despite Suppression" (in Chinese), press release, last modified June 18, 2014, https://goo.gl/sstk17.

6. "Civic Party Welcomes Democratic Party Joining Occupy Central" (in Chinese), *Apple Daily*, March 2, 2013.

7. "Opinion Letter to OCLP Troika," (in Chinese), last modified July 2013, https://goo.gl/iVUW4B.

8. The findings are collected from the following sources: "Democratic Party Was Hunted in Swearing Event for Occupy Central" (in Chinese), *Inmediahk*, February 5, 2014. Available at: https://goo.gl/Dzy8jD; "Yin-tung Cheung (General Marshal) Not Preferred to Surrender Today" (in Chinese), *Ming Pao Daily News*, December 3, 2014; "Voluntary Material Station in Admiralty Occupied Zone Rejects Any Hijacking" (in Chinese), *Ming Pao Daily News*, October 15, 2014; interview with leaders of Democratic Party, Civic Party; "Power Abuse in the Name of Law Enforcement" (in Chinese), official statement, last modified October 15, 2014, https://goo.gl/1iU5xM; interview with a leader of Confederation of Trade Unions, Labour Party; "Opinion Letter to OCLP" (in Chinese), last modified July, 2013, https://goo.gl/a8jLQn; "Responses to the Preliminary Proposal on Legislative Council Election by Alliance for True Democracy" (in Chinese), official statement, last modified July 18, 2013, https://goo.gl/UV55Wm; "Breaking the Political 'Winnow Basket' for Universal Suffrage and Striving for Autonomy by Civic Nomination" (in Chinese), official statement, last modified July 21, 2013, https://goo.gl/3uqRn2; "Voluntary Material Station in Admiralty Occupied Zone Rejects Any Hijacking" (in Chinese), *Ming Pao Daily News*, October 15, 2014; "Statement on Workers Supporting Occupy Central for Universal Suffrage," (in Chinese), last modified September 20, 2013, https://goo.gl/Ztmuv9; and interviews with NWSC officers and members.

9. King Chi Chan, "Post Umbrella Movement—Talking from the Appeal of Triple Strike by Alex Chow Yong Kang" (in Chinese), *Hong Kong Economic Journal*, December 22, 2014. Available at https://forum.hkej.com/node/119375.

10. Doug McAdam and Sidney Tarrow, "Ballots and Barricades: On the Reciprocal Relationship between Elections and Social Movements," *Perspectives on Politics* 8, no. 2 (2010): 537.

11. See R. B. Collier, *Paths Toward Democracy* (Cambridge: Cambridge University Press, 1999); J. J. Linz and A. Stepan, *Problems of Democratic Transition and Consolidation* (Baltimore: Johns Hopkins University Press, 1996); A. Stepan, *Arguing Comparative Politics* (Oxford: Oxford University Press, 2001), 174; O. G. Encarnacion, "Civil Society and the Consolidation of Democracy in Spain," *Political Science Quarterly* 53 (2001); and J. S. Dryzek and L. Holmes, "The Real World of Civil Republicanism: Making Democracy Work in Poland and the Czech Republic," *Europe-Asia Studies* 52, no. 6 (2000).

12. Linz and Stepan, *Problems of Democratic Transition*, 272.

13. See Collier, *Paths toward Democracy*. (Cambridge: Cambridge University Press, 1999); J. J. Linz and A. Stepan, *Problems of Democratic Transition and Consolidation* (Baltimore: Johns Hopkins University Press, 1996); A. Stepan, *Arguing Comparative Politics* (Oxford: Oxford University Press, 2001).

14. "Rating of Top Ten Political Groups," last modified February 23, 2017, http://hku pop.hku.hk/chinese/popexpress/pgrating/topten1.html.

15. Ming Sing and Lucy Cummings, *Constitutional Reform for Good Governance in the Hong Kong Special Administrative Region* (Hong Kong: Centre for Comparative and Public Law, 2010).

16. Ming Sing, *Hong Kong's Tortuous Democratization: A Comparative Analysis. Hong Kong's Tortuous Democratization: A Comparative Analysis* (London: Routledge Curzon, 2004).

17. "Catholic Monitors on Legislative Councillors," last modified December 15, 2015, http://www.legco-monitors.org.

18. "Survey Findings on Evaluation of Political Parties in Hong Kong," (in Chinese), last modified July 24, 2014, https://goo.gl/FtYGo3.

19. Christine Loh, *Underground Front: The Chinese Communist Party in Hong Kong* (Hong Kong: Hong Kong University Press, 2010), 209.

20. See N. H. Au, "Democratic Regression under Electoral Authoritarianism: Regime Consolidation and Elite Co-optation in Post-1997 Hong Kong" (MPhil thesis, the Chinese University of Hong Kong, 2015); Joseph Y. S. Cheng, "The 2003 District Council Elections in Hong Kong," *Asian Survey* 44, no. 5 (2004); and Bruce Kam-Kwan Kwong, "Patron-Client Politics in Hong Kong: A Case Study of the 2002 and 2005 Chief Executive Elections," *Journal of Contemporary China* 16, no. 52 (2007): 389–415.

21. Stan Hok-Wui Wong, "Resource Disparity and Multi-level Elections in Competitive Authoritarian Regimes: Regression Discontinuity Evidence from Hong Kong," *Electoral Studies* 33 (2013): 9, 200–219.

22. Wong, "Resource Disparity and Multi-level Elections," 7–8.

23. Ming Sing, *Hong Kong's Tortuous Democratization.*

24. Ngok Ma, "Political Parties and Elections," in *Contemporary Hong Kong Government and Politics: Expanded Second Edition*, ed. Wai-man Lam et al. (Hong Kong: Hong Kong University Press, 2012), 159–77.

25. Mair Biezen and Thomas Poguntke, "Going, Going, . . . Gone? The Decline of Party Membership in Contemporary Europe," *European Journal of Political Research* 51 (2012): 24–56; and Hoi Yu Ng, "What Drives Young People Into Opposition Parties Under Hybrid Regimes? A Comparison of Hong Kong and Singapore," *Asian Politics & Policy* 8, no. 3 (2016): 436–55.

26. Albert Ho, the former chair of DP, interview, June 5, 2016.

27. Wing-tat Lee, interview, September 2016.

28. Ming Sing, "Explaining the Mass Support for the UM," in *The Umbrella Movement: Civil Resistance and Contentious Space in Hong Kong*, ed. Ngok Ma and Edmund Cheng (Amsterdam: University of Amsterdam Press, 2019).

29. "Hong Kong Harmonious Society Public Opinion Programme 2012 Survey Result," Hong Kong Institute of Asia-Pacific Studies, accessed on November 3, 2017, http://www.cuhk.edu.hk/hkiaps/csp/download/Press_Release_20120306.pdf.

30. See https://goo.gl/sHJGKo, accessed on November 3, 2017.

31. See https://www.cuhk.edu.hk/hiiaps/tellab/pdf/telepress, accessed on November 3, 2017.

32. "Occupy Central and the Fight for Information freedom," last modified January 20, 2016, https://rsf.org/en/news/occupy-central-and-fight-information-freedom.

33. See https://goo.gl/u3WFeU, accessed on November 3, 2017.

34. See https://goo.gl/pLNS6k, accessed on November 3, 2017.

35. See https://www.thinkinghk.org/v508, accessed on November 3, 2017.

36. Yun Tong Tang, "A New Urban Movement Seeking Democratic Management of the City in Hong Kong: The Campaign to Preserve Lee Tung Street" (MPhil thesis, Hong Kong University of Science and Technology, 2013).

37. S. Nagy, "Social Inequality and the Rise of Localism in Hong Kong," *International Studies Review* 16, no. 2 (2015): 25–47.

38. Ming Sing and Yuen Sum Tang, "Mobilization and Conflicts over Hong Kong's Democratic Reform," in *Contemporary Hong Kong Government and Politics, 2nd ed.*, ed. Wai-man Lam et al. (Hong Kong: Hong Kong University Press, 2012), 137–58.

39. Ming Sing and Yuen Sum Tang, "Mobilization and Conflicts," 137–58.

40. "Supporting Motion: Trigger De-facto Referendum, College Students Support 5-district By-elections," *AM730*, March 18, 2010.

41. Francis L. F. Lee, and Joseph Man To Chan, *Media and Protest Logics in the Digital Era: The Umbrella Movement in Hong Kong* (New York: Oxford University Press).

42. "50% of Respondents Support Civic Nomination; Half Respondents Not Supporting All 3 Proposals; 27% of Respondents Will Vote on 6.22" (in Chinese), *Apple Daily*, May 12, 2014.

43. Based on the author's interviews with a student leader and a party leader.

44. "OCLP Once Considered Retreat Yet Vetoed by HKFS" (in Chinese), *Ming Pao Daily News*, October 5, 2014.

45. "Hong Kong Government asked Occupiers to Leave, but Joshua Wong Demanded Removing the Threshold of Chief Executive Election" (in Chinese), *Liberty Times Net*, October 10, 2014. Available at: https://goo.gl/BzrQf5; "Lester Shum: No Space for Exit Now" (in Chinese), *Ming Pao News*, November 10, 2014. Available at: https://goo.gl/K7tLxG.

46. Eason Chung, "The Meaning of Continuing Occupation" (in Chinese), *Pentoy*, November 6, 2014. Available at: https://goo.gl/k4P8R3.

47. "Investigation Result on Hong Kong Public Opinion and Political Development," (in Chinese), last modified December 18, 2014, https://goo.gl/RHuj33.

48. See the survey conducted by the Hong Kong Polytechnic University: https://goo.gl/s17jRj.

49. During the Umbrella Movement, the police injured 2,067 persons, including twenty-eight injuries to the head or other fatal spots. See http://www.inmediahk.net/node/1035184, accessed on August 27, 2017.

50. See https://goo.gl/y1FWr7, accessed on November 3, 2017.

51. "Scholarism Criticized Pan-democrats" (in Chinese), *Oriental Daily*, April 10, 2015.

52. "Joshua Wong: Supporting Political Reform Equals Betrayal of Umbrella Movement" (in Chinese), *Sing Tao Daily News*, April 17, 2015.

53. "Scholarism, HKFS and Dozens of Groups Issue Joint Statement Opposing Pan-Democrats Having Secret Talks" (in Chinese), *Ming Pao Instant News*, April 21, 2015. Available at: https://goo.gl/wEgjad.

54. See https://goo.gl/kp7dUa, accessed on November 3, 2017.

55. "Joshua Wong's New Political Party Demosisto Has Eyes Firmly on Seats in Legco," *SCMP*, April 16, 2016.

56. The sampling error is ± 3.1 percent and level of confidence is 95 percent. The response rate was 38 percent. The survey was conducted between September 5 and September 28, 2016, by the School of Journalism, the Chinese University of Hong Kong.

57. See https://www.hkupop.hku.hk/chinese/popexpress/pgrating/datatables/datatable44.html, accessed on November 3, 2017.

58. Ming Sing, "Explaining Support for Democracy in East Asia," *East Asia: An International Quarterly* 29, no. 112 (2012): 1–20.

59. See http://www.inmediahk.net/node/1029295, accessed on November 3, 2017.

60. Ming Sing, "Governing Elites, External Events and Pro-democratic Opposition in Hong Kong (1986–2002)," *Government and Opposition* 38, no. 4 (2003): 476.

8

HONG KONG'S HYBRID REGIME AND ITS REPERTOIRES

Edmund W. Cheng

On September 22, 2014, thirteen thousand students rallied in front of the Statue of Beacon at the Chinese University of Hong Kong. Protesting the NPCSC's August 31 decision that placed various restrictions on the election of the chief executive, the Hong Kong Federation of Students (HKFS) declared a week-long class boycott at universities. Scholarism further extended the boycott to secondary schools. Occupy Central leaders echoed this boycott by advancing the schedule of their civil disobedience campaign. Yet when protesters organized sit-ins on successive days at Tamar Park adjacent to government headquarters, the turnout stalled at several thousand protesters. There had been no indication that the scale of the protest would dramatically escalate.

The Hong Kong Special Administrative Region (SAR) regime and its allies and clients, however, responded quickly with coercive and intimidating forces. The Silent Majority of Hong Kong, a pro-regime civic organization, established hotlines to track and scrutinize teachers and students who had joined the class boycott. The Federation of Guangxi Community Organization, a pro-establishment clan association, secured the use of Tamar Park from authorities, which escalated the confrontation and pushed students toward the Civic Square outside of government headquarters. After the students stormed Civic Square on September 26, the police detained thirteen leaders and searched their apartments. When more than sixty thousand people marched to the protest site to support the students on September 28, the police fired eighty-seven cannons of tear gas. Unlike in other autocracies and democracies, tear gas had not been used against the Hong Kong citizens since the 1967 riots.[1] Countless indignant citizens soon dispersed into the streets. After the adoption of an attrition strategy that discredited and wore out the Umbrella Movement without offering concessions, political prosecution and countermobilization continued long after the Umbrella Movement ended.

This chapter analyzes the roots of the SAR regime's learning curve in managing popular contention and the mechanisms that have enabled the regime to develop its authoritarian structure and practices.[2] The chapter first defines Hong Kong's hybrid regime in terms of its liberal-autocratic and central-local contradictions and then discusses various state countermobilization strategies used to respond to mass protests.[3] It then examines how the hybrid regime's strategies of disciplinary exclusion, patron-client politics, ideological work, and attrition have mobilized or incentivized proregime and nonstate actors against dissent. On the one hand, the hybrid regime has co-opted formal institutions and has manufactured informal networks through which political crisis has been maneuvered by the regime to monitor the ruling class's factional quarrels and to further develop its authoritarian protocols. On the other hand, the party-state's local apparatuses have extended and refined their united propaganda and mass-line strategies to address the rise of activism in Hong Kong.[4] I use multiple documents and primary materials to unpack the black box of regime countermobilization.[5]

The Hybrid Regime and Its Learning Curve

Governed under the "one country, two systems" principle since the 1997 handover, the HKSAR is widely categorized as a hybrid regime or liberal autocracy.[6] There are two dimensions or sources of hybridity. The first involves the evolving relationship between the central government based in Beijing and the local government of Hong Kong. Constitutionally, Hong Kong has largely preserved its legally semiautonomous status, but politically, the Beijing government has actively sought to co-opt local elites and to intervene in local politics.[7] Hong Kong politics therefore always involves a competition between central and local imperatives and interests. This corporatist structure has laid foundations for the Basic Law, a mini-constitution ensuring that business tycoons and professional associations secure a majority to elect executive and legislative branches. Since the 1980s the Chinese Communist Party (CCP) has co-opted and granted autonomy to Hong Kong's business elite to earn their support and to thus guarantee stability and prosperity during the transition. But Hong Kong's increased economic dependence on Mainland China since the early 2000s has begun to limit local autonomy.

The second dimension of hybridity is the coexistence of civil liberties and executive domination. While regular and competitive LegCo elections, extensive civil liberties, and an independent judiciary exist, the pro-Beijing executive branch and political elite share a tight grasp over political power. For the pandemocratic opposition, taking issues onto the street has become an effective means to connect with voters and to bolster its leverage. Under classic typologies, such forms of liberal authoritarianism are highly unstable because civil liberties afford a window of opportunity for the opposition to align electoral with street politics and to contest the autocrats' power base.[8] The presence of a higher power has, however, rendered the SAR regime a resilient protectorate compared to its vanishing counterparts.[9]

If autonomy without sovereignty and liberalism with authoritarianism are structural features of Hong Kong as a hybrid regime, the regime is anything but static. Protest events have transformed power relations of this hybrid regime, which has also learned over time how to address protests. Since the historic July 1 rally of 2003, a series of mass protests have triggered elite defection and have established the precedent that popular protests can force the government to yield. The Beijing government began to view street politics as an organized attempt supported by foreign forces and coordinated by prodemocracy politicians aimed at subverting its sovereignty and regarding autonomy and sovereignty as zero-sum games. While concessions were temporarily offered, the Beijing government altered its policy of "non-intervention" to one of "pro-action" in the SAR.[10] In 2004, a CCP Politburo Standing Committee member was designated to head the Central Coordination Group for Hong Kong and Macau Affairs, leading to the formation of a coordinated strategy of coercion, cooptation, and penetration. Constitutionally, the Beijing government emphasized a narrative that the relationship between the central government and Hong Kong is one involving the delegation of power and not one of power sharing. Institutionally, the SAR government has proactively applied coercive force, legal tools, and gerrymandering against the opposition. Informally, the regime's administrative focus has shifted from the realm of civil administration to the Liaison Office.[11] The CCP's underground united front, mass-line, and propaganda organs developed in earlier years have been mobilized to co-opt elites, to penetrate society, and to discredit dissenters.[12] The following discussion analyzes the regime's repertoire of protest absorption and countermobilization.

Varieties of State Countermobilization Mechanisms

Mobilization is not exclusively carried out by protesters; states also countermobilize to respond to challenges from below or to deflect internal divisions.[13]

Traditionally, state mobilization has been considered unique to totalitarian or authoritarian regimes and to function as a series of top-down and standardized campaigns led by the party-state and coordinated through its mass organizations.[14] As electoral politics are emerging worldwide after the fall of communism, many authoritarian regimes have been forced to address citizens' rights and to adopt electoral procedures. The contemporary hybrid regimes' countermobilization mechanisms have interacted with existing institutional structures and outsourced agencies. While some agencies serve as a clear extension of state apparatuses, others are proxies for factional politics, and even more are an ambiguous outgrowth of rent seekers who use policy changes as opportunities. Owing to their informal status, these incentivized nonstate agencies can perform many tasks not easily accomplished by formal institutions.

Previous studies of regime protest responses have tended to follow the repression and concession nexus. Repression refers to the use of coercive force against defiance, and concession refers to the approval of certain protest claims; both are adopted to influence mobilization and public opinion.[15] Recent studies suggest that authoritarian regimes might adopt myriad strategies when protests do not threaten regime survival. They may prefer to tolerate or ignore such protests as the state operates formal institutions to bargain, regulate, or dismiss dissenting opinions, or they may use attrition tactics through which the state maneuvers the legitimacy of revered institutions such as the church and court to discredit protesters and to trivialize their protest claims. Outsourced informal actors such as gangs or countermovement groups may also be used to exhaust protesters and increase participation costs.[16]

In this paper we identity four countermobilization strategies adopted under the hybrid regime structure and mediated by multifaceted agencies. First, disciplinary exclusion maintains a corporatist alliance to ensure structural stability during upheavals. The central government abruptly punishes the defected elite to alert the capitalist class that aligning with the incumbent, rather than contesting it, is their only legitimate and available choice during a political crisis. Second, patron-client politics deepen collaboration between the state and capitalist class. With the assistance of the business elite, the party-state gradually extends its informal authorities and grassroots networks to co-opt professional associations, clan societies, and grassroots communities that were once governed by the civil administration. Third, ideological work serves as a discursive tool used to differentiate and regulate collective behaviors. Proregime mass media, politicians, and education program providers promote a nationalist discourse to construct a contrast between acquiescence/payoffs and dissent/penalties between loyal and disloyal subjects. Finally, attrition tactics combine formal institutions and nonstate agencies to suppress and attack activists. The government hence increases protest participation costs while preserving its established image as a neutral arbiter by maneuvering the legitimacy of the courts and by outsourcing its dirty work to proregime civil society groups. These four types of countermobilization mechanisms have produced "cumulative effects" through which the interplay between state and nonstate actors suppresses dissenting opinions and defers collective actions through Hong Kong's once highly autonomous social institutions and vibrant public sphere.

Disciplinary Exclusion and an Elite Alliance

A divided elite or alternative elite alliances often enhance political opportunities for social movements to emerge and diffuse. To repel challengers, regimes must maintain elite cohesion while preventing defection. This strategy is crucial for hybrid regimes, which generally are considered less legitimate than democracies and which cannot deploy their repressive apparatuses as readily as autocracies. While protests can undermine elite cohesion, they can also spur the formation of "protection pacts" among elites or provide them with nonmaterial resources such as norms, identities, and order.[17] Like other contemporary hybrids, the SAR regime upheld what Robertson calls "an air of invincibility" to persuade the business elite that their best prospect was to submit to rather than oppose the incumbents.[18]

The effectiveness and perceptions of a disciplinary action, however, cannot be fully articulated in an orderly manner without referring to the Beijing government's long-term united front work. Dating back to the transition years, the CCP had systematically co-opted Hong Kong's business elite to win their loyalty and support. After years of practice, whether the tycoons and their proxies are appointed, honored, or replaced in the national or provincial assemblies and in the annual awarding of titles would indicate the political proximity of business elites in the regime as a function and forecast of their status and well-being.[19] Competition between elite camps for political appointments in the NPC and Chinese People's Political Consultative Conference (CPPCC) are encouraged and mainly channeled through the CCP's United Front Work Department and the State Council's Hong Kong and Macau Office.[20] Any sudden removal of business elites from these top offices thus sends a clear and powerful message to all political agencies.

On July 1, 2003, more than half a million Hong Kong citizens marched through the streets to protest a proposed national security law and its encroachment on civil liberties. Although protests were not uncommon in Hong Kong at the time, participation in the early 2000s ranged from five hundred to thirty thousand people.[21] This historic rally created a crack in the stability of the ruling coalition when James Tien, chairman of the probusiness Liberal Party, resigned from the Executive Council the day after the rally and when his party withdrew its support for the national security bill. As the second largest proregime party of LegCo, its defection forced the government to withdraw the bill and the secretary of security to resign. Following another mass rally in 2004, the first chief executive also resigned. Subsequently, prodemocracy parties and the Liberal Party won a landslide victory in the 2004 LegCo elections.

While the defected elite's electoral gains could have divided the ruling class or even produced a relatively independent "third force," the regime responded quickly to forestall this outcome. First, the SAR government refused the Liberal Party's request to reintroduce a national security bill to reconcile its "wrongdoings." Moreover, members were summoned to Beijing to declare their patriotism, after which the party's manifesto lengthened the timeline to achieving universal suffrage. Worse still, the Liaison Office withdrew its grassroots support to the electorate, causing the party's defeat in the 2008 LegCo elections. Finally, several Liberal Party legislators who were national assembly members quit the party four days after the 2008 LegCo elections. Within five years, the Liberal Party's LegCo seats decreased from ten to three. Although this dissolution involved factional competition and cannot be fully attributed to a top-down order, it exemplifies the power of the regime's capacity to punish defection.

The 2014 Umbrella Movement presented another opportunity to further strategies of disciplinary exclusion. When the class boycott began on September 22, a delegation of seventy business elites was summoned to Beijing to meet with President Xi Jinping, who urged them to support the SAR government. On September 29, at the first media session attended by high-ranking government officials, Chief Secretary Carrie Lam revealed that Chief Executive C. Y. Leung was fully aware of "most of the actions taken against Occupy Central." By distancing herself from a highly unpopular decision and perhaps shifting the blame, she spurred speculation regarding a rift between the top leaders. Protest leaders were eager to exploit this emerging cleavage on how to end the political crisis. As Alex Chow, HKFS secretary-general, recalled, "several government middlemen approached us and implied a potential split among the elite."[22] The HKFS wrote a letter to Chief Secretary Carrie Lam on October 3 proposing a government-student dialogue:

> This unjust system . . . allows a Chief Executive who attacks protesters with tear gas and a legislative council that tolerates function constituency members who connive with the privileged class. . . . We believe that even you, as Chief Secretary, do not approve of such despicable acts of the Chief Executive.[23]

The next day, the chief executive accepted the protesters' proposal and asked the chief secretary to initiate a dialogue. The two top leaders did not seem to conceal their disagreements during the televised broadcast. Although the dialogue arrangement pacified the public and bought time for the regime, a side effect was a greater likelihood of elite fracturing and increased levels of uncertainty for Beijing and the ruling coalition. When the occupation continued to escalate and faced a deadlock, questions emerged regarding whether C. Y. Leung would step down as Beijing's concession, like his predecessor C. H. Tung had after massive protests that occurred in 2003 and 2004. On October 8, a journalist stationed in Beijing for over a decade published an article accusing C. Y. Leung of receiving millions from an Australian firm before his inauguration. This incident spurred speculations that Beijing, amid its anticorruption campaign and vested financial interests in the city, wanted to quickly end the political crisis.[24] Contrary to such expectations, *People's Daily*, the CCP's official mouthpiece, disregarded the scandal and strongly backed Leung, praising his performance in handling the protests and stressing that the central government was "very satisfied" with his work.[25] As OCLP leader Kin-man Chan admitted, middlemen connected to Beijing sent him a message that the central authority had ordered a policy of "no concession and no bloodshed," suggesting that the protesters should not expect to profit from the internal split and should quickly retreat from protest sites.[26]

Beijing's resolved attitude to uphold this uncompromising policy was further illustrated through the punishment of local elites. James Tien, a tycoon himself and a spokesman for other tycoons, urged Leung to resign on October 14. The CPPCC held a special meeting the next day and expelled Tien for violating its charter. Despite Tien's expulsion, top Chinese officials reassured him that he would remain part of the patriotic force. These nuanced outcomes imply that the power base of business elites cannot be eliminated under an existing statist-corporatist structure. Nevertheless, the tycoons stopped expressing their sympathy to students or challenging Leung in public and instead adhered to the official rhetoric that the movement was illegal and harmful to Hong Kong's prosperity and stability.

The effectiveness of disciplinary exclusion was further affirmed through elite nonaction during political crisis. Two moderate politicians of the administration, for instance, explained why they never considered resigning to protest police brutality or seeking a moment to become people's men at the peak of the Umbrella Movement:

> They are worried that resignation will only trigger Beijing's suspicion of foreign interference. The regime will exclude them and block other moderates. . . . They prefer to work within the system to lobby for restrained actions or to monitor the decision-making process.[27]

These moderates, despite understanding the causes of the movement, feared that if they expressed any dissenting public opinions or organized collective actions they would only provoke personal retaliation or justify Beijing's further intervention in local politics. They therefore chose to remain silent and to distance themselves from the protesters. Constrained by the SAR's central-local contradiction, the power struggle between hardliners and softliners common in Latin American and post-Soviet democratic transitions was hampered. What is unique about the Hong Kong case is that this contradiction is precluded by the asymmetric and much larger power held by the center versus the periphery. The careful practice of disciplinary exclusion observed also reflects the hybrid regime's adaptation, according to which punishment must be severe enough to issue credible threats to a few defectors but cannot be so severe that it triggers systemic defections among the entire ruling coalition. Although factional quarrels were far from reconciled, a temporary alliance was forged by designating street occupiers as a common enemy and Beijing authorities as the ultimate ruler. Elite cohesion thus provides structural stability, a necessary precondition for other innovative and situational responses to dissent.

Patron-Client Politics and Sectoral Penetration

As Beijing's government has long wished to deter Hong Kong's democratization, the politically conservative business elite has served as a natural and reliable partner in keeping prodemocracy forces from becoming the majority in the legislature. By providing Mainland connections and economic interests to the business elite, the regime aims to reinforce dependence and loyalty. The social-economic ties of the business elite also help the regime co-opt elite-sponsored clan societies, professional associations, or mass organizations, which are vital agencies of electoral countermobilization.

Between 2004 and 2016, Mainland China accounted for 43.7 to 50.8 percent (HK$1,806 to $3,860 million of Hong Kong's total trade. By 2016, investment from the Mainland accounted for about 25.7 percent or HK$3,241 billion of the total stock of Hong Kong's inward direct investment. Business patrons and their professional clients are intertwined with, if not crowded out by, state-owned enterprises and their subsidiaries. Increased economic interactions have amplified the merits of political patronage, motivating the business elite to seek direct access to Beijing authorities.[28] In addition to reinforcing patron-client politics through unified front work, the Liaison Office has furthered its sectoral penetration into grassroots communities and professional sectors through the application of mass-line strategies and bureaucratic control.

Since 2004 it has expanded its regional bureaus in response to constituencies in the LegCo elections. Each bureau is further divided into subsidiary teams to oversee several district council constituencies. By 2012 it was estimated to include twenty-five bureaus staffed by thousands of employees in Hong Kong.[29] To accommodate this elaborate operation, the Liaison Office purchased more than five hundred private commercial and housing apartments valued at more than $3 billion between 1999 and 2015. According to the Land Registry's records, the Liaison Office spent $70 million on Hong Kong properties within a year following the Umbrella Movement.[30] Similarly, the annual budget of the Democratic Alliance for the Betterment of Hong Kong (DAB), the largest proregime party, increased from $30 million in 2005 to $107 million in 2014; of this amount, approximately one-fourth came from membership fees, and one-half came from an annual fundraising event for which liaison officials served as patrons, business elites served as donors, and proregime parties served as benefactors.[31]

The SAR government has marginalized the opposition through a significant partisan bias in electoral redistricting. Through gerrymandering or the packing and cracking of opposition constituencies, the government aims to deter the re-election of prodemocracy incumbents.[32] While the SAR government leverages formal institutions, the party-state branch coordinates informal business operations.[33] The Liaison Office monitors and connects proregime political parties with grassroots organizations such as owners' associations and mutual aid committees. It also delegates resources through pro-Beijing political parties and their LegCo members and district councilors to sponsor tourism packages, banquets, training classes, legal consultations, medical checkups, festival gifts, and so forth. According to the investigative works of several journalists, proregime parties and intermediate associations must submit regular work reports to the Liaison Office in an election year to evaluate whether performance pledges are reached and whether resources are allocated efficiently.[34] By linking funding with accountability, the Liaison Office has established a hierarchical machine that regulates the once uncontested realm of grassroots politics. This bureaucratic monitoring and reward system shows traces of China's experience in maintaining stability.[35]

For instance, in 2014–2015, the DAB managed more than two hundred local branches offering 19,555 such events (53 events per day); in 2015–2016, the DAB recruited more than 31,000 members and 7,000 volunteers.[36] These everyday interactions have reinforced the authority of grassroots associations and have enabled proregime politicians to broaden social connections, assess public sentiment, exchange favors for votes, and develop solidarity among locals. Old and new professional organizations whose patrons are the business elite have taken a more proactive role to advance their social reach through public project procurement and social service provisions. Notable examples include the Internet Professional Association (1999) and the New Home Association (2010), which respectively target the social work and information technology sectors, traditionally strongholds of the pan-democrats. The latter is reported to have heavily subsidized new members to register as electorates of the information technology functional constituency. Over a short time the latter has operated with an annual budget of hundreds of millions, enabling it to recruit hundreds of social workers and to serve new immigrants from Mainland China.

These one-stop services and extended networks helped build trust and patronage with their commercial-cum-political clients.[37] Working-class citizens living in large public housing projects are easy targets for such collusion via the provision of goods, services, and conviviality; these penetration strategies have reinforced class divisions between proregime supporters and prodemocracy supporters in Hong Kong.[38] Members of the professional middle class such as social workers and IT experts are also increasingly subjected to more bureaucratic control and market consideration. While there is no clear evidence that these changes have affected their voting preferences, the proregime camp has steadily gained vote shares against pan-democrats in successive LegCo elections, increasing from 30 to 45 percent from 1998 to 2012 and remaining steady at this level of support. Since 2008 the proregime camp has controlled the majority and the chairmanship of all eighteen District Councils.[39] While this increase in the regime's infrastructural power has not destroyed the prodemocracy camp, it has acquired public resources and grassroots networks to limit the opposition's resource mobilization capacities and has generated widespread threats among social workers, Internet security experts, and NGO staff that their autonomous social realms or workplaces are increasingly being overloaded with political objectives, partly explaining why many of these individuals have become core participants of the Umbrella protests.

Ideological Work: Finding Loyal and Lawful Subjects

The hybrid regime's restructuring is not limited to the direct mobilization of voting. Indirect efforts are adopted to solicit resourceful collaborators to promote pro-China discourse. From the late 2000s the proregime business elite has gained control over all but one mass media corporation, leading to increased levels of censorship and self-censorship.[40] Some business elites are also designated as key service providers of curriculum programs and public events featuring patriotic education. By providing the elite with public funding and guiding elite-owned mass media, the regime spreads a nationalist and legalistic discourse to ultimately nurture loyal subjects but principally to maneuver patronage to demobilize dissenting behaviors.

PATRIOTIC EDUCATION

While political penalties and economic incentives have enticed elite compliance, Beijing has intensified its efforts to transform the Hong Kong population through various forms of patriotic education, and it has used cultural edification as a fundamental means to construct new identities and to transform hearts and minds. In 2007, in response to former Chinese president Hu Jintao's call to invigorate national education, former chief executive Donald Tsang proposed "new Hong Kongers" as a new identity that underpins patriotic sentiment toward the motherland and that instills a nationwide perspective that views Hong Kong from the eyes of the country.[41]

Primary agencies for enforcing education reforms are elite-sponsored mass organizations such as clan societies and grassroots and professional associations. Modeled on united front work with a long history in Hong Kong, these associations were developed to counterbalance prodemocracy NGO support in specific social sectors and network proregime groups by providing funding, cultivating exchanges, and establishing a hierarchy. Two notable developments, however, have occurred since 2003.

First, a new umbrella community of clan associations was created. Traditionally, clan associations have emerged organically according to the size and service demands of each clan or lineage. Apart from the Federation of Guangdong Community Organization and New Territories Association of Societies, most other clans are city- or prefecture-based. The 2010s witnessed the emergence of new provincial associations whose patrons are tycoons and members of the NPC or CPPCC. These associations have been encouraged to interact with their Mainland counterparts through tours and visits initiated and accompanied by Liaison Office officials.[42]

Second, youth have become targeted clients through activities of the Future Star Federation of Students (2005) and the Hong Kong Youth Exchange Promotion Association (2009), for instance. By providing billions in teaching grants each financial year, the Hong Kong SAR government recruited more than 160 primary and secondary schools to participate in the Putonghua education scheme between 2008 and 2012.[43] The SAR government, clan societies, and business chambers have financed hundreds of exchange tours to Mainland China each year for students of different ages. Perhaps the most controversial attempt to target youth was a plan to introduce moral and national education to primary and secondary schools in 2012 with criticisms that the curriculum could brain-wash students through its unreserved praise of communist and nationalist ideologies.

Converting targets such as the elite and youth into loyal subjects, however, may not be a policy priority. Over the years, it has become public knowledge that the majority of children of the business elite and of senior government officials are educated in international schools and overseas universities, which are not only exempted from patriotic curriculums but which are also exposed to liberal values, hence raising questions of how sincerely policy makers and service providers believe in the ideals of patriotic education. Similarly, youths' lived experiences with information and social media blockages during Mainland China trips have severely weakened the appeal of patriotic education and its capacities to transform "hearts and minds." The ideological battlefield, however, serves as a "public transcript" to educate providers and consumers of this official discourse. In particular, the transcript helps normalize the submission of businessmen and educators to their motherland/sovereign and standardize public services supporting patriotic programs from elite-sponsored intermediaries. The continuous and excessive implementation of patriotic programs, even though two-fifths of Umbrella protesters were recipients who reacted negatively and developed a strong local identity, reveal the contradictions of such a policy.[44] In light of this, the regime seems aware of policy limitations in altering the beliefs of the targeted audience, but it aims to reinforce such official discourse in the public sphere to restrain collective behaviors.

NATIONALISTIC AND LEGALISTIC FRAMES

People make sense of their lived experiences by placing them within a "frame" or schema that organizes selected ideas and that signifies objects and occurrences encountered.[45] To frame is thus a meaning construction and communicative process that "select[s] some aspects of a perceived reality and make them more salient in a communicating text."[46] As state-run and proregime mass media are compelled to report and analyze large-scale, eye-catching protests, the analysis of their framing helps to unpack the state's countermobilization strategies.

Nationalist framing that has blamed "foreign interference" for the Umbrella Movement has been emphasized by the Beijing government and by its official mouthpieces. By using the term "Occupy Central" in quotation marks, proregime mass media of Mainland China have expressed an official disapproval of the occupation and have regarded popular discontent as a malicious scheme orchestrated by foreign forces. The Ministry of Foreign Affairs described the movement as a "Hong Kong version of a color revolution" organized by manipulative politicians and anti-Chinese forces. The chief executive echoed that authorities held proof of "external forces' involvement."[47] *People's Daily* and *Global Times* identified "western countries such as the US and UK" and "forces for independence in Taiwan" as behind-the-scenes manipulators.[48] Without these external networks, the state insisted, a less-well-planned, large-scale, and resourceful occupation would have resulted. The framing of the Umbrella Movement as "an organized separatist movement plotting at regime change" fed growing nationalist sentiments on the Mainland and demobilized diffusion among China's dissenters. This frame thus externalized the cause of the subverting occupation to conspiracy theories that could not be easily verified but that could be effective in spreading fear and speculation.

Second, a legalistic framing that attacked the occupation as unlawful and economically costly and as creating social chaos has been perpetuated by the SAR government and by pro-Beijing newspapers, which have negatively depicted protest leaders as revolutionaries and young participants as victims of their illegal and misguided behaviors. Specifically, various proregime media sources have accused the movement of representing an organized attempt to cause disruption to China's financial center.[49] Testimonies estimating that economic costs had reached billions of dollars were provided on a daily basis. Described as a catastrophe that undermined the economy, cohesion, and order, the occupation was framed as a threat to the city's longstanding stability and prosperity.[50] A legalistic framing of "public disorder causing disrupted livelihoods" diverted attention away from protest claims to immediate costs, demobilizing public support. It also distinguished typical altruistically motivated participants from protest leaders with ulterior motives.

While both nationalist and legalistic frames have been applied to the movement's origins, its resolution has applied a legalistic frame. Table 8.1 provides a systematic overview of prognostic framing of the Umbrella Movement used in six state-run, proregime, and independent newspapers operating in Mainland China and Hong Kong. Among the eight solutions offered, the four state-run and proregime newspapers have overwhelmingly emphasized a need to restore law and order (58.5 to 85.6 percent). While the two independent newspapers have urged for a combination of incremental and structural solutions involving political accountability, constitutional reforms, and social programming, state mouthpieces have largely sought to maintain the status quo.

Nationalist framing has disregarded the spontaneous nature of the prodemocracy Umbrella Movement and has fabricated it as an act of proindependence separatism. In turn, legalist framing effectively discredited protest leaders when the regime later adopted more oppressive tactics to restore law and order.[51]

TABLE 8.1 Prognostic media framing of the Umbrella Movement

PRESS	INSTRUMENTAL					STRUCTURAL		
	RESTORE LAW AND ORDER n=279	DIALOG n=165	INVESTIGATION n=31	POLITICAL ACCOUNTABILITY n=23	BEIJING INTERVENTION n=16	CONSTITUTIONAL REFORM n=28	SOCIAL PROGRAM n=28	CIVIC ENGAGEMENT n=29
State-run								
People's Daily	64.7	29.4	0.0	0.0	0.0	0.0	5.9	0.0
Global Times	62.5	20.0	0.0	5.0	0.0	5.0	2.5	5.0
Proregime								
Ta Kung Pao	85.6	6.1	5.3	0.0	0.0	0.0	0.0	3.0
Oriental Daily	58.2	10.4	0.0	0.0	22.4	1.5	6.0	1.5
Independent								
Ming Pao	15.7	49.7	9.7	0.0	0.5	2.7	10.8	10.8
Apple Daily	10.9	8.7	6.5	41.3	0.0	32.6	0.0	0.0

Source: Data (n=599) included headlines and editorials in the six newspapers that covered the Umbrella Movement between September 28 and December 18, 2014. For each article, two trained coders examined the text and counted the total number of instances of each framing code. Intercoder reliability coefficient is 0.77.

A tactful interplay between nationalist and legalistic frames has constructed an official discourse that has been discursively discouraging if not functionally demobilizing to mass mobilization and public deliberation.

Attrition Tactics: Litigation and Outsourced Confrontation

Whereas the previous tactics are used as regular mechanisms for pre-empting protest and dissent, this section discusses what occurred during and after the protests. As an Occupy Central leader admitted, middlemen told him that Beijing authorities had ordered the policy of "no concession and no bloodshed," which was later leaked through the *New York Times*.[52] This policy stopped the SAR government's hardliners from continuing with direct repression but also restricted softliners from giving concessions. By revealing how the regime incentivized and benefited from outsourcing coercive actions, we show that attrition in terms of litigation and countermovements serves as an integral part of the regime's protest responses.

TARGETED PROSECUTION

During the Umbrella Movement, the High Court granted four civil injunctions to evict the occupied sites; two were granted to taxi driver groups and a minibus operator group in Mongkok, and two were granted to an investment company and a bus company in Admiralty. Despite a lack of evidence that the authorities *initiated* these private filings of injunctions, these associational groups had close ties with the proregime camp owing to their corporatist linkages to the government. Two senior staff members of transport companies told us that the company was approached by an intermediary who relayed the government's message that "something could be done by the company to end the protests." One company member refused to participate, while the other prepared an injunction document.[53] The company that refused to assist was coincidentally removed from the government's list of subsidiary programs in the following financial year. Moreover, the lawyer who applied for an injunction on behalf of the minibus group is a DAB member and was appointed to a university governing council one year after the movement. The investment company, which owns the CITIC Tower to which the injunction would apply, is a joint venture controlled by the Chinese state-owned CITIC group.

Although the SAR government had legal grounds to have the police clear the occupation of traffic arteries, it chose not to apply its default legal power. Instead, the two highest-ranking officials, the chief executive and chief secretary, urged protesters to obey court orders or have police assist bailiffs in enforcing orders by making arrests when necessary.[54] Rather than using coercive power, the regime leveraged the institutional legitimacy of the judiciary to increase costs of protest participation and to demobilize the public from supporting the occupation. Although there is no evidence that the government directly used the courts against protesters or that the courts ruled with bias, proregime groups certainly played key roles in the application of injunctions, and the police fully supported their enforcement. The outcome of this coincidence, if not collaboration, was the end of the protracted Umbrella Movement.

The use of injunctions rendered the legal system a third-party actor and shifted burdens of protester clearance from the police to the judiciary. Injunctions not only helped reframe the protests from a form of political contention to court disputes, but they also introduced an additional qualification of the protests as unlawful. In effect, judicial injunctions gave rise to criticisms from the mass media and professional organizations that the defiance of court orders would erode the rule of law and thereby jeopardize protesters' civic image.[55] Injunctions also created divisions among protest leadership figures on whether protesters should heed the legal consequences of a contempt of court order or submit themselves to penalties according to demands and principles of civil disobedience.

While the number of arrests has increased, most protesters have not been prosecuted. In the wake of the Umbrella Movement, 1,003 protesters were arrested for unlawful assembly during protests, but as of June 2015, only 5 percent had been prosecuted, and only 34 percent of these protesters were found guilty, which is lower than the 2014 conviction rate of 49.7 percent.[56] Constrained by an independent judiciary, the regime could not move from targeted arrests to mass arrests. The percentage of illegal assemblies ending with a prosecution has indeed remained constant from 2003 through the ongoing prosecutions of Umbrella Movement activists in 2014 and of Mongkok rioters in 2016.

While the government was not able to fully influence the court's verdicts, it has practiced pre-emptive and severe prosecution procedures and endorsements to achieve its goal of disciplining protesters. First, penal codes used against protesters were chosen for their severe penalties. Protesters charged with assaulting a police officer before 2005 were consistently prosecuted under the Police Ordinance (Cap 232 section 61), which allows for suspended sentences. After 2006, the secretary of justice opted for the Offences against the Person Ordinance (Cap 212 section 36b), which makes imprisonment mandatory.[57] Second, six legislators who were elected in the 2016 LegCo elections and who endorsed relatively radical platforms were disqualified through oath-violating litigation. Following the SAR government's unprecedented legal challenges faced in November 2016, the NPCSC reinterpreted Article 104 of the Basic Law on what constitutes a "sincere and solemn" oath-taking process, and the interpretation was applied retrospectively. Subject to this binding legal interpretation, the court disqualified all the plaintiff legislators. Third, young protest leaders with minor offenses who had been traditionally exempted from prosecution were targeted. Sixteen activists who had participated in various protest events in 2014 were convicted for civil disobedience actions and were sentenced to community service and probation in 2015. While these verdicts observed precedents of a common-law system, the secretary of justice appealed.[58] Eventually, all sixteen activists were sentenced to six to fourteen months in prison. As both verdicts were reached at the Court of Appeal, they had a binding effect on the hundreds of court cases on illegal assembly and police assault pending in the lower courts in years to come.

By leveraging legal authority to punish protesters, the regime effectively had a chilling effect on civil society. Compelled by the trustworthiness and respect of legal institutions in Hong Kong, the regime claimed impartiality while also discouraging discussions regarding justifications for arrests and prosecution. Student activists and prodemocracy politicians who were designated offenders were subjected to strong financial and psychological pressures but wielded few political tools to gain public sympathy and to contest the regime.

OUTSOURCED COUNTERMOVEMENT

Defined as opposing movements that make "contrary claims simultaneously to those of the original movement," countermovements often develop tactics similar to targeted social movements.[59] In hybrid regimes, they are often linked to state authorities in the form of elite alliances or sponsorship while striving to appear as citizen-based grassroots movements. Moreover, countermovements can employ situational repertoires to appeal to different social groups of society to disrupt the organizational inertia of target movements.[60] Threats of countermovements have often impeded target movements' energies, have neutralized their claims, and have increased risks of protest participation, thereby facilitating movement demobilization. Such actions have also showcased the regime's popularity, have developed large organizational networks, and have mandated the official framing of dissent.

Although countermovements have emerged in Hong Kong only recently, they have swiftly become a notable force in the dynamics of contentious politics. Proregime mass organizations in Hong Kong have historically operated underground.[61] Despite their abundant resources, strong sectoral networks, and strength in local elections, these groups are less capable than pan-democrats in terms of shaping public discourse and mobilizing public support, leaving civil society largely dominated by the prodemocracy camp.[62] Only from 2010 have an increasing number of state-endorsed civil society associations appeared and claimed to represent the silent majority who treasure the core values of Hong Kong as much as activists do.

Figure 8.1 shows that protest mobilization and countermobilization have interacted with one another, causing the diffusion of proregime, nonstate actors and shaping their forms and repertoires. While both groups are responding to a strict change in policy and support the regime, the latter appears to be more spontaneous and autonomous. State-endorsed groups have gradually been replaced with citizen-based groups peaking in 2015, the year following the Umbrella Movement.

State-endorsed groups have tended to form ad hoc umbrella alliances to support government policies or projects. In demonstrating their clear and strong linkages with the state and the pro-Beijing establishment, state-endorsed groups have preferred peaceful repertoires such as parades and signature campaigns to appeal to a broader constituency. For example, the Alliance of Constitutional Development was initiated by leading proregime figures and was supported by

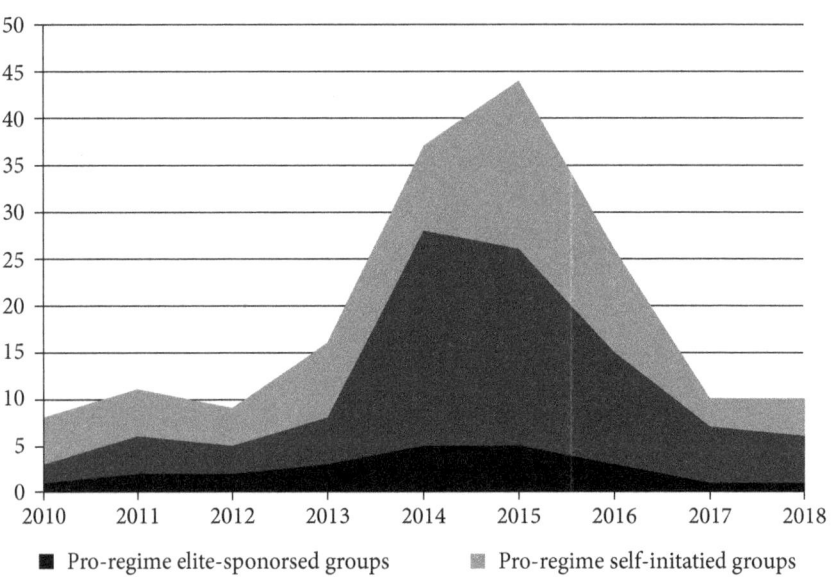

FIGURE 8.1. The ecology of mobilization and countermobilization in Hong Kong.

Source: Author compiled. Compiled by (1) identifying the major citizen-based groups that have engaged in mobilization and have been featured in the mass media and (2) mapping the smaller groups through cross-checking the major groups' extended networks in their social media platforms.

forty-four large and conventional organizations including trade unions, political parties, clan societies, and youth associations. In January 2010, the organization claimed to have collected 1.6 million signatures in support of the SAR government's constitutional reform. In contrast, citizen-based groups have emphasized their independent and spontaneous nature in response to certain social movement organizations or what they perceive to be deviant phenomena. Although they openly preach their proregime agendas, citizen-based groups tend to conceal their institutional linkages to proregime political or business elites. For this purpose, a wide range of repertoires such as parades, demonstrations, verbal abuse, assaults, sieges, and acts of harassment can be deployed according to situations and audiences involved. Compared to state-endorsed groups that have typically relied on united front networks and mass media channels to mobilize supporters and to deliver their messages, these citizen-based groups have used social media platforms to promote their causes.

Despite these differences, both state-endorsed and citizen-based groups are highly organized. Our participant observation results show that most protesters have fixed working hours, follow a common dress code, and use standardized protest slogans. A process tracing the rise and fall of these countermovements shows that groups that manage to capture media attention place pressures on activists, or attract new members are rewarded with new resources and crowd out space available for other less successful groups or new groups to emerge. In contrast, those that cannot fulfill these key performance requirements quickly disintegrate or vanish. While these groups are not directly linked to the regime, they are an ambiguous outgrowth in response to a hardline approach to dissent or are linked to organizations with abundant resources and a strong interest in steering civil society to toe the party line.

The most representative example of a state-endorsed civil society group is the Silent Majority for Hong Kong. Led by a group of journalists, businessmen, and scholars, this group strove to combat Occupy Central by adopting tactics such as demonstrations and petitions to mobilize the conservative middle class against protesters, thus promoting the official rhetoric that civil disobedience disrupts order and livelihoods. Its one-week petition in September 2013 is said to have collected 1.83 million signatures, including the signatures of ranking officials of the Liaison Office, of government secretaries, of senior civil servants, and of business elites. The seemingly credible and impartial signatures they collected were then cited by authorities to show popular support against Occupy Central. Established by the same group of professionals, digital media outlet HKG Post endorsed nearly every government policy and criticized prodemocracy politicians and activists of the post-Occupy era. According to Qsearch data, HKG Post recorded the second highest level of engagement of all digital media websites in

Hong Kong in late 2016.[63] In December 2016, leaders of the Silent Majority of Hong Kong received the NPC chairman's "full recognition" in Beijing. Chairman Zhang, also the chair of the leading small group in charge of Hong Kong affairs, praised these civic leaders in their efforts to create a platform to allow "the majority of Hong Kong people to express their views" and to "spread positive energy."[64]

Other countermovement groups such as Caring Hong Kong Power and Voice of Loving Hong Kong have been more aggressive. Advocating for physical contention and large-scale rallies to exhibit their strengths, these groups appeal to the grassroots populace but avoid revealing their organizational lineages and linkages. A recent investigative report, however, found that many of their "demonstrators" are sent by the provincial Youth League, are paid by clan societies, and are recruited from the Mainland.[65] In contrast, SpeakoutHK is an indigenous propaganda outlet that emerged during the Umbrella Movement. Established by the United Foundation, chief campaigner for the former chief executive, the organization soon emerged as an unofficial mouthpiece for the SAR administration. Using populist language and false data supplemented with insider information, the site has reached a segment of the population that could not be reached previously. Internet traffic suggests that it had the highest engagement rate of all online media websites from October to December 2016, which amplified the regime's public support.[66] Like similar operations of authoritarian China, many of these social media accounts are fake and operated by remunerated commentators.[67] They have also created biased representations of public opinion and have challenged the optimistic notion that the virtual space may be conducive to the growth of civil society. Instead, these confrontational tactics have inevitably provoked more extreme reactions and have effectively encouraged contention between people. One prodemocracy LegCo member described ways in which the recurrence of countermovements has weakened protests.

> By encouraging recurring affrays in people's neighborhoods, they dragged everyone through the mud. Countermobilizers were ostracized by many citizens, who also blamed the protesters. The logic is simple: why did these counter-movements occur? Because the protesters occupied roads or disrupted order. Orderliness and insecurity also made people feel impatient and threatened. In our contingencies, voters often came to us and demanded that we end the crisis.[68]

Despite drawing negative impressions through their violent confrontations, anti-Occupy protests helped create a physical and visual specter of chaos and violence at protest sites. Casual protesters were threatened from returning, newcomers were discouraged from joining, and parents obtained evidence convincing them to prohibit their children from participating in peaceful protests.

Conclusion

The Umbrella Movement began with a spectacular start when hundreds of thousands of protesters spontaneously mobilized against police violence and occupied streets and lanes for more than two months. This unprecedented outcry, however, was gradually enervated through the regime's multiple adaptive responses against dissent. This chapter examines countermobilization mechanisms adopted by Hong Kong's hybrid regime to absorb and suppress dissent, thereby producing cumulative effects in expanding state power into the once relatively autonomous public sphere and social realm.

First, this chapter shows how the hybrid regime has adopted multiple countermobilization mechanisms to absorb, erode, and suppress dissent. First, disciplinary exclusion maintains an elite alliance to ensure structural stability during political upheavals. The central government abruptly punishes the defected elite to signal to the capitalist class that aligning with the incumbent rather than contesting it is their only legitimate and available choice during political crises. Second, patron-client politics help consolidate the regime's sectoral penetration. With the assistance of the business elite, the regime gradually extends its party-state apparatuses and proregime political parties to co-opt professional associations, clan societies, and grassroots communities, which were traditionally governed by the civil administration and dominated by prodemocracy forces. Third, ideologies serve as a discursive tool for differentiating and regulating collective behaviors. Proregime mass media, politicians, and education program providers promote a nationalist discourse to construct a parallel between acquiescence and payoffs for loyal subjects and between dissent and penalties for disloyal subjects. Finally, attrition tactics combine formal institutions and nonstate agencies to suppress and attack activists or amplify levels of contention between people. The government in turn increases protest participation costs while preserving its established image as a neutral arbiter by maneuvering the legitimacy of the courts and by outsourcing its dirty work to proregime civil society groups.

These four types of countermobilization mechanisms have produced cumulative effects through which the interplay between state and nonstate actors suppresses dissenting opinions and defers collective actions in the once highly autonomous social institutions and vibrant public sphere. These mechanisms, which were rooted in Beijing's ruling strategies of combining united propaganda and mass-line fronts but that were amplified during and after the Umbrella

Movement, illustrate a mechanical perspective of the robustness of contemporary authoritarianism. Contrary to the conventional view that the rule of law, civil society groups, and social media platforms are defenders of an open society if not prerequisites for democratic transition, these revered institutions and nonstate agencies are either maneuvered and incentivized to serve as intermediaries of countermobilization in times of state need.

In a nutshell, the decentralized structure of the hybrid regime's countermobilization machine has the advantage of allowing improvisation, thereby becoming readily adaptive to the activists' changing repertoires. But as the machine counts on the fragmented agents' interpretation and encourages their competition to marginalize the dissentients, it often provokes unintended consequences. Their countermobilization repertoires have not only eroded the revered institutions and caused backfire from the democratic opposition, but also unavoidably deviated from the regime's agenda to create a united force and observe the mass-line opinions. As a result, the countermobilization machine, despite its effectiveness, also features a structural contradiction. Whether or not other eventful protests in the future may contest its weak spot remains to be seen.

NOTES

1. Hong Kong police fired tear gas at gangs in 1984, at unidentified forces in 1989, at Vietnamese refugees in 1995, and at Korean farmers in 2005; none of these targeted peaceful protesters.

2. Graeme B. Robertson, *The Politics of Protest in Hybrid Regimes: Managing Dissent in Post-Communist Russia* (Cambridge: Cambridge University Press, 2010).

3. David S. Meyer and Suzanne Staggenborg, "Movements, Countermovements, and the Structure of Political Opportunity," *American Journal of Sociology* 101, no. 6 (1996): 1628–60.

4. See Ching Kwan Lee and Yonghong Zhang. "The Power of Instability: Unraveling the Microfoundations of Bargained Authoritarianism in China," *American Journal of Sociology* 118, no. 6 (2013): 1475–1508; Christine Loh, *Underground Front: The Chinese Communist Party in Hong Kong* (Hong Kong: Hong Kong University Press, 2010); Edmund W. Cheng, "Street Politics in a Hybrid Regime: The Diffusion of Political Activism in Postcolonial Hong Kong," *China Quarterly* 226 (2016): 383–406.

5. First, I analyzed official records of government bureaus. Second, I conducted twelve semistructured interviews with politicians, activists, and journalists who are sponsors, targets, or intermediaries of regime actions and who thus have access to firsthand information. Third, I applied a participation observation approach during various episodes of countermobilization to uncover their logics and networks. Finally, I used print and social media data to map the official framing of protest events and the emergence of state-endorsed and citizen-based countermovements.

6. Hsin-chi Kuan and Siu-kai Lau. "Between Liberal Autocracy and Democracy: Democratic Legitimacy in Hong Kong," *Democratization* 9, no. 4 (2002): 58–76.

7. Ngok Ma, "The Making of a Corporatist State in Hong Kong: The Road to Sectoral Intervention," *Journal of Contemporary Asia* 46, no. 2 (2016): 247–66.

8. Vincent Boudreau, *Resisting Dictatorship: Repression and Protest in Southeast Asia* (Cambridge: Cambridge University Press, 2009).

9. Ming Sing, *Hong Kong's Tortuous Democratization: A Comparative Analysis* (London: Routledge, 2004).

10. Cheng, "Street Politics," 388.

11. A ranking officer of the Liaison Office called for the creation of a "second ruling office" to "fully, openly and legally" assist in local governance. See Er-ban Cao, "Governing Force in Hong Kong under the Condition of One Country, Two Systems," *Xuexi shibao*, January 28, 2008.

12. Loh, *Underground Front*.

13. Meyer and Staggenborg, "Movements."

14. Juan J. Linz, *Totalitarian and Authoritarian Regimes* (Boulder, CO: Lynne Rienner Publishers, 2000).

15. See Mark Irving Lichbach, "Deterrence or Escalation? The Puzzle of Aggregate Studies of Repression and Dissent," *Journal of Conflict Resolution* 31, no. 2 (1987): 266–97; Doug McAdam, "Tactical Innovation and the Pace of Insurgency," *American Sociological Review* 48, no. 6 (1983): 735–54.

16. Lynette H. Ong, "Thugs-for-Hire: State Coercion and Everyday Repression in China." *China Journal* 80, no. 1 (2018): 94–110; Samson Yuen and Edmund W. Cheng. "Neither Repression nor Concession? A Regime's Attrition against Mass Protests," *Political Studies* 65, no. 3 (2017): 534–57.

17. Dan Slater, *Ordering Power: Contentious Politics and Authoritarian Leviathans in Southeast Asia.* (Cambridge: Cambridge University Press, 2010), 47.

18. Robertson, "Managing Society," 530.

19. Leo F. Goodstadt, "China and the Selection of Hong Kong's Postcolonial Political Elite," *China Quarterly* 163 (2000): 721–41.

20. Loh, *Underground Front*, 28–33.

21. Francis L. F. Lee and Joseph M. Chan, "Making Sense of Participation: The Political Culture of Pro-Democracy Demonstrators in Hong Kong," *China Quarterly* 193 (2008): 88.

22. Protest leader, interview, September 2, 2015.

23. Hong Kong Federation of Students, *An Open Letter to Ms Carrie Lam Cheng Yuet-Ngor*, October 2, 2014. https://www.hkfs.org.hk/an-open-letter-to-ms-carrie-lam-cheng-yuet-ngor-chief-secretary-for-administration-from-hkfs/.

24. "Hong Kong Chief Executive CY Leung Faces Questions Over Secret $7m Payout from Australian Firm," *Sunday Morning Herald*, October 8, 2014.

25. "Jianjue guanche 'sange jianding buyi'" [Firmly implement the three unswerving perseverance], *People's Daily Editorial*, October 2, 2014.

26. Protest leader, interview, March 16, 2016.

27. Interviews with foreign reporters who spoke to the politicians in early October, October 5, and November 21, 2014.

28. Brian C. H. Fong, "The Partnership between the Chinese Government and Hong Kong's Capitalist Class: Implications for HKSAR Governance, 1997–2012," *China Quarterly* 217 (2014): 195–220.

29. "Sai Wan Ruling Hong Kong, The Liaison Office Goes Aboveground" (in Chinese), *Hong Kong Economic Journal*, March 2, 2017. Available at goo.gl/oUXucC.

30. Land Registry Public Records.

31. "Annual Report of the DAB, 2014–2016," *Ming Pao*, April 17, 2014.

32. Stan Hok-Wui Wong, "Gerrymandering in Electoral Autocracies: Evidence from Hong Kong," *British Journal of Political Science* (2017): 1–32.

33. Andrew G. Walder, "Local Governments as Industrial Firms: An Organizational Analysis of China's Transitional Economy," *American Journal of Sociology* 101, no. 2 (1995): 263–301.

34. Interviewswith journalists, September 15, 2016.

35. Lee and Zhang, "The Power of Instability."

36. "Annual Report of the DAB, 2014–2016."

37. Interviews with social workers, August 11, 2016.

38. Stan Hok-Wui Wong, "Resource Disparity and Multi-level Elections in Competitive Authoritarian Regimes: Regression Discontinuity Evidence from Hong Kong," *Electoral Studies* 33 (2013): 200–219.

39. Wong, "Resource Disparity," 205.

40. Francis L. F. Lee, and Angel M. Y. Lin, "Newspaper Editorial Discourse and the Politics of Self-Censorship in Hong Kong," *Discourse & Society* 17, no. 3 (2006): 331–58.

41. Donald Yam-kuen Tsang, "2007–08 Policy Address: A New Direction for Hong Kong," accessed on October 15, 2015, https://www.policyaddress.gov.hk/07-08/eng/docs/policy.pdf.

42. "Sai Wan Ruling Hong Kong."

43. "Scheme to Support Schools in Using Putonghua to Teach the Chinese Language Subject," Standing Committee on Language Education and Research, last accessed October 15, 2018, http://www.language-education.com/eng/pbt_pmic_faq.asp.

44. Edmund W. Cheng and Wai-yin Chan. "Explaining Spontaneous Occupation: Antecedents, Contingencies and Space in the Umbrella Movement," *Social Movement Studies* 16, no. 2 (2017): 222–39.

45. David A. Snow, Rens Vliegenthart, and Catherine Corrigall-Brown, "Framing the French Riots: A Comparative Study of Frame Variation," *Social Forces* 86, no. 2 (2007): 385–415.

46. Robert M. Entman, "Framing: Toward Clarification of a Fractured Paradigm," *Journal of Communication* 43 (1993): 52.

47. "A Hong Kong–Version Colour Revolution: Beijing's Harshest Warnings Yet on Occupy Protests," *South China Morning Post*, October 2, 2014.

48. "'Zhanzhong' po xianggang shi min gao han qing chang" ("Occupy Central" caused the public to call for clearance of protest sites) (in Chinese), *Global Times*, October 15, 2014; *People's Daily*, "Weihu xianggang fanrong wending" (Protect the stability and prosperity of Hong Kong), (in Chinese), October 1, 2014.

49. *Ta Kung Pao*, "Zhanzhong sanchou ke tao luangang zuize nantao" (Three clowns of the "Occupy Central" can escape from Hong Kong without responsibilities) (in Chinese), October 29, 2014.

50. *Oriental Daily*, "Zhanzhong yinfa houyizheng" (Occupy Central caused aftershocks), October 9, 2014; *Headline Daily*, "Meizhengfu shuxia jigou muhou bengshui" (US government–related organization provides financial support behind the scenes) (in Chinese), October 14, 2014.

51. Interviews with student activists, September 2, 2015; interview with occupy central leader, March 18, 2016.

52. Interview with occupy central leader, March 16, 2016; *New York Times*, October 17, 2014.

53. Interviews with senior executives of transportation companies, August 20 and 27, 2015.

54. "Hong Kong Police Set to Implement Court Order on Protesters," *Global Times*, November 12, 2014.

55. "Above All, Hong Kong Society Must Abide by the Rule of Law," *SCMP Editorial*, November 2, 2014.

56. "Minutes of Legislative Council Meeting on March 25, 2015," Hong Kong Legislative Council, accessed on October 15, 2018, http://www.legco.gov.hk/yr14-15/chinese/counmtg/hansard/cm20150325-translate-c.pdf; "Legco Discussion Document

CB(4)1386/16–17(07)," Hong Kong Legislative Council, accessed on October 15, 2018, http://www.legco.gov.hk/yr16-17/chinese/panels/ajls/papers/ajls20170718cb4-1386-7-c.pdf.

57. Interviews with politicians and activists, July 2 and August 22, 2015.

58. *SJ v Yan Shen* CAAR 10/2010; *HKSAR v Wong Yuk Man and Chan Wai Yip*, HCMA 453/2013.

59. Meyer and Staggenborg, "Movements."

60. Jennifer Earl, "Tanks, Tear Gas and Taxes: Toward a Theory of Movement Repression," *Sociological Theory* 21, no. 1 (2003): 44–68.

61. Loh, *Underground Front.*

62. Agnes Ku, "The Public Up against the State: Narrative Cracks and Credibility Crisis in Postcolonial Hong Kong," *Theory, Culture & Society* 18, no. 1 (2001): 121–44; Eliza W. Y. Lee, "Civil Society Organizations and Local Governance in Hong Kong," in *Repositioning the Hong Kong Government: Social Foundations and Political Challenges*, ed. Stephen W. K. Chiu, and Siu-lun Wong (Hong Kong: Hong Kong University Press, 2012), 147–64.

63. Tommy Cheung, "The Pro-Establishment Is Winning Online Opinion Battle" (in Chinese), *HK01*, December 13, 2016, available at https://goo.gl/UA3k3B.

64. "Senior Chinese Official Praises Anti-Independence Campaign by 'Silent Majority' Activist Robert Chow," *Hong Kong Free Press*, November 29, 2016. Available at goo.gl/EEEQu1.

65. "Dujia diaocha: Shenzhen yigongdui fugang fan gangdu" [Excusive investigation: Shenzhen's voluntary team traveled to attack Hong Kong independence] (in Chinese), *Initium*, December 6, 2016, available at goo.gl/Nppz85.

66. Cheung, "The Pro-Establishment Is Winning."

67. Gary King, Jennifer Pan, and Margaret Roberts, "How the Chinese Government Fabricates Social Media Posts for Strategic Distraction, Not Engaged Argument," *American Political Science Review* 111, no. 3 (2017): 484–501.

68. Interview with LegCo member, February 3, 2017.

9

PROTEST ART, HONG KONG STYLE

A Photo Essay

Oscar Ho

FIGURE 9.1. Invented by a high school girl as a do-it-yourself paper umbrella, the yellow umbrella became a popular creation, appearing throughout the occupied zones of the Umbrella Movement.

FIGURE 9.2. Tens of thousands of Hong Kong citizens responded to the call to join the "Occupy Central" demonstration for "real democracy."

FIGURE 9.3. Eighty-seven tear gas grenades were fired, and many, including young children, were injured.

FIGURE 9.4.   A confrontation between the demonstrators and police near the Government Headquarters.

FIGURE 9.5.   A student in Mongkok trying to stop the police from entering the occupied zone.

FIGURE 9.6. Innocent faces at the Admiralty, holding hands in solidarity as the police moved in.

FIGURE 9.7. Shaving one's hair is a gesture of showing determination. Exhausted and hurt after the police attack, demonstrators stayed on.

FIGURE 9.8. The number of occupation participants increased after the tear gas attack; many stayed overnight and made the streets their home.

FIGURE 9.9. Umbrellas destroyed were turned into quilts; tents were built or brought in for shelter.

FIGURE 9.10. The village at the Admiralty.

FIGURE 9.11. A map was made at the exit of the subway station at the Admiralty next to the occupied zone. The map indicated some of the key spots such as the library, the study corner, medical and supplies centers, toilets, and other services.

FIGURE 9.12. As more and more people moved in, a village was formed. Volunteers built a study corner with a library, and volunteer tutors helped students with their homework.

FIGURE 9.13.   The atmosphere of the community formed at the occupied zone was not always tense and confrontational. There were also moments of fun and games. Here, the youngsters play the rock-paper-scissors game to determine work assignments.

Creative Expressions

One of the most outstanding achievements of the Occupy Movement was its artistic creation during the occupation, inside and outside of the occupied zones. The movement triggered an unprecedented outburst of creative expressions, turning the occupied zones into giant theaters and galleries that provided new definitions of political/community art. The long period of occupation in which many young people were idle together encouraged and stimulated the making of images, writing, singing, and other creative acts to voice their desire, to draw attention from the public and the media, or simply to relieve their frustration over the betrayal and the deceptive promises of "one country, two systems."

Protest art, not the artwork by professional artists who were normally too consciously making "art," is a democratic act in which anyone can make art the way they like. It was the creative expression coming from the ordinary folks out of their need to express that was most outstanding. The forms of creative expressions ranged from dance, music, and image making to primal expressions such as body painting, tattooing, street performance, or traditional and newly invented rituals, making the occupied zone dazzlingly spectacular and lively. Outside the occupied zone, there were also countless images, texts, and animations delivered via websites, e-mail, and Facebook.

FIGURE 9.14.   Mui Chuek Yin, a well-known local dancer, spontaneously dances with friends on the street at the Admiralty.

FIGURE 9.15.   Creative works large and small could be seen everywhere at the occupied zones.

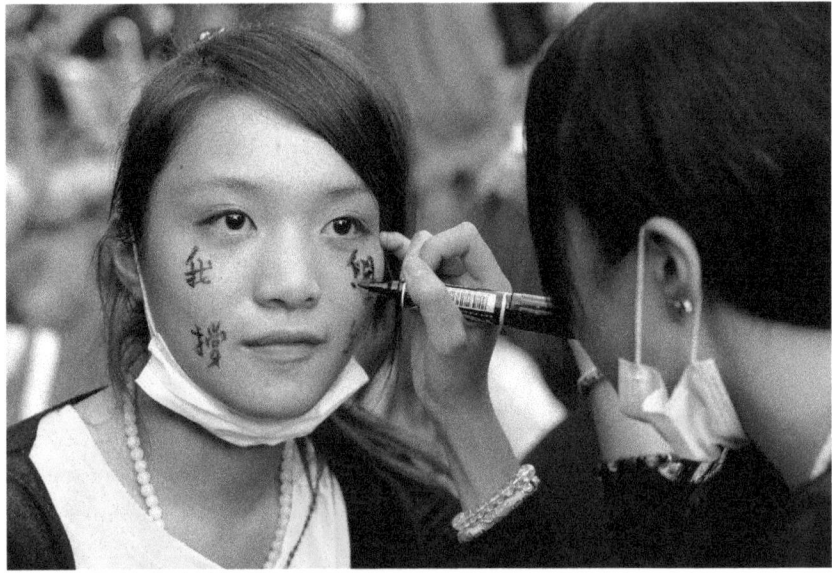

FIGURE 9.16.   A young demonstrator writing "I support students" on her face.

FIGURE 9.17.   The early stage of the Lennon Wall.

FIGURE 9.18.   Because the yellow umbrella was broadly recognized as a symbol of the movement, demonstrators frequently used it as a notebook for writing statements and drawing images.

One of the landmark artworks at the Admiralty was a collective installation along a stairway at the Government Headquarters. The impressive installation was afterward named the Lennon Wall, referring to the John Lennon–inspired wall in Prague during the 1980s social movement in Czechoslovakia. It began with a few stickers on which individuals wrote statements and pasted on the wall. As more and more people pasted their wishes and comments, the wall grew to be a monumental expression of the people, while individual messages could still be heard if one swam around that ocean of colorful stickers.

The occupation zones that transformed into colorfully diversified spaces for personal and collaborative expression reflected the poststructural spirit of the movement and the eclecticism of Hong Kong's culture, which is always willing to utilize and appropriate anything from anywhere provided it is serviceable, and if possible, attached with a touch of cynical fun.

To give birth to such an explosion of creativity, certain conditions were required. The urge to express oneself was the most forceful driving source that bypassed all conventions normally restricting creative expression. The seventy-nine days of occupation created a stable communal platform for such expression, like a giant canvas that was an ideal nurturing ground for creative interaction and stimulation.

FIGURE 9.19.   Workshops in folding yellow paper umbrellas were organized at the occupied zones where the umbrellas were freely distributed. Large and small installations with the little paper umbrellas appeared everywhere, echoing the aesthetic of the "small but collective monumental."

FIGURE 9.20.   A young girl resting on her bed with a poster of Buddha and the message "If Mongkok is lost, so will Admiralty" over her bed.

Running the risk of being overly generalized and ignoring the complex mixture of the participants at the three occupied zones, one may say that the three occupied zones each had their own characteristics. The Admiralty, where the government is headquartered, consisted of many students and academics, and Causeway Bay, a popular shopping district, had a strong middle-class presence. As for Mongkok—a unique district that mixes shopping, karaoke, street performance, bookstores, and underground activities within a highly condensed area—its distinctive characteristics created a population of working-class laborers, housewives, students, and people from marginal communities. It was the most diversified, complex, and culturally interesting zone. The strong presence of the working class and the rebellious spirit at the Mongkok occupied zone made the political arts there outstandingly colorful.

The ability to create commonly identified icons that highlight certain shared values and beliefs is essential to political art. Iconic images from popular culture—which are clear, direct, and loaded with easily understood meaning—are popular among young people. Images from Western, Japanese, and local popular cultures were employed, ranging from Hollywood superheroes to Winnie the Pooh and the Hongkongers' beloved Japanese creature Totoro.[1] They were instruments of empowerment and for building solidarity. One of the most devoted defenders was a gentleman known as Captain America, whose shield was frequently captured by the press.

FIGURE 9.21. Parents brought their children to the zone as part of family education.

FIGURE 9.22. Superheroes such as Spider Man and Captain America appeared at Mongkok and were popularly received as representations of power against evil and injustice.

A group of young people who called themselves the "Spider Kids" climbed up the Lion Rock, a steep mountain that stands tall in the middle of Kowloon, and hung an enormous "I want real universal suffrage" banner. The banner could be prominently seen from most parts of Kowloon. Such a superheroic act surprised the government and excited many. Although the banner was dismantled the next day, its image was permanently displayed on the Internet. With the advancement of digital media, any propaganda act, even one lasting only a few minutes, could be the subject of a picture and generate a powerful influence. The Spider Kids became mythical figures with their superhero act. Very soon, similar banners large and small appeared all over the city—on the streets, at schools, and on private homes—making the Lion Rock a new political icon for democracy.

The adaptation of popular culture not only created commonly identified images and values, but it also generated a sense of humor with a touch of cynicism, which is typical of Hong Kong's pop culture. Starting at the turn of the century, when street protest became a common activity in Hong Kong, a new concept called "happy confrontation" was invented. This was a belief that political confrontation could be undertaken in a celebrative mode and that street demonstrations could take the form of a carnival.

FIGURE 9.23.   Many went to Lion Rock and took pictures with the banner. Lion Rock became the holy mountain for many supporters of the movement.

FIGURE 9.24.   A game corner along with angry posters calling for a real election at the Admiralty.

Of course, there were people who disagreed with such a concept, especially for the Umbrella Movement, which was full of hardship, conflicts, and brutal attacks. The conflict became apparent when some people were playing Ping-Pong and having barbecues at the occupied zones, disregarding the attacks from the police and other progovernment groups. Nevertheless, throughout the occupation, such humor and cynicism could be easily found, especially at Mongkok. The demonstrators were fully aware of the power of making an emotional appeal and of agitation with a touch of humor.

The use of popular culture with a Hong Kong touch was exemplified by such absurd ways of dealing with abuse such as singing "Happy Birthday." During the occupation at Mongkok, progovernment groups, some of them employing gangsters, frequently moved in and used the most abusive language, if not downright physical acts attacking the occupants. Insisting on nonviolent resistance, the occupants retorted by collectively singing "Happy Birthday." Such a simultaneous, absurd response totally dumbfounded the attackers and many times successfully stopped the abuse. Such absurd tactics could only be found in Hong Kong because it comes straight from the "Mo lei tau" (totally doesn't make sense) culture best reflected in the popular films of Stephen Chow.[2]

The all-embracing culture of the post-1949 generations reflects a lack of cultural identification to which to turn and, simultaneously, a distrust of any

FIGURE 9.25.   At Mongkok, the garbage cans were turned into cartoon figures, creating a sense of humor within a heavily oppressed atmosphere.

governing authority. At the same time, the use of religious icons and rituals reveals another dimension of Hong Kong's cultural identification. Such identification bypasses the communist Chinese experience and returns to a rural religious tradition that was brought in and preserved by the older generations from Guangdong on the one hand and that echoes the colonial culture and education on the other. While much of China's religious tradition was wiped out after 1949, Hong Kong is one of the few places where various Chinese religious traditions have been practiced and preserved. In certain areas, Hong Kong is more traditionally Chinese than is China. For example, at the beginning of each year, one of the most important events about the city's future is the message[3] given to a government representative by Che Kung, a god of southern China who has a historical linkage with Hong Kong.[4]

This link between religious ritual and politics in cosmopolitan Hong Kong emerged in the Umbrella occupation too. Soon after the occupation of Mongkok, a shrine of the popular god Kwan Tei[5] was established to protect the demonstrators and became an important spot in the Mongkok zone. At a time when there were joint attacks from the police on the one side and commissioned gangsters on the other, the presence of Kwan Tei was needed because he is the god of brotherhood, righteousness, and justice. Ironically, both the police and gangsters traditionally worship Kwan Tei as their guardian god. Its presence at Mongkok was not

FIGURE 9.26. Kwan Tei temple at Mongkok.

only a reminder to the attackers of the virtues that Kwan Tei represented but also served as the supreme spiritual power protecting the righteous from evil attacks, whether from gangsters or the police.[6]

At the other side of the Mongkok zone was the St. Francis Chapel, where regular services and prayer meetings were held. It was later transformed from a small altar to a proper worship space where people gathered and prayed. In the middle of the altar was the picture of Jesus, and next to Jesus was the picture of the Archangel St. Michael, the "great prince who stands up for the children of your people."[7] Represented by the dragon on which he is stepping, St. Michael is not only the Satan slayer but also the patron saint of the police in Catholic tradition. There was a battle on earth as in heaven.

The two gods frequently appeared as major characters in the movement's creative expressions, mostly in comics, but also in other art forms, including a popular computer game in which Kwan Tei would come out to help fight against the police and gangsters at critical moments. On Connaught Road, the main street at the Admiralty, a religious motto was written: "In Hoc Signo Vinces" (in this sign you will conquer). With an ancient reference to a message Constantine I received from Jesus in a dream, the motto was once again being used to reassure participants of the promise of final victory. The sophistication in utilizing religious symbols and mottos was further elaborated by religious rituals.

FIGURE 9.27. Chapel at Mongkok

Gesture/rituals commonly appeared during the movement, such as holding up hands to signify "nonviolent" resistance or crossing hands to say "no." There were also the traditional folk religious rituals of "Three Kneeling Down and Nine Kowtow" performed by secondary school students to show their determination and humility and make their appeals to god.

FIGURE 9.28.   Holding both arms up was a common gesture during police attacks to show the movement's peaceful, nonviolent nature.

FIGURE 9.29.   Even after the occupied zones were cleared, religious rituals continued. Christmas carols, with lyrics rewritten to call for universal suffrage, were sung on the streets of Causeway Bay.

Religious rituals and ceremonies were common in Mongkok. Rituals such as the parade to welcome the landing of Kwan Tei from heaven or the bearing of suffering through the ritual of walking the "Fourteen Stations of the Cross" of Jesus were introduced to evoke spiritual power among the believers and to reassure the people of the promises of ultimate triumph.

FIGURE 9.30. Group of students taking an after-school picture to record the historical event in which they participated.

FIGURE 9.31. Dawn of December 17, exhausted and sad, some demonstrators sit and wait for the police to move in and arrested them.

FIGURE 9.32.   The day of retreat, December 17, 2014.

Mixing religion with popular culture as tools for propaganda and for entic-
ing spiritual power, the Umbrella Movement's creative expressions began a new
chapter of political art with its rich, sometimes primal application of icons and
symbols. It fully reflected the eclectic characteristics of Hong Kong culture, which
combines the transient mindset of a refugee culture that preserves some aspects
of Chinese and colonial cultures, as well as the rootlessness of the Hong Kong–
born generations. It also evinced the poststructural nature of the Umbrella Movement that allowed everyone the chance to express themselves without inhibition.

NOTES

1. Totoro is the character from the 1988 animation film *My Neighbor Totoro* by the
Japanese director Hayao Miyazaki. The film was popular in Hong Kong, and the image of
Totoro holding an umbrella is well known to Hongkongers.

2. Hong Kong film director whose mindless, absurd comedies have been extremely
popular in Hong Kong and Greater China during the 1990s and who was frequently
regarded as a typical representation of Hong Kong culture.

3. The message, which is called "chim" in Cantonese, is similar to O-mikuji Japanese at
a Japanese shrine, where one prays and randomly receives a message about the question
asked.

4. Che Kung was originally a general of the South Sung dynasty who accompanied the
last emperor in his flight from the Mongolian attack. He died on his way to Hong Kong.

5. Also known as Kwan Kung, a character of courage, royalty, fidelity, and justice from
the classic Chinese novel *Romance of the Three Kingdoms*. Later, he became a god endorsed
by both the Taoists and the Buddhists and was popularly worshiped.

6. On October 17, when the police attempted to clear Mongkok, they had to stop when
they reached Kwan Tei temple. Their fear of offending Kwan Tei was apparent.

7. Daniel 12:1, King James Version.

10

TAIWAN'S SUNFLOWER OCCUPY MOVEMENT AS A TRANSFORMATIVE RESISTANCE TO THE "CHINA FACTOR"

Jieh-min Wu

Historic events strike the world unexpectedly; social scientists cannot precisely predict the occurrence of a particular event, but when one does happen, we can explain why and how it happened with appropriate mechanisms and causal narratives.[1] The Sunflower Occupy Movement broke out in March 2014, shaking Taiwan's political landscape and its relations with China. The Sunflower Movement preceded the Umbrella Movement in just a few months. These two campaigns fought for democracy and autonomy from China, both were mobilized by civil forces and led by the youth, and activists from both places interacted frequently for mutual empowerment. The former caused the suspension of a trade agreement between Taiwan and China, a severe blow to Beijing's irredentism, while the latter failed to achieve the goal of direct election of the chief executive.

Before the Sunflower Movement, a pessimistic atmosphere had overwhelmed people striving for political autonomy, as an ascendant China kept swaying the political direction of the island. Since the mid-2000s, Beijing had adroitly employed its resources and cooperation with the Kuomintang government to absorb Taiwan further into the Chinese economic sphere, thereby leveraging economic dependence for political ends. Both sides signed a Services Trade Agreement (STA) in 2013, intended to deepen cross-strait economic integration, but without due consultation with Parliament and civil society. Until early 2014, things had been set firmly on a path favorable to Beijing's irredentist agenda. Overnight, though, that seemingly inexorable trend slowed; a majority of Taiwanese publicly embraced the occupation of Parliament, and the movement interrupted CCP-KMT cooperation and loosened a structure once deemed unbreakable. But how did this historic event happen, and why?

The Occupy Movement crystalized a subtle change in public perception of the "China factor." Hitherto deepening economic and social exchange with the Mainland had not brought the average citizen the benefits promised by the CCP-KMT cooperation platform. Instead, most of the economic advantages were reaped by the KMT's top leadership. Moreover, the STA, if implemented, would have posed a threat to Taiwan's disadvantaged industries and national security. The perception of a "China threat" loomed large in opposition to that of the "China opportunity." This helps to explain the legitimacy of Occupy as an act of civil disobedience, an unprecedented collective action initiated by youth and social movement groups at a time of political crisis. This chapter will demonstrate that momentum for a contentious mobilization against CCP-KMT cooperation had been accumulating for several years before the outbreak of the Sunflower Movement, thanks to the activism of civic groups. That movement in turn transformed social attitudes toward China.

First, the chapter accounts for the movement's emergence and immediate impact, and analyzes strategic interactions in light of short-term political opportunity. It then illustrates the "long path to the Sunflower Movement" by focusing on the turn of discourse, the surging protest cycle, and new protest repertoires leading to the Occupy actions. Thirdly, it elucidates the transformative nature of the movement. The final section will compare the cases of Taiwan and Hong Kong in terms of youth politics, civil society, and the China impact. The data used were collected through analysis of public opinion surveys, content analysis, in-depth interviews, and participant observation in Taiwan and Hong Kong from 2008 to 2016.

The Outbreak of the Occupation

At around ten past nine on the evening of March 18, 2014, some two hundred students, together with social movement activists, stormed into the Legislative Yuan (Taiwan's Parliament) and sat in the chamber for twenty-four days, further motivating nationwide protests. This action was intended to protest against the ruling Kuomintang's forcing through the ratification of a trade pact with China the previous day. The Cross-Strait Services Trade Agreement had been signed the previous summer, prompting enormous criticism from the opposition and civil society—even from an ex-adviser to then president Ma Ying-jeou—over concerns regarding its undemocratic "black-box manipulation" and potential damage to vulnerable industries and national security. Civil and student organizations had fought it ever since, demanding that the government conduct a comprehensive consultation with wider society before initiating the legislative process. The KMT had, as a result, signed an agreement with the opposition that "the STA should be subject to reviewing and voting article by article." Ma's government, however, broke its promise, determined as it was to pass the agreement hastily by using its parliamentary majority.

Process and Immediate Impacts

News of the occupation spread swiftly through social media and TV. Within hours, thousands of citizens had rushed to the scene, surrounding the Parliament compound to "defend" the students while NGO activists set up logistical support outside. The police tried at first to evict the occupiers, but in vain, and the speaker of the Legislative Yuan, Wang Jin-Pyng, decided not to summon additional forces to eject them. The core leadership of the protesters soon formed and demanded "retraction of the STA" and "enactment of an Oversight Law regulating the cross-Strait agreements."

On March 23, President Ma held a press conference, saying that he agreed with the principle of "reviewing and voting article by article" but refusing to retract the STA. Ma also condemned the occupation as illegal, while the protesters claimed it as an act of civil disobedience. On the evening of that same day, several groups of militant protesters, impatient with the stalemate and irked by Ma's intransigence, dared to escalate matters by trying to occupy the main building of the Executive Yuan.[2] This move was met with a fierce reaction by riot police, resulting in hundreds of injuries and scores of arrests. When photos and footage of the police beating unarmed protesters circulated in the following days, needless to say, the political crisis heightened. The violent crackdown enraged the public and triggered a massive demonstration in front of the Presidential Palace on March 30. Half a million citizens turned out, the largest rally in Taiwan's history. At this stage, the occupation enjoyed its highest approval in public opinion polls.[3]

President Ma remained uncompromising in the face of growing public discontent. The protest leaders were also faced with increasing pressure as the stalemate became a war of attrition, while their approval ratings began to dwindle. Both sides were competing for public support and legitimacy while seeking exit strategies. But fortune favored the occupiers. Through rounds of communication (about which the details remain unclear), on April 6 Wang Jin-Pyng announced as speaker that he would not convene the interparty negotiation on the STA until the aforementioned Oversight Law had been enacted; this amounted to an indefinite suspension of the review of the trade pact and came close to the occupiers' demands.[4] The next day, the leadership decided to end the occupation on April 10.

The movement delivered a severe blow to President Ma, to his ruling Kuomintang, and to CCP-KMT cooperation. When a Chinese official in charge of Taiwan affairs visited the country afterward, he encountered protests wherever he went and was forced to truncate his schedule. Consequently, that year's annual CCP-KMT forum was suspended. In November, the KMT lost the local elections to the Democratic Progressive Party (DPP), which would go on to win the 2016 presidential and legislative elections.

Political Opportunity in Short-Term Perspective

With hindsight, speaker Wang honored his "tacit pact" with the movement, and the STA has not been ratified thus far.[5] Wang's decision was widely believed to have been motivated by his power struggle with President Ma, who had since the previous year alienated Wang by accusing him of illegal lobbying and attempting to bring him down. The Ma-Wang split within the KMT had in effect created a political opportunity for the movement. But the protesters evidently did not realize it as an opportunity to be exploited at the time of launching the occupation; they only discovered it ex post facto during the movement.[6]

From a short-term perspective, the struggle between Ma and Wang was key to shaping the dynamics of the Sunflower Movement. Let us illustrate the multilateral interaction step by step. To begin with, since 2005 the KMT had adopted a rapprochement with its arch-rival CCP, based on the so-called "1992 Consensus" (the one-China principle), aiming at slowing the tide toward Taiwanese independence. When the KMT won the presidential election in 2008, it began to implement the mutually agreed cooperation agenda, including signing the Economic Cooperation Framework Agreement (ECFA) in 2010. The disputed STA of 2013 was one subsequent pact within the ECFA. Beijing proceeded by offering "concessionary policies" to Taiwan, but the so-called "peace dividends" were nothing but political prizes granted to a cross-strait government-business coalition. Under the monopolized CCP-KMT platform, the DPP had virtually no say on issues concerning Mainland affairs until the outbreak of the Sunflower Movement. During President Ma's tenure (2008–2016), civil society kept a watchful eye on KMT policies insofar as they touched upon predatory developmental projects, democratic careening, and an overly pro-China stance. Civil groups and the social movement sector maintained a conditional, issue-by-issue coalition with the DPP. As the DPP was sidelined by the KMT, it was civic activism that created "opposition momentum" over many issues such as anti-land-grab protests, environmental protection, labor disputes, and

China policies. When the occupation took place, DPP legislators immediately jumped in to "protect the students" and helped facilitate talks between occupiers and authorities. The outbreak of the movement suddenly launched the DPP back to the table, offering it an opportunity to adopt a firmer anti-STA stance. Amid complex and multiple strategic interactions, the previously emergent Ma-Wang struggle provided the opportunity for an exit strategy in favor of the occupiers.

One might be tempted to attribute the pivotal dynamics of the Sunflower Movement to the Ma-Wang struggle in the light of political opportunity structure theories in the literature of contentious politics.[7] If we adopt a long-term perspective, however, the intra–ruling bloc's split becomes just a partial factor; we need a longitudinal viewpoint to better understand the process of social mobilization against the KMT government and, more critically, the "China factor." First, in the broader sense of "social movement," the Sunflower Movement was a continuation of the anti-STA movement that had germinated upon the signing of the trade agreement in 2013. Second, the fight against China's threats can trace its roots back to the 1990s. Ever since Ma Ying-jeou took office in 2008, protests about China had occupied a significant part of the protest cycle. Meanwhile, public discourse on the China factor emerging before the Sunflower Movement paved the way for a "consensus mobilization" for self-defense against China's aggressive interventions.[8] Moreover, the Ma-Wang split should not be construed merely in terms of personal animosity: in fact, the conflict stemmed from a deeper structure of factional and ethnic politics. On Taiwan's political scene, Wang Jin-Pyng embodied the indigenous factions within the KMT, the so-called "nativists," while Ma Ying-jeou represented the Mainlander elite who emigrated to Taiwan in 1949 and had ruled the country for half a century. During the authoritarian period (1949–1986), the KMT purposefully cultivated local native factions, a tool of divide-and-rule. Since democratization, though, there had been intermittent advocacy for the "nativization" of the KMT, a euphemism for the dissolution of the Mainlander-centered political dominance. Ma, however, as a second-generation Mainlander party head, "sees the rejuvenation of the party, that is, to eliminate the negative influence of the local factions, as his mission. This deems a big trouble between Wang and Ma because Ma's strategy clashed with the idea of nativization."[9] Ma's antagonistic moves against Wang were depicted by nativists as "Mainlanders bullying the Taiwanese."[10] The ethnopolitical rift within the KMT represented a longstanding Mainlander-native chasm in the state-society relationship. Above all, a short-term perspective, though an apt account for a denouement favorable to the protesters, cannot fully explain the dynamics of the movement.

The Path to the Sunflower Movement

The Sunflower Movement was a culmination of resistance to China's political influence and to the KMT government's democratic careening. It arose from a changing political atmosphere and a wave of interconnected social protests in preceding years. This section analyzes the path leading to that final eruption.

A Discursive Turn: Pinpointing the China Factor

China, a constant presence for the Taiwanese people during the Cold War, was a mirror image of the Kuomintang émigré regime's ideology. Defeated by the communists on the Mainland in 1949, the KMT fled to Taiwan, proclaimed itself the sole legitimate government of China, and with its anticommunist propaganda pledged to "recover the Mainland" until the late 1960s. A fictional version of China served to legitimize dictatorship. Taiwan only began to get a feel for the *actual* China toward the end of the 1980s, when the ban on visiting the Mainland was lifted and businesspeople began to invest there. The Taiwanese felt the heat of a rising China during the 1996 presidential election, when the PLA launched missiles near Taiwan in an attempt to derail the process. Beijing feared that the direct election of a Taiwanese president symbolized the practice of popular sovereignty. Once Beijing had enacted an irredentist claim on Taiwan, the issue of the "China threat" surfaced. Since then, Beijing has intervened in every national-level election in Taiwan.

With the DPP winning presidential power for the first time in 2000, Beijing turned to the KMT as a confederate in reining in this "indigenous regime," and the two arrived at a collaboration pact in 2005 in the form of the so-called "CCP-KMT cooperation platform," which would promote the image of the "China opportunity." At the same time, apart from this approach of direct menace (though often failed or insufficient), China added a new modus operandi: exerting pressure indirectly through economic incentives by way of a cooperative KMT, local political figures, and Taishang (Taiwanese people doing business both in Taiwan and China).[11] The case of these Taishang is particularly illuminative. Beijing called this strategy "using business to encircle politics." Beijing utilized economic integration to set up cross-strait networks and cultivate "local collaborators," who spoke on behalf of Chinese interests at critical junctures. In 2012, echelons of tycoons loudly supported the "1992 Consensus" during the presidential campaign, helping to induce "economic voters" to re-elect Ma Ying-jeou.[12] And China indeed altered some people's preferences through this maneuver.[13] Beijing also encouraged Taishang to buy news outlets and placed "embedded marketing deals" in Taiwan's news media. The case of the "Want Want *China*

Times Group" was spectacular, serving as it did as an "agent" for outsourcing paid news on behalf of the Chinese authorities. The Control Yuan investigated the company's behavior and rectified the relevant government agencies, but the paid news deals continued.[14] The contested Cross-Strait Services Trade Agreement was a continuation of such an economic united front strategy.

The China threat had become a daily reality, but how was the social movement sector to deal with this emerging situation? Problems were debated: was China a rival state to fight against? How was this adversary to be named? In the old KMT textbook propaganda, its arch-enemies were the "Communist bandits" who robbed the Mainland. Such state ideology had gradually been phased out since the 1980s, but the "anticommunist" mantra was still engraved in people's minds. In effect, China is no longer a communist regime but a booming capitalist state (though with rampant corruption and without democracy); the KMT and the CCP are not enemies; instead, both parties cooperated to stymie Taiwanese independence. "Anticommunist" discourse was not an appropriate frame for the movement. A new concept was needed to grasp the reality. The concept of the "China factor" is crucial to the civic movement in its resistance to Chinese interference. Yet it took a while for the term to emerge into public discourse. As early as 2009, a few journalists and scholars had called attention to the term,[15] but it was not frequently used until 2012 simply because "China" remained a taboo term, prohibited by both Beijing and the KMT: both see giving the Mainland the cognomen "China" as tantamount to asserting Taiwan as a separate political entity. Until Ma's presidency, the KMT's official stance was to call China "the Mainland," which dovetailed nicely with the official line of the People's Republic of China.[16] Furthermore, any mention of "China" in cross-strait affairs or any sharp critique of the Chinese state would be dubbed irrational "China-phobia" under the Chinese nationalism upheld by both CCP and KMT. An inevitable outcome of this enduring ideological hegemony was self-censorship, even for the movement's activists.

The "China factor" first became a catchphrase in the civic movement's fight against Chinese penetration in 2012. A banner reading "Face Up to the China Factor" appeared that year in a parade (the Anti-Media Monopoly Movement) protesting against the Want Want *China Times* Group. The slogan pointed to the fact that Beijing was using Taishang to manipulate public opinion. Some of the organizers of the protest recalled that there was an intense debate within the group before a consensus was reached on adopting the term "China factor."[17] One student leader described how China factor discourse was suppressed:

> Looking back at the movements in those years, [I observed] there was a
> weird atmosphere. The Wild Strawberry Student Movement [in 2008]

was triggered by the visit of [the Chinese official in charge of cross-strait exchanges] Chen Yun-Lin, but its appeals entirely avoided mentioning China. . . . The DPP was crying out for Taiwanese independence. . . . However, the students thought, "It was vile." . . . Everybody was self-censoring, not to call for Taiwanese independence. . . . Up until July 2012 [during the Anti-Media Monopoly Movement], everybody plainly knew that there was the China factor operating behind the scenes, but did not speak out squarely.[18]

So the cause of independence was for young activists still taboo in 2012. More significantly, this recollection suggests the complicated play of *identifying* the actor, *naming* the rival, and *framing* the movement. And the power of a movement comes from an accurate signifier that hits the mark.

"China factor" discourse differed from conventional Taiwanese independence advocacy in several ways. First, it proposed a new way of analyzing existential China by emphasizing influence mechanisms such as Taishang; by contrast, traditional calls for independence stressed ethnonational identity. Second, it allowed for empirical studies of political economy and economic statecraft by analyzing cross-strait capital activities and cross-border class issues, previously unseen by the public eye.[19] Above all, it focused on self-defense for liberty and democracy without resorting to the hoary old language of "anticommunist struggle," which proved unsavory to younger generations.

Public discourse was thus able to pinpoint China's influence, opening up the way for the subsequent campaign against the Services Trade Agreement. The new perspective served as a "master frame" in social movement theories.[20] It bridged widespread discontent and political threats and opportunities.[21] The actors would not have been able to grasp the factor of "operating behind the scenes" without such an apt cognitive frame. On the eve of the Sunflower Movement, most people had a sense of China's overwhelming influence, and the contestation over the Services Trade Agreement revealed Beijing's grand strategy toward Taiwan and offered a critical momentum for the movement to shake off the suppression of talk of the China factor.

The Surging Protest Cycle and Innovative Repertoires

In 2008, the KMT took power back from the DPP. Ma Ying-jeou won landslide elections for president and Parliament by running on a platform of a better economy, to be achieved preferably by means of improving relations with the Mainland. Since the return of the KMT, however, an array of quasi-authoritarian measures in the economic sphere had resurfaced, including predatory

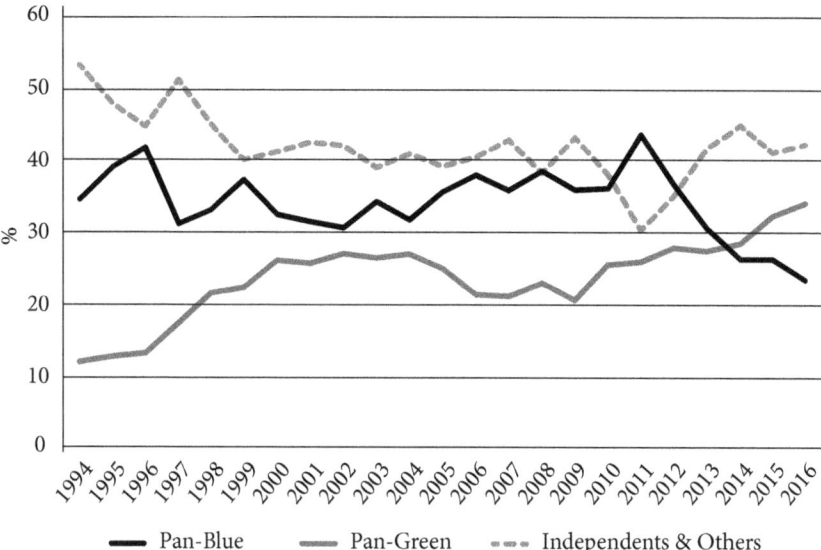

FIGURE 10.1. Trend of party preferences in Taiwan, 1994–2016
Source: TEDS, NCCU.

development projects, aggressive urban renewal, looser environmental standards, and ignoring unemployed workers' grievances. Social protests screamed out in response. In his second term (2012–2016), Ma expressed an even stronger determination to draw Taiwan closer to the Mainland, yet his "lean-to-China policies" did not deliver the promised economic gains for the average citizen but instead caused acute societal anxiety over being infiltrated by Chinese political influence. The steady drip of unpopular policies eroded support for the KMT government. Figure 10.1 indicates a trend in voters' preference for the "blue camp" (with the KMT as leading party) over the "green camp" (led by the DPP). Noticeably, the KMT's popularity had begun to plummet since 2012, two years before the explosion of the Sunflower Movement. This erosion of popularity signified an imminent crisis for the KMT.

Societal grievances and mounting discontent quickly fermented into a surging cycle of collective protest accompanied by episodic rallies over China and CCP-KMT cooperation prior to March 2014. Several major incidents amid this protest cycle helped to forge organizational capacities and solidarity indispensable for the massive mobilization in the subsequent Sunflower Movement:

- The Chen Yun-lin Incident, November 2008. The first ever visit of a Chinese envoy to Taiwan led to several days of massive protest. The police confiscated demonstrators' ROC (Republic of China, the current national title of Taiwan) flags and cracked down on protesters with a ferocity unseen for two decades. This further led to a months-long student movement, the so-called "Wild Strawberry," and gave rise to civil groups who later played a significant role in the rallies resisting China's encroachment.

- The Kadeer Documentary Incident, 2009. The Chinese authorities demanded that the Kaohsiung government withdraw a documentary about the exiled Uyghur leader Rebiya Kadeer from an officially sponsored film festival. Local politicians and tourism interest groups collaborated in exerting pressure. Protests by the opposition DPP and civil organizations helped the local government to successfully resist pressure from Beijing.

- The Chung Ting-Bang Incident, 2012. Chung Ting-Bang, a Taiwanese practitioner of Falun Gong, traveling to China to visit relatives and was arrested on a charge of "jeopardizing national security." Numerous NGOs in Taiwan and abroad interceded on his behalf, and Chung was released nearly two months later.

- The Anti-Media-Monopoly Movement, 2012. This movement was mobilized to fight the Want Want *China Times* Group and its owner's blunt pro-China speeches, as mentioned above. Composed of several waves of street protest, the movement went on for an entire year. It also provoked heated debate as to the role of the Chinese government. Activists were divided over whether the protest's major target was the "capital factor" or the "China factor," though in retrospect these proved to be conflated simply because Beijing deployed a stratagem of "commercialized United Front Work" using Taishang to manipulate public opinion. Finally, a core group of the movement's organizers persuaded others to adopt the "China factor" as a framework. This Anti-Media-Monopoly Movement involved many civil and student organizations and may be considered as a rehearsal of the necessary social solidarity that preceded the Sunflower Movement.

- The Anti–Services Trade Agreement Movement, 2013–2014. This trade agreement was signed on June 21, 2013. That same day, several civil and social movement groups began protests, and in July they formed an anti-STA umbrella organization, the Democratic Front (DF), which led discourse and mobilization through to the eruption of the Sunflower Movement. Later, a nationwide student organization, the Black Island Nation Youth Front (BINYF), was established, with opposition to the STA as its primary raison d'être. Members of the BINYF were active in protests leading up to the Sunflower Movement and afterwards. The DF, as a key node in the network, acted as a bridge for mutual trust and cooperation among the various member groups under the umbrella. Trust and coalition were deemed preconditions for efficient mobilization for the twenty-four days of occupation.

So the above protests anticipated the final eruption. But how to account for the conflation of the China-related and non-China-related movement sectors in those years of evolution?

We found a transitivity effect that linked actors in different issue areas. Using network analysis, the author's research team found that the Sunflower Movement, defined as an "event," stood at the peak of interconnected events during the protest cycle from January 2012 to April 2014, while anti-nuclear-power protests and human rights activities, among others, helped to expand and intensify movement networks. The Sunflower occupation brought together a wide range of groups with diverse foci and formed a large-scale, cross-issue coalition.[22] Probing deeper, the movement solidarity necessary for a large-scale event like the Sunflower Movement had already come into existence among groups and activists through networks, in which the mutual trust, tacit understanding, and shared cultures of NGO activists made possible an unprecedented mobilization.[23]

We can also quantitatively measure the cumulative effect of social protest mobilization on the eve of the Sunflower Movement by taking March 2014 as a cutoff point. The author conducted a protest event analysis and documented a total of 1,494 events from January 2012 (the year in which protests against China-related issues became frequent) to March–April 2014 (the months of Sunflower Occupy), with a total of 1,430,111 participants.[24] Table 10.1 indicates the "explosiveness" of the Sunflower Movement, contrasting March–April 2014 with the preceding twenty-six months. In the period January 2012–February 2014, we recorded a sum of 1,277 protest incidents, of which merely 4.9 percent related to China, whereas in March–April 2014 alone, 94 incidents were concerning China, which amounted to 43.3 percent of all incidents. Regarding the scale of mobilization, from January 2012 to February 2014, China-related issues accounted for just 2.9 percent of all protest participants, whereas in March–April 2014 China-related actions attracted 198,057 participants, 62.7 percent of all participants, eclipsing all other protests. One can almost feel the calm before the storm. China-related protests seemed less tangible than other issues before March 2014. As argued above, however, the general protest cycle had prepared massive rallying against the China factor in terms of movement networks, mobilization skills, and innovative repertoires.

Further focusing on the timespan of the Sunflower Movement (March 18 to April 10, 2014), we found that because of the tensions at play within the

TABLE 10.1 Frequencies and scale of protest incidents, January 2012–March 2014

	FREQUENCIES: COUNT OF INCIDENTS		SCALE OF MOBILIZATION: PARTICIPANTS	
	CHINA-RELATED INCIDENTS	ALL OTHER INCIDENTS	CHINA-RELATED INCIDENTS	ALL OTHER INCIDENTS
Jan. 2012–Feb. 2014	62 (4.9%)	1,215 (95.1%)	32,313 (2.9%)	1,081,730 (97.1%)
March-April 2014	94 (43.4%)	123 (56.7%)	198,057 (62.7%)	118,008 (37.3%)

movement, counteractions on the ground, including people opposing "China interference" and others upholding "mother China," were recorded as consisting of up to twenty-two occurrences during that short period. One might wonder, given such tense mobilization and countermobilization, whether China-related protests were more violent than others? This hypothesis is refuted statistically.[25] Furthermore, we find that China-related events tend to be more innovative in action repertoire.

The Sunflower Movement employed a broad spectrum of repertoires. The means of collective protest are embedded in specific cultures and tend to be stable within a protest cycle. Within the trend of escalating confrontation with the Ma government, particularly over its predatory development projects and China policies, we can observe that a variety of repertoires—e.g. occupation as civil disobedience, shoe throwing, and demonstrations by ostensible passersby—became the prevailing tactics. Throwing shoes and occupation are certainly not local inventions, but borrowed through a learning process under globalization. In the process of appropriation, these need to be put into continual practice to become localized repertoires.

Long before the current idea of occupation entered the horizon of Taiwanese activists, the "blockade" was commonly used in environmental protests, with residents blocking the gates of polluting factories. Occupation in the wave of Arab uprisings and antiausterity campaigns (2011 to 2013) featured demonstrations in public spaces such as plazas and parks, using camping and horizontal direct democracy as major repertoires.[26] In its local innovation, "occupation" conveys a brand new tactic, though suggestive of the conventional means of blockade, intended to interrupt the normal operation of government agencies by breaking into buildings and obstructing official work. The core idea is to make heavily guarded central government offices the focus of protest.

The young protesters experimented with this notion of occupation in several episodes before occupying Parliament. On August 15, 2013, during the Dapu anti-land-grab campaign, a small group of protesters from the "Taiwan Rural Front" raided the Executive Yuan. They dressed up as tourists from the Mainland, with the police being on low alert for such characters. They broke into the sealed compound of the Executive Yuan and threw eggs and paint, but they failed to get into the main building. This surprise attack was carried out under the slogan "Tearing Down the Government," in reprisal for the government's demolition of citizens' properties. Three days later, the same group launched an even bolder action. Hundreds of youths occupied the plaza surrounding the Ministry of the Interior overnight. A couple months later, another group, its members overlapping with the above organization, attempted to occupy a landmark city gate near the Presidential Palace. The action failed because the police had gotten wind of it and deployed a heavy guard beforehand, but the protesters learned from it. They did not carry out these actions in anticipation of the occupation of Parliament; such a line of argument is causally flawed. In retrospect, however, this series of actions had unintentionally prepared a contingent condition: the youngsters repeatedly practiced the repertoire of occupation and cultivated the skills and the mutual trust necessary for the occupation.

The Art of Occupation

On March 18, 2014, the occupation was triggered by the KMT's legislative gambit lacking due process. It was unexpected, but it was neither uncoordinated nor chaotic, decided as it was at a time of sudden political crisis. In fact, the entire movement combined a coordinated leadership and a variety of horizontal and direct actions. A core group took the initiative on the evening of March 18, scores of social and civic movement groups joined in immediately, and thousands of citizens had rushed to the scene by the wee hours. This massive gathering made it difficult for the police to evict the students in the Parliament chamber at that moment without large-scale reinforcement. Inside Parliament, the youngsters displayed the power of collective action, muscular but nonviolent, forceful but innovative. For instance, they stacked the legislators' chairs into barricades to block the entrances into the chamber right after they had ejected the guards. They immediately set up communication channels with activists outside and with news media and broadcast the ongoing action via social media. The occupation was so powerful because it outright negated the legitimacy of the KMT-dominated Parliament, which was abruptly incapacitated as if a central nerve of the body politic were severed. This may explain why the Ma government decided to immediately crack down on the attempt to occupy the Executive Yuan, the center of national administration, with overwhelming police force on the night of March 23.

The twenty-four-day occupation demonstrated spontaneity and creativity. With the occupation secured, a full set of the necessary *personnel* for battle—decision-making and coordination meetings, multiple-language translation teams, and a picket section—were all in place inside Parliament. Outside, participants engaged spontaneously in a division of labor for matériel, including a food supply (a "battlefield kitchen" volunteered by catering chefs, among others), lavatories and shower facilities, stage equipment, camping gear, Internet services, medical care, legal and psychological counseling, and even garbage recycling. This was done mostly without vertical coordination with the core leadership inside the Parliament. There were also plenty of satirical posters and artwork created on the spot. Noticeably, a new genre of "deliberation on the street" was practiced. Measures of deliberative and participatory democracy had been a frequent feature in Taiwan, but this discussion on the Services Trade Agreement took the form of an unprecedented outdoor deliberation that involved thousands of participants. The movement pulled together a variety of previous repertoires and transformed them in creative ways, redefining street actions. "Passersby demonstrations" were one such action whose significance was reinvented. Initially, a pro-China party used it to disturb the occupiers, but then the occupiers used it to confront the police. Besides, the occupation of Parliament inspired many spontaneous protests nationwide. In this way, the movement embodied a certain degree of "order-in-anarchy" because its organizational character was a mixture of structured leadership and direct, decentered action. Unsurprisingly, problems of miscommunication and mistrust, line struggle, and emotional outbursts emerged; overall, however, the movement displayed spontaneity, solidarity, and self-control.

Transformative Effects

As argued by William Sewell, "Events may be defined as that relatively rare subclass of happenings that significantly transforms structures. An eventful temporality, therefore, is one that takes into account the transformation of structures by events."[27] The Sunflower Movement stands as one such rare event in which powerful collective action ruptures the structures confining a country. "Structures" here refers to two kinds of structure that constrain the space of individual and collective action but also induce action within this space: the structure of political rules, and that of ideology. This popular upsurge brought about tremendous impact, not merely transforming the political landscape of Taiwan but also diverting the political direction of the country from the KMT's pro-China policy, thus interrupting the course of a decade-long CCP-KMT cooperation. It is still too early to discuss the long-term transformations initiated by the movement, but some short-term outcomes have been advanced and deserve analysis.

Changing Structures of Political Rules and Ideology

The movement damaged the KMT's legitimacy by exposing its undemocratic dealings with Beijing, and it broke off the CCP-KMT cooperation platform. Opinion polls show that the ruling party began to lose its lead during 2012–2013; the occupation delivered a fatal blow, and the KMT's popularity continued to deteriorate since the Sunflower Movement (see figure 10.1 above). At the end of 2014, the KMT suffered unprecedented losses in local elections. The opposition DPP took four of six municipalities, while the capital, Taipei, was won by an independent supported by the Green camp. It is telling that the KMT's candidate for Taipei City, Sean Lien, was depicted during the election as a key member of the privileged cross-strait group and a second-generation wealthy son in silk pajamas. Sean Lien's father, former KMT chairman Lien Chan, had facilitated cooperation with the CCP in April 2005, just one month after Beijing had passed the "Anti-Secession Law" aimed at Taiwan. Since then, Lien Chan and his entourage had frequently visited China in conjunction with business tycoons, political notables, and religious leaders. It was widely reported that this "trans-strait politico-business group" reaped the bulk of the "peace dividends" while disregarding Taiwan's national security and sovereignty. The exposing of the Lien family's China ties was critical to Sean Lien's defeat.

Even more tellingly, a dramatic turnaround in public trust in both parties regarding prospective negotiation with the Chinese government occurred within a short period. According to a 2013 survey, when the KMT was already on the downward slope in terms of party preferences, it still enjoyed a commanding 50 percent of trust, compared to the DPP's 35 percent (see table 10.2 below). But by 2015, the year following the Sunflower Movement, the KMT had lost its trust to the DPP; by 2016, the DPP had reversed its previous disadvantage. As a result, the CCP-KMT platform lost all credibility, and it is not difficult to pinpoint the relationship between the two: the KMT had been the local agent in implementing the CCP-KMT cooperation agenda and had to suffer a loss of the people's trust when the people decided that the China opportunity was an empty promise and that the China threat turned out to be tangible. This may help to explain the discursive turn of the China factor at the popular level and the surging, contentious wave in defiance of the Ma government. In this sense, the Sunflower Movement represents a social resistance movement against the PRC.

The movement has simultaneously transformed the structure of political forces in Taiwan and across the strait. The propaganda war over the "1992 Consensus,"

TABLE 10.2 Public trust in the parties regarding political negotiation with China (%)

YEAR	2013	2105	2016
Trust in KMT	50	37	33
Trust in DPP	35	44	51
Trust in both	2	2	2
Trust in neither	11	14	10
Others	2	3	4
Sample size	1220	1252	1206

Question asked: If Taiwan is to conduct political negotiations with Mainland China, would you trust a KMT Government or a DPP Government more?"

Sources: compiled from China Impact Survey (CIS) 2013, 2015, 2016, Academia Sinica, Taiwan.

a salient feature of the 2012 presidential election, ceased to be effective in the 2016 campaign. The author's research found that the effect of the 1992 Consensus was by 2016 negligible compared to 2012.[28] Meanwhile, attitudes toward the Sunflower Movement became a significant factor in explaining voters' choices in 2016. Those who approved of the movement tended not to vote for the KMT's candidate. The power of the movement laid bare the rhetorical (in)validity of economic prosperity suggested by the 1992 Consensus. Henceforth, Taiwan's civil society became a determinant in cross-strait affairs. It is no exaggeration to say that civil resistance defeated Chinese interference in the 2016 election, while the movement simultaneously broke loose the structures of political rules and ideology.

Youth Politics and the Rejuvenation of Taiwanese Independence

Young activists are major actors in this wave of contentious politics. It is intriguing to discover how they have become politically engaged, how they have negotiated their political identities, and how the Sunflower Movement has transformed them. We examine the quantitative changes in national identity over the period under study. Figures 10.2 and 10.3 compare people's attitudes toward "independence" and "unification" in four waves of surveys within a span of five years. If we look at the averages, the overall trends in pro-independence or pro-unification have not changed substantially. When we break down the samples by age group, however, we find that support for independence has increased from 43 to 56 percent for those aged twenty to thirty-four years. There is no similar change in other age groups (figure 10.2). In addition, unification has for a long time been unattractive, and it is particularly unappealing to Taiwan's youth. For the majority of people, "unification" means a passive annexation by the PRC rather than an active choice. We do not find a drastic drop in support for unification in this group, perhaps because it is already below 10 percent. Nonetheless, the elderly show a faster decline in their taste for unification (figure 10.3). To sum up, we have observed a rejuvenatory trend for Taiwanese independence, precipitated by the Sunflower Movement.

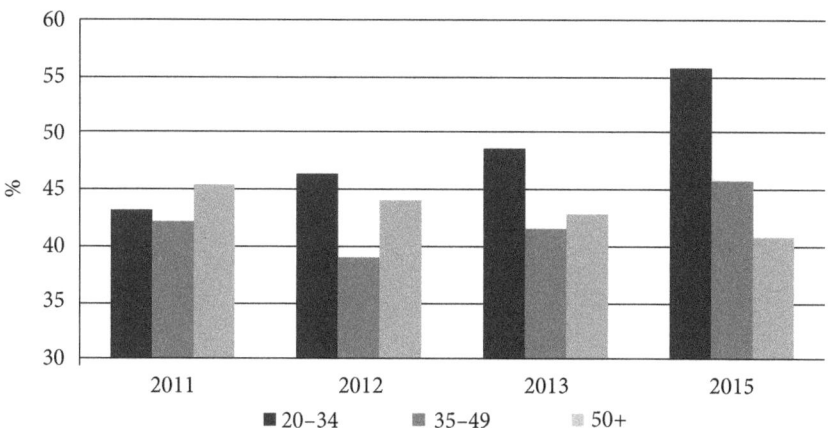

FIGURE 10.2. Trend of pro-independence by age groups, 2011–2015

Source: CIS, Academia Sinica.

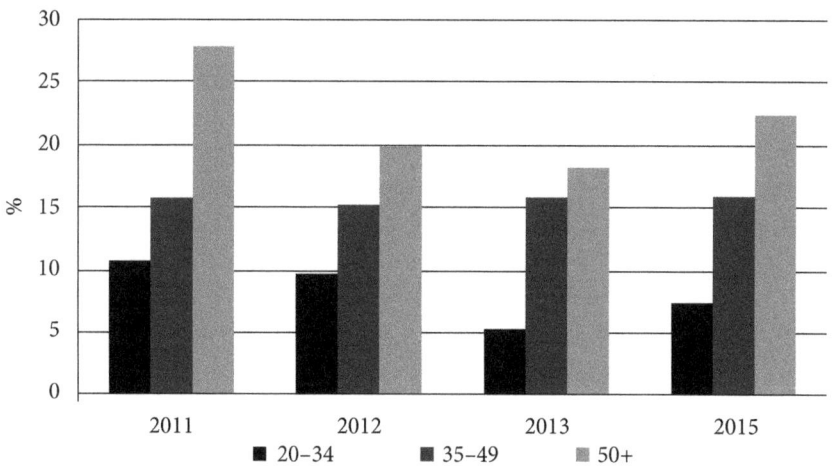

FIGURE 10.3. Trend of pro-unification by age groups, 2011–2015

Source: CIS, Academia Sinica.

Along with protest movements, youngsters' rising support for Taiwanese independence has given birth to a new term: "born independentist." It suggests that younger generations support the idea of independence as a consequence of their "natural disposition," through their lived experience of the world and their educational upbringing in schools that are no longer China-centric. This simple image of the "born independentist," however, may be misleading, as reflected upon by one activist:

> It's true that we often hear the phrase *tianrandu*, but I think that when it comes to the issue of independence, we need to return to the idea of sovereignty. [We are now in a situation of] de facto independence; we are mutually exclusive with the communist regime. As yet, [the formation of independence consciousness] requires a process of transformation for the so-called *tianrandu* generation. Rigorously speaking, they should be called "*tianrantai*" [born Taiwanese]; they identify themselves as Taiwanese, but they may approve of the Republic of China [the current national title of Taiwan, yet unrecognized by world powers] as a sovereign state, and may even regard themselves as Chinese at the same time. So, to be exact, they are the *tianrantai* generation; a majority of them do not understand the predicament of Taiwan's sovereignty status.[29]

This activist rejected the formula of an "independent ROC statehood on Taiwan" acceptable to generations "born Taiwanese." In his reflection, a born independentist means one who has a conscious aspiration after a Taiwan independence movement, while a born Taiwanese would not necessarily embrace such a pursuit. This makes a meaningful distinction between strong and weak national identity. The former entails seeking de jure independence, sovereignty, and international recognition, while the latter can be contented with a politically unconscious, emotional affiliation.

We may further define the average born Taiwanese as possessing a "thin" Taiwanese identity as opposed to the "thick" Taiwanese identity of active advocates of independence. To acquire a thick identity means that one needs to strive for his or her understanding of a Taiwanese consciousness, just as prior generations did under the KMT's ideological hegemony. In fact, we found that many young movement members engaged themselves in a soul-searching process. They re-educated themselves through learning Taiwanese history not from school textbooks but from relived experiences, by interviewing democracy pioneers, compiling their biographies, and producing documentary films. For example, one group of postgraduates and college students formed a study club; they read Su Bing's book on Taiwanese history, first published in the 1960s and subsequently banned during the authoritarian era. Su Bing, a self-made historian and a revered veteran of the Taiwanese independence movement, was long exiled abroad before coming back to Taiwan after democratization. These young activists learned of Taiwan's history under colonialism and dictatorship through interviews with Su Bing, and they published his biography. And this story is just one of the many instances of how younger generations have come to grasp their thick Taiwanese identity. For them, participation in waves of protests gradually nurtured their political maturity, and then the Sunflower Movement provided a mammoth "laboratory" for them to test their convictions and capabilities. The movement, above all, empowered the youth politics of the present age.[30]

What makes this rejuvenated cause for independence distinct from that of prior generations? First, this is a jump from quantity to quality. Demographically, the trend in supporting independence among the young is upward, but, more significantly, the young as a generation are actively searching for their own imagining of statehood, unafraid of expressing the idea of independence during the Sunflower Movement. One movement leader, quoted above, criticized the way in which so many activists in 2012 still eschewed the word "independence." This was more so for the older generations, when Taiwanese independence was treated as a stigma by the KMT regime. That the young openly and collectively embraced the idea of an independent statehood in various forums during the movement is a new phenomenon; momentum has shifted from "independence in hidden transcript" to "independence in public performance." Besides, this transformation is taking the form of collective action, rather than the individual expression observable in the old days. Now the cause of independence is not only destigmatized, but even accorded a new cachet, symbolizing youth and aspiration. No wonder that Beijing hastily pronounced a refocusing of its Taiwan policy on youth work after the Sunflower Movement.

Second, the meaning of independence has transformed from domestic to external contention. Before Taiwan was democratized, independence meant "shaking off the KMT émigré regime," but since the onset of political transition, people came to realize that the pursuit of independence had to run up against an external rival—China—on top of the fact that the China-centric KMT still defied independence. It is well known that CCP-KMT cooperation hinged on fighting the common enemies of Taiwanese independence and an indigenous regime. Hence, an essential difference between the Sunflower and the Wild Lily generation lies in the presence of the China factor. The Wild Lily Student Movement that erupted in 1990 fought the Long Parliament elected decades earlier on the Mainland and called for genuine democracy. This movement targeted KMT authoritarian rule. The *real* China had not yet loomed large at that juncture.

Globalization always makes a dent in a local movement, but it made less of an impact on the Wild Lily generation than on the present one. The Wild Lily cohort was influenced by contemporary pioneers of "Third Wave Democracy" such as in the Philippines and South Korea, as well as being inspired to some extent by the 1989 Tian'anmen Movement. Nonetheless, that generation was more or less domestically oriented, compared to subsequent generations. Members of the Sunflower generation, thanks to the Internet and social media among other factors, turned a keen eye toward current world and regional affairs, such as the situation in Hong Kong, Japan, Okinawa, Tibet, the Arab Spring, Occupy Wall Street, Ukraine, and beyond. The heightened China influence and concomitant geopolitical changes have further pulled Taiwan's youth closer to their counterparts in neighboring countries. Take for example the frequent interactions between the students of Hong Kong and Taiwan. The millennial movement cohorts in both societies have kept up constant exchanges in recent years, in large part stirred by ever-aggressive Chinese interference. Many Sunflower activists stated that they contacted Occupy Central and Umbrella activists during their protest careers, and vice versa. Quite possibly, it is fears over such links that motivated Beijing and the Hong Kong authorities to make their pre-emptive attack on the so-called convergence of Taiwan and Hong Kong independence movements. That aside, we can observe some of the effects of mutual influence between the movements in both these places, such as their action repertoire and their framing of the rivalry. The movements in both places seem to embody a sort of isomorphism, as it were, under the same coercive mechanism created by Beijing and, consequently, the mechanism of mimicry in response to pressures imposed by the China factor, inter alia.

Comparing Taiwan and Hong Kong

The Sunflower Movement was a rare transformative event in Taiwan's history of contentious politics. It developed from a long-term accumulation of enormous social forces, and the occupation action detonated the historical moment. It transformed political structures, discourse, and ideology. In this final section, I will discuss three themes by putting the protest movements in Hong Kong in perspective.

Emergent Youth Political Movement

Both Hong Kong and Taiwan have endured political transformation in the shadow of China. Not incidentally, in 2014 both polities experienced historic resistance movements in reaction to Chinese influence, but with divergent outcomes; both the Umbrella Movement and the Sunflower Movement were transformative, but with different political impacts. The generational shift in Taiwan's identity politics turned out to be more immediately visible than in Hong Kong. The thick Taiwanese identity is anchored in a national consciousness distinct from the Chinese, whereas in Hong Kong it remains in a tug-of-war between Chinese identity and Hongkonger identity. The option of an exclusively "Chinese identity" has withered to a negligible level in Taiwan; by contrast, in Hong Kong, though Chinese identity has declined steadily from a peak of 38.6 percent in 2008, it remains at a significant 20.9 percent as of 2017.

In the aftermath of the Umbrella Movement, many have turned to localism, and some have even embraced the cause of independence. The identity struggle, however, still concerns the young population as well as the movement circles. Given the recent development of radicalized youth politics, two kinds of localism—civil-local identification and ethnic-local identification—are keenly in competition.[31] Is the ongoing trend of identity politics in Hong Kong following a path of "indigenization" similar to that of Taiwan over the years? Despite the comparability, we should not assume there is an isomorphic development in identity formation between both polities. In Hong Kong, certain variables, such as the degree of state repression of the opposition and movement solidarity, can be volatile. For the present, the cause of Hong Kong independence is at an embryonic stage and has an uncertain future.

The Sunflower Movement opened up a new space for youth politics in Taiwan. In its wake, several political parties having connections with the civic movements were established, and they involved much young talent. Besides, scores of activists were absorbed by the ruling DPP or joined the new government. Conspicuously, the New Power Party won five seats (out of 113) in its first parliamentary campaign, a victory hitherto unseen in Taiwan's electoral politics. In part inspired by the success of New Power Party, the young activists in Hong Kong organized new parties and devoted themselves to elections at different levels, and they achieved salient gains. Fearing such a trend, Beijing used "convergence of Taiwan and Hong Kong independence movements" as an excuse to purge the emergent youth movement. The Hong Kong authorities, under increasing pressures from Beijing, have disqualified prodemocracy and localist candidates and lawmakers and severely clamped down on the localist advocates following the protest events since 2014.

The power of social resistance grows out of a historical depth in the protest movement. The Sunflower Movement, set within the contentious politics genre, was an unprecedented event in Taiwan in terms of its scale and duration, its repertoires, and its political horizons. With the youth power, it cut off a nerve center of the state machine, which made the Wild Lily Movement moderate.

Taiwan's youth involvement in national politics developed hand-in-hand with the democracy movement over a span of three decades. There existed a deep-rooted network of trust and solidarity. The Sunflower Movement inherited this cherished network and further brought the solidarity to a new height. In Hong Kong, the Umbrella Movement, precipitated by students' hunger strike, rocked the whole world and dwarfed the scale of the Sunflower Movement. Yet the effort to consolidate the achievement of the Umbrella Movement was troubled by line struggle, leadership competition, and a lack of solidarity.

The Civil Society in Contentious Politics

This section compares the differential embeddedness of the protest movements in civil society in both polities. For Taiwan, we need to trace the historical formation of civil society at least from the later period of quasi-colonial, authoritarian rule in the 1970s. Many civil society organizations today are characterized by autonomy and contentiousness. Genuinely civil organizations, as opposed to those cultivated by the regime under state corporatism during authoritarian rule, had been consciously keeping a distance from the state. They, therefore, turned out to be autonomous from, contentious to, and confrontational with the KMT regime. Inheriting that legacy, the Sunflower Movement was deeply embedded in a contentious civil society tradition. Following the 2016 power transfer, the civil society still kept alert to the DPP government, though a natural ally under the KMT rule.

Hong Kong developed a vibrant civil society of its own under British colonialism, configured by the traditional South China social structure, colonial state cooptation, and Cold War geopolitics. A form of "collaborative colonialism" evolved.[32] A new wave of social protests emerging in the 1970s was led by grassroots "group interests."[33] They pioneered the status of "Hong Kong citizenship,"[34] which built a foundation for the subsequent political movement concerned with the issue of sovereignty transfer to China in the 1980s and 1990s.[35] Yet the idea of Hong Kong citizenship is different from a distinct national identity.

Within the historical context, civil society organizations in Hong Kong appeared to be "cooperative" with the government, since many of them were created for social service functions and maintained via state sponsorship. Overall, they were intrinsically moderate and decorous in political inclination. Hence Hong Kong's organized civil society tends to be less confrontational with the state than that of Taiwan, because, first of all, it lacks a sustained historical consciousness of confronting the colonial state (be it British or, arguably, the current Chinese-imposed regime) and because Hong Kong's civil society lacks the support of a strong and unified opposition within the political society, as the pan-democrats appear fragmented and weak. Without a strong and unified opposition, the civil society could not have the benefit of "political protection" extended by the democrats when contesting the state; without a confrontational civil society, the opposition would not attain a "strategic depth in the political battlefield" to push for the state's concessions. Strong opposition parties and robust civil society could form a "reciprocal protection," which was significant in Taiwan's democratization.

This may explain why some of the localist rallies that stressed militancy and valiant confrontation with a repressive state apparatus tended to disconnect from organized civil society, and therefore why radicalized political contention with Beijing for self-determination or independence lacks a strong ally in society or in the opposition. The Fishball Revolution, a violent interaction between the localists and police in February 2016, was a remarkable case of such disconnectedness from the "establishment" in the civil society. The Fishball Revolution changed part of the grammar of the previous collective protests, but it also triggered a series of harsh punishments by the state.

In the Shadow of China

Besides the above predicaments, a fundamental obstacle for Hong Kong's democracy movement comes from its relationship with China: Hong Kong as a political unit under Chinese sovereignty. The condition of stateness matters. Beijing merely claims sovereignty over Taiwan, but tightly holds sovereignty over Hong Kong.

According to political scientists Linz and Stepan, "Democracy requires statehood. Without a sovereign state, there can be no secure democracy."[36] The authoritarian center is unwilling to let a subunit under its jurisdiction establish democracy. That would bring trouble for itself since democratic legitimacy demands application to all citizens under a state's territorial jurisdiction, and a democratic subsystem would encourage other areas to seek democratization. This thesis succinctly summarizes Hong Kong's democracy movement over the course of two decades. The current situation looks even more pessimistic. In the wake of Occupy Central and the Umbrella Movement, Beijing has further turned the screws on Hong Kong. It is not only that the promise of "one country, two systems" is on the verge of bankruptcy, but much-cherished freedom and the rule of law are also jeopardized. The Chinese government has disseminated authoritarian control into Hong Kong. Many parastate organizations and pro-Beijing political factions have been organized to counter the democracy movement in recent years, helping to fracture the civil society and making scarce social solidarity further fragmented. As a result, a consensual Hong Kong identity would be difficult to firm up.

In contrast, contingent on a high degree of stateness, Taiwan consolidated its electoral democracy before the arrival of an ascendant China, but when Hong Kong began to strive for universal suffrage, the uncompromising China factor kept on holding back the pursuit of democracy. With Beijing not countenancing local democracy within a national authoritarian setting, the China factor effectively trumped and determined the outcome of Hongkongers' resistance in round one.

In the final analysis, the Sunflower Movement embodied the confluence of the crescendo of Taiwanese identity, the rejuvenated cause of independence, and public awareness of Chinese interference. The framing of the China factor as a major rival of the resistance movement proved pivotal and consequential. Long before the Sunflower Movement, Beijing had placed local collaborators in every aspect of the society (businesses, NGOs, religion, the media, education, legislature, and government) to speak for Chinese interests. This audacious United Front Work was observed by many people, but most would not dare expose it to the public because such a critique could be stigmatized as an irrational sentiment of "China-phobia." "China" was a taboo till then. The Sunflower Movement brought the KMT-CCP "black box" to light, forcing people to face up to the China Factor, and shed off the shackles of fear and self-censorship in one blow. In this way, the eventful protest not only stalled the passage of the STA and disrupted the Beijing irredentist agenda, but it also transformed the longstanding China-centric cultural hegemony. It, therefore, set the stage for a new wave of the youth movement.

NOTES

The author thanks Cheng-yu Lin, Mei Liao, En-en Hsu, I-lun Shih, and Kuei-min Chang for research assistance and Ching Kwan Lee, Ming Sing, and reviewers for their suggestions for revision.

1. See Jon Elster, *Nuts and Bolts for Social Sciences* (New York: Cambridge University Press, 1989), and William H. Sewell Jr., *Logics of History: Social Theory and Social Transformation* (Chicago: University of Chicago Press, 2005) for the methodological significance of explanatory mechanism and the causal narrative in eventful sociology, respectively.

2. For the process of this action, see "Report on the Executive Yuan Incident on March 23rd, 2014" (in Chinese), accessed December 27, 2016, https://goo.gl/9unwJo.

3. See Ming-sho Ho, "The Dynamics and Contingency of Movement-Government Standoffs: Hong Kong's Umbrella Movement and Taiwan's Sunflower Movement Compared," (2016:25, Table 1), paper presented at the 2016 annual conference of the Taiwanese Sociological Association, November 26–27, 2016, National Dong-Hwa University, Hualien.

4. Jieh-min Wu, "The Path to the Sunflower Movement: How Taiwanese Civil Society Has Resisted the China Factor" (in Japanese), *Nihon Taiwan Gakkaihou* 17 (2015): 1–36; Ming-sho Ho, "Occupy Congress in Taiwan: Political Opportunity, Threat, and the Sunflower Movement," *Journal of East Asian Studies* 15 (2015): 69–97.

5. Wang stepped down as speaker in 2016 after the KMT lost its majority.

6. The author's participant observation and interviews with the movement activists in December 2016, Taipei.

7. Sidney G. Tarrow, *Power in Movement: Social Movements and Contentious Politics* (New York: Cambridge University Press, 2011); Charles Tilly and Sidney Tarrow, *Contentious Politics* (New York: Oxford University Press, 2015).

8. "Consensus mobilization" means a movement's attempts to convince people of the plausibility of a cause or viewpoint as espoused by that movement. See Bert Klandermans, "The Formation and Mobilization of Consensus," in *From Structure to Action: Comparing Movement Participation Across Cultures,* ed. B. Klandermans, H. Kriesi, and S. Tarrow (Greenwich, CT: JAI Press, 1988), 173–97.

9. Interview with a DPP official, September 2013, Taipei.

10. NOWnews 2013/09/17. See http://www.nownews.com/n/2013/09/17/943649. Note that Ma launched his attack on Wang when the latter was abroad for his daughter's wedding, a move said to be "insidious."

11. Jieh-min Wu, "The China Factor in Taiwan: Impact and Response," in *Handbook of Modern Taiwan Politics and Society*, ed. Gunter Schubert (London: Routledge, 2016), 425–45.

12. Jieh-min Wu and Mei Liao, "From Unification-Independence Divide to the China Factor: How Changing Political Identity Influences Voting Behavior" (in Chinese), *Taiwanese Sociology* 29 (2015): 87–130.

13. William Norris, *Chinese Economic Statecraft: Commercial Actors, Grand Strategy, and State Control* (Ithaca, NY: Cornell University Press, 2016).

14. The Control Yuan is a national investigatory agency, parallel to the Legislative Yuan, which monitors other branches of government.

15. Hsin-fei Lin, "Report to Director, We Have Bought the 'China Times'" (in Chinese), *Commonwealth Magazine* 416 (2009): 35–38; Jieh-min Wu, "The China Factor and Its Impact on Taiwan's Democracy" (in Chinese), *Reflexion* 11 (2009): 141–57.

16. As soon as it was inaugurated, the Ma government forbade government agencies from using the term "China." See http://hk.crntt.com/doc/1006/6/4/1/100664190.html.

17. Interview with a social movement activist, December 2014, Taipei.

18. Interview with a student leader of the Sunflower Movement, July 2016, Taipei.

19. Wu, "The China Factor in Taiwan."

20. Doug McAdam et al., eds., *Comparative Perspectives on Social Movements: Political Opportunities, Mobilizing Structures, and Cultural Framings* (Cambridge: Cambridge University Press, 1996); Robert D. Benford and David A. Snow, "Framing Processes and Social Movements: An Overview and Assessment," *Annual Review of Sociology* 26, no. 1 (2000): 611–39; David A. Snow, "Framing Processes, Ideology, and Discursive Fields," in *The Blackwell Companion to Social Movements*, ed. David A. Snow, Sarah A. Soule, and Hanspeter Kriesi (Malden, MA: Blackwell Publishing, 2004), 380–412.

21. Tilly and Tarrow, *Contentious Politics*, 31–35.

22. En-en Hsu, Jieh-min Wu, Tsung-tang Lee, and I-lun Shih, "Explaining the Social Movement Solidarity in the Sunflower Movement" (in Chinese), paper presented at the 2016 annual conference of the Taiwanese Sociological Association, November 26–27, 2016, National Dong-Hwa University, Hualien.

23. The author's participant observation and interviews with the movement activists in December 2016, Taipei.

24. Here the number of incidents counted are subtracted by the missing cases where the scales of participants are unknown. Recompiled from Jieh-min Wu's research data on "Social Protests in Taiwan, 2008–2016" a research project sponsored by the Ministry of Science and Technology, Taiwan (ROC).

25. Cheng-yu Lin, Jieh-min Wu, and Mei Liao, "The Overall Trends of the Collective Protests in Taiwan: 2012–2014" (in Chinese), paper presented on the 2016 annual

conference of the Taiwanese Sociological Association, November 26–27, 2016, National Dong-Hwa University, Hualien.

26. See James L. Galvin, *The Arab Uprisings: What Everyone Needs to Know* (New York: Oxford University Press, 2012); W. Lance Bennett and Alexandra Segerberg, *The Logic of Connective Action: Digital Media and the Personalization of Contentious Politics* (New York: Cambridge University Press, 2013); and David Graeber, *The Democracy Project: A History, a Crisis, a Movement* (New York: Spiegel & Grau, 2013).

27. Sewell, *Logics of History*, 100.

28. Jieh-min Wu and Mei Liao, "The China Factor in Taiwan's Elections: The '1992 Consensus' and the 2012 and 2016 Presidential Elections," unpublished paper, 2016.

29. Interview with a Sunflower Movement activist, May 2016, Taipei.

30. Note that neither do the young activists all share this ideal-typical description, nor do all of them share the same *Weltanschauung*. But this ideal type is becoming mainstream.

31. Sebastian Veg, "The Rise of 'Localism' and Civic Identity in Post-Handover Hong Kong: Questioning the Chinese Nation-State," *China Quarterly* 230 (2017): 323–47.

32. Wing Sang Law, *Collaborative Colonial Power: The Making of the Hong Kong Chinese* (Hong Kong: Hong Kong University Press, 2009).

33. T. L. Lui, "The Traits of Hong Kong's Public Sphere under British Colonialism," workshop on The Development of "Tradition" and "Civil Society": Comparing Taiwan, Hong Kong, and China. December 12–13, 2015, Hsin Chu: National Tsing Hua University.

34. T. L. Lui and Stephen Chiu, "Social Movements and Public Discourse on Politics," in *Hong Kong's History*, ed. T. W. Ngo (London: Routledge, 1999), 108–11.

35. Lui, "The Traits of Hong Kong's Public Sphere."

36. Juan J. Linz and Alfred Stepan, *Problems of Democratic Transition and Consolidation* (Baltimore: Johns Hopkins University Press, 1999).

HONG KONG'S TURN TOWARD GREATER AUTHORITARIANISM

Ming Sing

The Umbrella Movement of 2014 in Hong Kong shocked the world and captured global attention. It was prominent by its long duration, grand scale of participation, and a radical turn in movement tactics from the past in this cosmopolitan city. The movement has been hailed by many in the world, as so many Hong Kong people had the courage to challenge bluntly the largest dictatorial regime on earth for democracy. That said, the democracy movement has hit a bump, with Beijing not budging on democratization. What is worse, Beijing and the HKSAR government have patently tightened their control over Hong Kong's freedoms and genuine electoral contestation in the aftermath of the movement.

Soon after the termination of the Umbrella Movement, Beijing doggedly stuck to its hardline policy on Hong Kong by dramatically raising the political cost for those challenging its suppression of Hong Kong's democratization. There were mass arrests of the movement's leaders. The successful prosecution of some arrested ones have led to the imprisonment of some famous leaders of the movement, including Joshua Wong and Alex Chow. To pre-empt another large-scale Occupy Movement, Beijing and the HKSAR government have also curbed Hong Kong's press freedom and academic freedom and have undermined the electoral competition.

Undermining Hong Kong's Freedoms and Electoral Competition

Beijing for a long time has endeavored to turn Hong Kong's media into its mouth-pieces. In 2016, the Chinese government and corporations secured control of stakes in 31 percent of mainstream media outlets in Hong Kong, which has allowed Beijing to commit all sorts of media interferences.[1] Consequently, in April 2016, Reporters without Borders found that Hong Kong's press freedom fell pre-cipitously from a rank of 18 in 2002 to 70 in 2015. The ranking was predicated on forty-three benchmarks, including violations directly aimed at journalists (mur-ders, imprisonment, physical attacks, and threats) and at the news media (censor-ship, confiscation of newspapers and magazines, searches, and harassment).[2]

In 2018, the Hong Kong public's evaluation of press freedom in Hong Kong fell to the lowest level since the Hong Kong Journalists Association's annual survey began in 2013. The study cited the mounting pressure from the central government as the culprit that adversely undermined Hong Kong's press free-dom. Half of the journalists surveyed regarded Beijing as one of the primary fac-tors shaping press freedom—a jump from 38 percent in 2017—supplanting the HKSAR government as one of the top three factors, while 63 percent replied that central government officials "favored one country before two systems," leaving them uneasy when reporting on voices with different views.[3]

Academic freedom has also had a setback during recent years. In the after-math of the Umbrella Movement, political pressure was applied to Hong Kong's universities, in particular over senior academic appointments. In January 2015, a former official of the State Council underscored "the 'national interest' must be considered when Hong Kong considered its education policy."[4] After the Umbrella Movement, a worrying trend of top-down backlash that restrains academic free-dom became noticeable. The trend includes liberal-minded academic figures being removed from their posts, having their promotions blocked, or extra-legal campaigns initiated to assist in their removal from universities. Occupy convener Benny Tai was, for instance, an academic facing extra-legal action.[5] Of no less importance, the government has appointed more pro-Beijing figures to govern universities. At the same time, universities' heads have been under pressure to curb the freedom of speech on campuses concerning the political independence of Hong Kong. And there is a highly visible trend for some local universities to limit freedom of speech without any legal basis when independence was dis-cussed on campuses.

Last but not least, for many nondemocratic or authoritarian regimes, states attempt to suppress political opposition by excluding or marginalizing political opposition. Apart from the hardline tactic like imprisoning opposition leaders and electoral fraud, banning the opposition parties and candidates from running elections is a common soft tactic launched by the regimes.[6]

In Hong Kong, to stifle the growth of prodemocracy opposition including the new political parties initiated by the young activists and student leaders, Beijing has "reinterpreted" Hong Kong's mini-constitution to compel the courts to disqualify elected prodemocracy legislators because of a controversial oath taking. Soon after that, the HKSAR government also disqualified many localists from running the elections. The localists stressed the protection of the Hong Kong people's interest as their top priority, and some localists also advocated the political independence of Hong Kong. More recently, the government has disqualified even the self-determinists from joining the electoral race. The self-determinist activists included many student leaders of the Umbrella Movement, who belonged to the newly established party of Demosistō formed in 2016. The Demosistō campaigned for democratic self-determination and autonomy from the CCP's control via direct actions, popular referendums, and nonviolent methods.[7] Though the party does not push for Hong Kong independence, it plans to hold a referendum by 2026 to allow the Hong Kong people to express their preferences on Hong Kong's political future after 2047.[8]

In short, all the aforementioned measures testify to Xi Jinping's pursuit of a hardline policy, as revealed in its increasingly blatant measures to curb freedoms and meaningful electoral competition to ensure Beijing's absolute control over Hong Kong. The attainment of genuine universal suffrage in the near future has become a far-fetched dream for Hong Kong people. Instead, the prodemocracy community and activists have been besieged by the battle of defending Hong Kong against the perceptible erosion of its freedoms and its turn to greater authoritarianism.

NOTES

1. "One Country, Two Nightmares: Hong Kong Media Caught in Ideological Battleground—2016 Annual Report," last modified July 2016, https://www.hkja.org.hk/ebook/e_Annual_report_2016/mobile/index.html#p=1.

2. Ming Sing, "Politics and Government in Hong Kong," in *Global Encyclopedia of Public Administration, Public Policy, and Governance* ed. Ali Farazmand (New York: Springer, 2018).

3. "Hongkongers Say Press Freedom Has Dropped to Its Lowest Point—Survey," last modified April 12, 2018, https://www.hongkongfp.com/2018/04/12/hongkongers-say-press-freedom-dropped-lowest-point-survey/.

4. "The Six-Monthly Report on Hong Kong: 1 January to 30 June 2015," last modified July 2015, https://assets.publishing.service.gov.uk/government/uploads/system/uploads/attachment_data/file/447070/6MR_2015_Jan-Jun.pdf.

5. "Growing Push to Limit Academic Freedom in Hong Kong after Occupy Protests, Says New UK Watchdog Report," last modified January 23, 2018, https://www.hongkongfp.com/2018/01/22/growing-push-limit-academic-freedom-hong-kong-occupy-protests-says-new-uk-watchdog-report/.

6. Andreas Schedler, "The Nested Game of Democratization by Election," *International Political Science Review* 23, no. 1 (2002): 106; Henry Hale, "Hybrid Regimes: When Democracy and Autocracy mix," in *The Dynamics of Democratization: Dictatorship, Development and Diffusion*, ed. N. J. Brown (Baltimore: Johns Hopkins University Press, 2011), 23–45.

7. See https://goo.gl/kp7dUa, accessed on November 3, 2017.

8. "Joshua Wong's New Political Party Demosisto Has Eyes Firmly on Seats in Legco," *SCMP*, April 16, 2016.

Contributors

Chris K. C. Chan is an associate professor in the Department of Sociology at the Chinese University of Hong Kong. His research focuses on employment relations, labor activism, and civil society in Hong Kong and mainland China.

Edmund W. Cheng is an associate professor in the Department of Public Policy at the City University of Hong Kong. His research interests include contentious politics and political sociology, public opinion, Hong Kong politics, and Global China. He is the coeditor of *An Epoch of Social Movements* (Chinese University Press, 2018) and *The Umbrella Movement: Civil Resistance and Contentious Space in Hong Kong* (Amsterdam University Press, 2019), and his articles have appeared in *China Quarterly, China Journal, Political Studies,* and *Social Movements Studies.*

Alex Yong Kang Chow was the secretary-general of the Hong Kong Federation of Students during the Umbrella Movement. He is a founder of Community Citizen Charter Movement and the Community Press Crowdfunding Scheme in Hong Kong. He also serves as a member of NOYDA (Network of Young Democratic Asians), which aims at building regional platforms for activism and young activists. He is currently a PhD student in geography at the University of California, Berkeley. He has an MSc in city design and social science from the London School of Economics and Political Science, and graduated from the University of Hong Kong with majors in comparative literature and sociology. His research interests include cities and community building, alternative urban/rural economy, social movements and the state, colonialism and postcolonialism, religion and spirituality, political ecology, and technology.

Oscar Ho (CRS) is an associate professor in practice and director of the MA Programme in Cultural Management at the Chinese University of Hong Kong. He was previously the exhibition director of the Hong Kong Arts Centre, senior research officer in cultural policy for the Hong Kong government, and the founding director of the Museum of Contemporary Art in Shanghai. He has curated many exhibitions on the art of Hong Kong and Asia. He is also one of the founding directors of the Asia Art Archive and founder of the Hong Kong chapter of the International Art Critics Association. He has written for local and international publications such as *Art Journal, Art in Asia Pacific,* and *Art Forum.*

Wing Sang Law is an adjunct associate professor of cultural studies at Lingnan University, Hong Kong. He received his PhD from the University of Technology in Sydney, Australia, and his research interests include historical and cultural studies of colonialism, Hong Kong's cultural formation and citizenship, and cultural theory. He is the author of *Collaborative Colonial Power: The Making of the Hong Kong Chinese* (Hong Kong University Press, 2009) and his articles have appeared in *Inter-Asia Cultural Studies, Positions. East Asia Culture Critique, Traces: A Multilingual Series of Cultural Theory and Translation, Social Transformations in Chinese Societies, Renjin Review, Taiwan: A Radical Journal of Social Studies, Reflexion,* among others.

Ching Kwan Lee is a professor of sociology at University of California–Los Angeles. Her research interests include labor, political sociology, globalization, development, China, Hong Kong, the Global South, and comparative ethnography. She is the author of three award-winning books on China's turn to capitalism through the lens of labor: *Gender and the South China Miracle: Two Worlds of Factory Women* (University of California Press 1998), *Against the Law: Labor Protests in China's Rustbelt and Sunbelt* (University of California Press 2007), and *The Specter of Global China: Politics, Labor and Foreign Investment in Africa* (University of Chicago Press 2017). Her articles have appeared in *American Journal of Sociology, American Sociological Review, Theory and Society, New Left Review, China Quarterly,* and *Journal of Asian Studies.*

Francis L. F. Lee is the director of and a professor at the School of Journalism and Communication, Chinese University of Hong Kong. He focuses on journalism studies, political communication, public opinion, and media and social movements. He is the lead or sole author of *Media and Protest Logics in the Digital Era: The Umbrella Movement in Hong Kong* (Oxford University Press 2018), *Talk Radio, the Mainstream Press and Public Opinion in Hong Kong* (Hong Kong University Press 2014), and *Media, Social Mobilization, and Mass Protests in Post-Colonial Hong Kong* (Routledge 2011). He is currently chief editor of *Chinese Journal of Communication* and associate editor of *Mass Communication & Society.*

Ming Sing is an associate professor in the Division of Social Science at The Hong Kong University of Science and Technology. His research interests include the comparative study of democracy and democratization, political culture, civil society, quality of life, and Hong Kong politics. He obtained his DPhil from Oxford University in sociology and is the author or editor of four books, plus over thirty articles in *Journal of Politics, Journal of Democracy, Democratization, Government and Opposition,* and *Social Indicators Research,* among others. He has also been an active commentator in local and international media on Hong Kong politics.

Jieh-min Wu is an associate research fellow at the Institute of Sociology, Academia Sinica, Taiwan. His research interests include political sociology, social movements, and political economy. He is the author of *Rent-Seeking Developmental State in China: Taishang, Guangdong Model and Global Capitalism* (National Taiwan University Press and The Harvard-Yenching Institute Academic Book Series, 2019) and *Third View of China* (Rive Gauche Publishing House, 2012); and the coeditor of *Anaconda in the Chandelier: Mechanisms of Influence and Resistance in the "China Factor"* (Rive Gauche Publishing House, 2017) and *China's influence: Centre-Periphery Tug of War across Indo-Pacific* (under submission to Weatherhead East Asian Institute, Columbia University).

Samson Yuen is currently an assistant professor in the Department of Political Science of Lingnan University. Trained as a political scientist, he studies state power, civil society, contentious politics, and local governance in authoritarian and hybrid regimes, with a specialization in the Greater China region. He has published articles in *Political Studies, Journal of Contemporary China, China Information, Social Movement Studies, Hong Kong Studies,* and *China Perspectives.* He received his MPhil in comparative government and a DPhil in politics from Oxford University.

Index

DISCARD

CPSIA information can be obtained
at www.ICGtesting.com
Printed in the USA
LVHW071426281019
635569LV00015B/84/P